Accounting and Finance for the Hospitality Indu

To Elaine and Samantha

Accounting and Finance for the International Hospitality Industry

Edited by
Peter J. Harris
Oxford Brookes University

Butterworth-Heinemann
Linacre House, Jordan Hill, Oxford OX2 8DP
A division of Reed Educational and Professional Publishing Ltd

⭐ A member of the Reed Elsevier plc group

OXFORD BOSTON JOHANNESBURG
MELBOURNE NEW DELHI SINGAPORE

First published 1995
Reprinted 1996
Paperback edition 1997

British Library Cataloguing in Publication Data
A catalogue record for this book is available from
the British Library

ISBN 0 7506 3586 X

Printed and bound in Great Britain by Hartnolls Ltd, Bodmin, Cornwall

Contents

Peter J. Harris MSc, MHCIMA, CDipAF, FBHA
Principal Lecturer
School of Hotel and Catering Management
Oxford Brookes University, UK

Geoff S. Parkinson BSc, FCA, FHCIMA, FBHA
Managing Director, BDO Hospitality Consulting and Partner, BDO
Stoy Hayward Chartered Accountants, UK

Paul Fitz-John MBA, FCA, MIMgt
Principal Lecturer
Department of Finance and Law
Bournemouth University, UK

Paul Collier BSc, FCA
Senior Lecturer
Department of Economics
University of Exeter, UK
and
Professor Alan Gregory MSc, FCMA, Cert Ed
Department of Accounting and Finance, University of Glasgow, UK

Tracy A. Jones BSc, MPhil, MHCIMA
Senior Lecturer
Department of Leisure Management
Cheltenham and Gloucester College of Higher Education, UK

Jacqueline Brander Brown, BA (Econ), ACA, ABHA
Senior Lecturer
Department of Accounting and Finance
The Manchester Metropolitan University, UK

Preface

The main purpose of this book is to present new and interesting research and other findings and developments in the field of accounting and finance as it relates to the work of managing enterprises and organizations in the international hospitality industry. Although the focus is on hotels the content can readily be interpreted in a broader context. Many hospitality organizations contain hotel services components such as the provision of rooms, food and beverage facilities and, therefore, the examples and illustrations can be related to restaurants, licensed house management, hospital and university services, clubs and so on.

The content contains contributions from experienced researchers, university and college lecturers, practising accountants and consultants and senior managers associated with the international hospitality industry in the UK and abroad. The material is drawn from their own work and experience and relates directly to the management of hospitality undertakings.

Most books written for the hospitality industry tend to concentrate on the application of accounting and financial management in a theoretical context. In contrast, this work presents new findings and developments drawn from a combination of live fieldwork and practical experience. In this context it is anticipated that the readership will include: practising managers and financial controllers in hospitality organizations, professional accountants and consultants, postgraduate candidates studying for master's degrees in hospitality management and final-year undergraduate students of hospitality management who elect to take an accounting option.

The contents are arranged in four parts. The purpose of this is to provide a general structure by grouping similar kinds of areas together. However, it will be appreciated that some contributions could be judged to fall into one or more parts and, therefore, to some extent, the groupings are arbitrary.

Part I focuses on the analysis and evaluation of performance. Methods of analysing past financial and operating performance are considered together with an examination of approaches used to predict the potential failure of a business.

Part II places emphasis on matters of planning. Analytical methods and techniques are applied to cost and project planning and the assessment of risk in terms of attaining projected revenues. Consideration is given to the development of a framework for financial planning and to the current and future management accounting practices of hotel groups.

Part III concentrates on the use of accounting and control information in relation to decision-making and human behaviour. This includes an investigation of a framework for management information needs and emerging developments in the use of information in marketing decisions.

Part IV examines issues concerned with financial managers and with the financial management of hospitality organizations. It also examines the financial implications of hotel management contracts from the European and North American perspectives.

Notwithstanding the classification or grouping of the material presented here, the range of topics brings together a rich fund of knowledge and experience from contributors who operate internationally throughout the world. Without their generosity and commitment to the sharing and dissemination of information, a book of this kind would not be possible; a debt of gratitude is owed to them all.

Acknowledgement is also due to a number of my colleagues who have eased the production of the final publication: Sue Wilkins for collating and standardizing the text; Tom Anstey and Chris Murphy for help with reading material off disks; Liz Drewett for word-processing; and to my other colleagues for their support and tolerance throughout the preparation of the manuscript. Finally, thanks go to Jacquie Shanahan of Butterworth-Heinemann who as usual has been considerate and supportive throughout.

As always, my single wish is that the reader finds the content to be of practical use.

Peter Harris
Editor

Contributors

Raymond Schmidgall received his BBA degree in accounting from Evangel College in 1967. He received his MBA in 1969 and PhD in 1980, both in accounting, from Michigan State University. In 1973 he received his CPA from the State of Michigan.

His industrial experience includes three years of public accounting for international and statewide firms. In addition, he was financial controller for the American Hotel and Motel Association's (AH&MA's) Education Institute for two years.

Professor Schmidgall has authored four textbooks on hospitality accounting and finance. In addition, he has published articles in *Lodging, Club Management, Bottomline, The Consultant, Restaurant Business* and the *Cornell Hotel and Restaurant Administration Quarterly*. His current research is being conducted in the areas of accounting for bartered transactions and small-business financing.

Dr Schmidgall is Secretary of the Association of Hospitality Financial Management Educators, a member of the AH&MA's financial management committee, chairperson of the International Association of Hospitality Accountants communications committee; he serves on the editorial board of the Council on Hotel, Restaurant and Institutional Education's (CHRIE's) *Hospitality Research Journal*, and is treasurer of International CHRIE, and a member of several professional accounting associations.

Debra Adams is a senior lecturer in Accounting in the Department of Service Industries at Bournemouth University, UK. A graduate of Dorset Institute (now Bournemouth University), she holds a BSc in catering administration and is a qualified member of the Chartered Institute of Management Accountants. She joined Forte hotels as an accounting trainee in 1985, holding management accounting positions in the hotels division and in the Ring & Brymer contract catering division. She has published several articles and case studies in hospitality accounting, and has been external examiner for the Hotel, Catering and Institutional Management Association (HCIMA) and for the British Association of Hotel Accountants (BAHA). Her current activities include chairmanship of the BAHA Education Committee and the preparation of a new text in hospitality accounting.

Elisa S. Moncarz is Professor of Hospitality Accounting and Finance in the School of Hospitality Management at Florida International University in Miami, Florida. Born in Havana, Cuba, she spent 10 years in New York, where she received degrees in public accountancy and became a certified public accountant. She has extensive auditing, Securities and Exchange Commission (SEC) and tax experience that includes over six years with the international Certified Public Accountants (CPA) firm which is now Ernst & Young. She has co-authored two textbooks on accounting and finance and has written numerous articles published in the *FIU Hospitality Review, International Journal of Hospitality Management, Bottom Line* and the *Cornell, Hotel and Restaurant Administration Quarterly*. She has served as consultant and speaker for several organizations in the USA and Latin America. Her current research interests include the areas of operational analysis, restructuring and financial failure in the hospitality industry.

Richard N. Kron, president of Kron Hospitality Consulting, Inc., has managed and/or consulted with hotel operators throughout the USA, the Caribbean, South America and Japan, including Hyatt, Marriott, Hilton International, Sheraton, Sonesta, Holiday Inn, Ritz-Carlton and numerous non-affiliated hotels. He was a manager of Pannell Kerr Forster's Management Advisory Services division from 1986 to 1991. He also managed hotels and restaurants for 16 years prior to receiving an MSc degree in hotel and food service management from Florida International University. His extensive operations and consulting experience has given him expertise in the performance of operational analyses of hospitality firms.

Past speaking engagements include the Caribbean Hotel Association annual conferences, International Association of Hospitality Accountants, Florida International University and Florida Restaurant Association. His current interests include the development of hotel control systems and management operational reviews for hotels and resorts.

Angela Maher is a lecturer in human resource management for the hospitality industry in the School of Hotel and Catering Management at Oxford Brookes University. She contributes to a wide range of courses at undergraduate, postgraduate and HCIMA levels within the school and has also lectured at the Institute for Tourism Studies in Malta. Her research interests are in a number of areas related to human resource management and accountancy and, more specifically, she is concerned with investigating ways to account for the value of human resources. She holds a BA from Oxford Brookes University and is currently working towards the completion of a PhD on the latter subject and has presented a conference paper on some of the initial research findings. Other areas of interest include equal opportunities in employment, Japanese management styles and trade unions in the hospitality industry.

Peter Harris is principal lecturer in accounting and programme director of the master's degree in international hotel management at Oxford Brookes University. He was trained in the hospitality industry and held management positions in hotels, restaurants and banqueting operations. He has published a number of books and articles on hospitality accounting and has carried out numerous consultancy assignments for leading hotel organizations in the UK and abroad. He is director of the BAHA programme of continuing professional education and a visiting professor at the Institut de Management Hotelier International (Cornell University-l'Ecole Supérieure de Sciences Economiques et Commerciales) programme in France.

Geoff Parkinson is managing director of BDO Hospitality Consulting and a partner with BDO Stoy Hayward, a leading firm of consultants and accountants. He graduated from the University of Surrey in hotel and catering administration and subsequently qualified as a chartered accountant, since which time he has specialized in providing consulting advice to clients planning investments in the hotel, tourism and leisure sectors. He has travelled extensively during his career in consulting, has authored a number of publications on the financial aspects of the sector and is a frequent lecturer and conference speaker.

Paul Fitz-John had professional accountancy practice experience whilst qualifying as a chartered accountant. This was followed by 20 years' commercial experience in retail and distribution companies, broken by a year on the full-time MBA programme at Cranfield University. His commercial experience included five years as group financial director of the largest distributor of catering equipment in the UK.

For the last 10 years he has been a principal lecturer in financial management and management accounting at Bournemouth University, specializing in the hospitality and retail industries. He teaches extensively on undergraduate and postgraduate programmes and is a visiting lecturer on the BAHA Continuing Professional Education programme at Oxford Brookes University.

Paul Collier is a senior lecturer at the University of Exeter and an academic fellow of the Institute of Chartered Accountants in England and Wales.

Following his degree in management at the University of Aston in Birmingham, he worked with Touche Ross & Co., chartered accountants, for 10 years, specializing in computer auditing. Subsequently, he has lectured first at the Aston University Management Centre and then at the University of Exeter. His research interests have included: international financial management especially focusing on the management of currency risk by multinational companies in the UK and US; the implications of information technology for accountants and accountancy education; computer fraud and abuse through the Woolwich Centre for Computer Crime Research; and corporate governance research into the role of audit committees. His research output has appeared in a number of monographs, and academic and professional journals including *Accounting and Business Research, Policy and Society, Artificial Intelligence Review, Journal of Information Technology, Accounting Education, Managerial Auditing Journal, Accountancy* and *Management Accounting.*

Alan Gregory is Professor of Accounting and Finance, University of Glasgow. He has worked as a management accountant in industry, before taking up an academic career. After initially teaching professional accountancy students, he completed an MSc in accounting and finance at the London School of Economics, and lectured at Brighton Polytechnic, City Polytechnic, the University of Exeter, before joining Glasgow.

His research interests have included divisional manager performance evaluation, investment appraisal, acquisitions and mergers, and stock market efficiency. His research papers have been published in journals which include the *Economic Journal, Accounting and Business Research, Journal of Business Finance* and *Accounting and Journal of Business Law.* He is the author of *Valuing Companies* (Woodhead-Faulkner) and his research interest in this area is continuing with an Institute of Chartered Accountants of England and Wales (ICAEW) Research Board-funded project which is investigating the valuation practices of professional accounting firms.

Tracy A. Jones is senior lecturer in the department of leisure management, Cheltenham and Gloucester College of Higher Education, UK.

She worked in various sectors of the industry before returning to college to complete her HCIMA qualification. As part of this course she was awarded the Greene, Bellfield-Smith Award for achieving the highest marks nationally in the finance examination. She remained at Oxford Polytechnic (now Oxford Brookes University) and completed a BSc (Hons) in hotel and catering management.

Between 1987 and 1990 she was a post-graduate teaching assistant in the School of Hotel and Catering Management, Oxford Polytechnic, where she was awarded an MPhil degree for her research into the financial and operating information needs of managers in hotel companies.

In 1990 she joined Cheltenham and Gloucester College of Higher Education. Her main teaching areas are finance and accounting, within the hospitality programmes in the department.

Jacqueline Brander Brown is an associate of the Institute of Chartered Accountants in England and Wales and of the British Association of Hotel Accountants, having spent some eight years as an accountant, both in professional practice and as a financial controller with De Vere Hotels. She is currently a senior lecturer in the department of accounting and finance at the Manchester Metropolitan University, where she is the Departmental Research Coordinator and also has responsibilities for developing the management accounting elements of all three years of the undergraduate degree. Her research interests include the design of effective management accounting and control systems, particularly with regard to the needs of service industries and she is in the process of completing a PhD programme at Oxford Brookes University.

Nina J. Downie is a lecturer in operations management in the School of Hotel and Catering Management at Oxford Brookes University. She returned to education following extensive managerial experience in hotels and restaurants. Having successfully completed a BSc Hons degree at Oxford Brookes University as a mature student, she also attained membership of the Chartered Institute of Marketing. Her research interests focus on the use of accounting information for management decision-making in hotels. She has worked with a number of organizations, including the Savoy Hotel Group and the Institute for Tourism at Bourgas, Bulgaria.

Cathy Burgess qualified in hospitality management at Leeds Polytechnic (now Leeds Metropolitan University) and then joined EMI Hotels, which later became Thistle Hotels, as a management trainee. She spent 13 years in various operational and financial management positions within the hotel and catering industry, latterly as a financial controller. In 1989 she was appointed senior lecturer in accounting at Oxford Brookes University, teaching financial management to degree and master's students, and was course director of the master's degree in hotel and catering management. She maintains close links with industry through research and consultancy and as a Council and Education Committee Member of the British Association of Hotel Accountants. Her current research interests include investigating the factors relating to the success of international hotel groups.

Ian Graham is a native of Edinburgh, Scotland and currently lives in Waterloo, Belgium. He is a graduate in hotel and catering administration from the University of Surrey, and qualified as a chartered accountant during training periods with Horwath Consulting and Peat Marwick Mitchell (now KPMG).

He is a finance director with 20 years' experience in the hotel industry throughout Europe, Middle East, Africa and the Indian subcontinent, including periods living in Togo, Syria, Jordan, England, Scotland and Germany, before taking up his present position. His experience encompasses joint ventures, capital expenditure appraisals, information technology systems development and management, franchise and management contract administration, project cost management, strategic planning, budgeting and forecasting, multicurrency treasury and tax management, and many aspects of financial reporting to USA, UK and European standards.

Howard Field is director of International Hotel & Leisure Associates Ltd., independent advisers to the hotel and leisure industry, and managing director of FM Recruitment, specialist financial management recruitment consultants for the sector. Advisory assignments have included acting as chief executive of UK hotel-owning partnerships involving Sheraton, Marriott and Holiday Inn operations in the UK and France.

He is chairman of the International Committee of the British Association of Hotel Accountants, of which he is an honorary fellow, a founding member and past treasurer. He is visiting lecturer at Oxford Brookes University and London South Bank University, specializing in the subject of hotel management contacts for undergraduates and postgraduates.

He qualified as a chartered accountant in 1965, since when positions held include hotel unit financial controllerships with UK and international groups; consultant with Horwath UK; vice-president – finance with Commonwealth Holiday Inns of Canada in their European division, and group financial controller with the Savoy Hotel Group.

Paul Beals is a professor and director of the Statler hotel management programme at Canisius College, the first American undergraduate programme to create a course of study to prepare asset managers for the hotel industry. He holds master's and doctorate degrees in hotel administration from Cornell University and has served as executive editor of *The Cornell Hotel and Restaurant Administration Quarterly* and as director of the Institut de Management Hotelier International, a joint graduate-level programme between Cornell's Hotel School and l'Ecole Supérieure de Sciences Economiques et Commerciales (ESSEC), one of France's most prestigious business schools. His publications, primarily in the area of hotel development, have appeared in the *Journal of Real Estate Finance, Real Estate Review, The Cornell Hotel and Restaurant Administration Quarterly* and *L'Hôtel Revue*. A member of Phi Beta Kappa and the Council on Hotel, Restaurant and Institutional Education, he is currently a contributing editor to *Hospitality and Tourism Educator* and the *International Journal of Contemporary Hospitality Management*.

Frank Croston is managing director of Pannell Kerr Forster Associates (PKFA), responsible for the direction of the hotel and leisure consultancy in Europe, the Middle East and Africa. Frank has been with PKFA since 1983.

Having graduated in hotel and catering Administration, he pursued a career within the financial side of the industry. Prior to joining PKFA, Frank worked for Grand Metropolitan and Caledonian Hotel Management in the UK and Africa respectively.

His current role involves responsibility for the direction of a wide range of consultancy services offered to the hotel and leisure industry, and he has directed assignments in more than 50 countries. He has undertaken a number of strategic development reviews for international hotel groups, and has led several assignments to prepare comprehensive operations policies and procedures manuals. In addition, he has addressed numerous industry conferences and seminars and has been invited by several hotel groups to address internal management meetings.

As well as being a fellow of the HCIMA, Frank is currently vice-chairman of the British Association of Hotel Accountants.

Part I   Financial Analysis

1 Performance measures used in hotel companies

Raymond S. Schmidgall

Introduction

The overall objective of hotel companies is to provide satisfaction for their stakeholders. The stakeholders vary from guests, to employees (including management), to owners, to suppliers, to financial lenders, to the community where the hotel is located. Each stakeholder group seeks different 'rewards' from the hotel companies. First, the hotel guest often seeks quality services at a reasonable price. The services include but are not limited to food, beverages and lodging. The employees of the hotel companies seek monetary rewards including wages and fringe benefits, as well as non-financial rewards such as promotions and recognition. Management's desires are similar to employees; however, they often include additional financial rewards such as capital in the employer's company stock. Other stakeholders include the community in which the hotel is located and creditors including lenders of funds on both a long and short-term basis to the hotel. The community desires the hotel to be a credit to its environment and to 'serve' the area. Suppliers desire to receive cash payments for their services on a timely basis while lenders seek the repayment of their funds, including interest. Finally, the owners who take the ultimate risk seek a fair return on their investment. This return takes two forms: first, dividends from the hotel to the owners are the return on their capital investment. The second reward is the increase in the value of the owners' investment. This reward is easily measured by hotel companies whose capital stock is trade on stock exchanges such as the New York Stock Exchange, the London Stock Exchange or the Tokyo Stock Exchange.

In order for a hotel company to meet the desires of its stockholders (owners) the hotel must generate profits, that is revenue must exceed expenses. In essence this is the bottom line if the overall objective of a hotel company is to be satisfied. This chapter discusses performance measures used in hotel companies to determine and help ensure the achievement of the desired net income of a hotel company. First, the three major financial statements are presented and illustrated, followed by financial ratios used to reduce the statements to indicators of success.

Financial statements

The three major financial statements include the balance sheet, the income statement, and the statement of cash flows. These statements are prepared at the end of the accounting period and are based on generally accepted accounting principles.[1]

The balance sheet, illustrated in Figure 1.1, reflects assets and claims to assets of the hypothetical Mayfair Hotel. Assets simply are items of value to the hotel company. The first claims to assets are by the creditors and these claims are referred to as liabilities. The claims which must be paid within a relatively short period of time are labelled as current liabilities while other obligations of the hotel company at the balance sheet date are long-term liabilities. The residual claims to assets are by the owners and are revealed in the owners' equity section of the balance sheet. The claims to the assets equal the assets; thus this is the reason why this financial statement is called the balance sheet.

Assets are classified as current, investments, and property and equipment, as shown in Figure 1.1. The balance sheet is a static statement as it is prepared as of a given date, the last day of the accounting period. This statement reflects the accounting equation of assets equal liabilities plus owners' equity. The balance sheet of the Mayfair Hotel reveals assets of $1,176,300 and liabilities and owners' equity for the same amount on December 31, 19X2.

The financial statement which reflects operations of the Mayfair Hotel is the income statement, as illustrated in Figure 1.2. The income statement includes both revenues (sales) and expenses. The income statement illustrated in this chapter contains considerable detail and reflects activity by areas of responsibility. The top section of the income statement contains the revenue, payroll and related costs, other direct expenses, and departmental income of the rooms department and indicates departmental income of $605,000 for 19X2. The second section reflects the operations of the food and beverage department. The top portion of the income statement down to

Figure 1.1   Balance sheets

Balance sheets
Mayfair Hotel
December 31, 19X0, 19X1, 19X2

Assets	19X0	19X1	19X2
Current assets:			
Cash	$ 17,000	$ 18,000	$ 21,000
Marketable securities	81,000	81,000	81,000
Accounts receivable (net)	100,000	90,000	140,000
Inventories	17,000	20,000	18,000
Prepaid expenses	13,000	12,000	14,000
Total current assets	228,000	221,000	274,000
Investments	22,000	35,000	104,000
Property and equipment:			
Land	78,500	78,500	78,500
Buildings	800,000	840,000	870,000
Furniture and equipment	170,000	170,000	172,000
	1,048,500	1,088,500	1,120,500
Less:			
Accumulated depreciation	260,000	300,000	345,000
China, glassware, silver, linen, and uniforms	11,500	20,500	22,800
Total property and equipment	800,000	809,000	798,300
Total assets	$1,050,000	$1,065,000	$1,176,300
Liabilities and owners' equity			
Current liabilities:			
Accounts payable	$ 60,000	$ 53,500	$ 71,000
Accrued income taxes	30,000	32,000	34,000
Accrued expenses	70,000	85,200	85,000
Current portion of long-term debt	25,000	21,500	24,000
Total current liabilities	185,000	192,200	214,000
Long-term debt:			
Mortgage payable	375,000	375,000	400,000
Deferred income taxes	40,000	42,800	45,000
Total long-term debt	415,000	417,800	445,000
Total liabilities	600,000	610,000	659,000
Owners' equity:			
Common stock	55,000	55,000	55,000
Paid-in capital in excess of par	110,000	110,000	110,000
Retained earnings	285,000	290,000	352,300
Total owners' equity	450,000	455,000	517,300
Total liabilities and owners' equity	$1,050,000	$1,065,000	$1,176,300

Figure 1.2   Income statements

Income statements
Mayfair Hotel
For the years ended December 31, 19X1 and 19X2

	19X1	19X2
Total revenues	$1,300,000	$1,352,000
Rooms:		
Revenue	$ 780,000	$ 810,000
Payroll and related costs	135,000	145,000
Other direct expenses	62,500	60,000
Departmental income	582,500	605,000
Food and beverages:		
Revenue	430,000	445,000
Cost of sales	142,000	148,000
Payroll and related costs	175,000	180,000
Other direct expenses	43,400	45,000
Departmental income	69,600	72,000
Telephone:		
Revenue	40,000	42,000
Cost of sales	30,000	31,000
Payroll and related costs	10,000	10,500
Other direct expenses	5,000	4,500
Departmental income	(5,000)	(4,000)
Rentals and other income	50,000	55,000
Total operated departments income	697,100	728,000
Undistributed operating expenses:		
Administrative & general	105,000	108,500
Marketing	51,500	55,000
Property operation & maintenance	65,250	67,500
Energy costs	80,250	81,500
Total undistributed operating expenses	302,000	312,500
Income before fixed charges and management fees	395,100	415,500
Management fees	65,000	66,000
Rent	20,000	20,000
Property taxes	20,000	24,000
Insurance	5,500	6,000
Interest	54,000	60,000
Depreciation	60,000	61,000
Income before income taxes	170,600	178,500
Income taxes	51,180	53,550
Net income	$ 119,420	$ 124,950

'total operated departments income' reflects activities of the profit centres, that is areas of activity that generate revenue and incur expenses resulting in profit (labelled as income in this illustration).

The next section of the income statement contains the operating overhead expenses and is labelled 'undistributed operating expenses.' This section is often divided into four lines including administrative and general, marketing, property operation and maintenance, and energy costs. Additional lines are provided for human resources, data processing, guest transportation, and entertainment for large hotels which have separate departments for these areas of responsibility. In general, these areas of responsibility are referred to as service centres since their objective is to provide services to other departments of the hotel. A detailed schedule is generally prepared for each profit and service centre and should contain sufficient detail to allow the department head to monitor expenses and revenues properly, if any, of their department.

The difference between income from the profit centres and the undistributed operating expenses is 'income before fixed charges and management fees' (sometimes referred to as gross operating profit – GOP). Expenses subtracted from this figure are based for the most part on decisions of the board of directors rather than management. The board decides whether to use a management company or hire managers as employees. The board determines the size of the hotel and its equipment which will be depreciated and how it is financed, which results in interest expense when funds are borrowed. Other fixed charges, such as fire insurance and property taxes, relate to the property and equipment. Thus, fixed charges are often referred to as capacity overhead. Income taxes based on income before taxes are subtracted to determine the hotel's bottom line.

The income statement illustrated in this chapter is prepared for internal purposes, that is, to be used by the general manager and department heads.[2] A much more abbreviated statement is prepared for outsiders such as creditors and even stockholders. The income statement is a dynamic statement as it covers a period of time. In relation to the balance sheet, the results of operations are recorded as a change in owners' equity on the balance sheet at the end of the accounting period.

The third and final statement to be discussed is the statement of cash flows. This statement reflects the cash flows of the hotel company for a period of time. The three major sections of this statement reflect cash flows from operating, investing and financing activities. The statement of cash flows is illustrated in Figure 1.3, again using the hypothetical Mayfair Hotel. The operating activities show the reconciliation of net income for the accounting period to cash flows from operations. The first item shown in this section is net income followed by items to determine cash flow from operations such as depreciation and so on. The net cash flow from operating activities for 19X2 is $157,450.

Figure 1.3   Statement of cash flow

Statement of cash flow
Mayfair Hotel
December 31, 19X1 and 19X2

	19X1	19X2
Net cash flow from operating activities		
Net income	$ 119,420	$ 124,950
Non-cash expenses included in income:		
Depreciation	60,000	61,000
Deferred income taxes	2,800	2,200
Changes in non-cash current accounts:		
Accounts receivable	10,000	(50,000)
Inventories	(3,000)	2,000
Prepaid expenses	1,000	(2,000)
Accounts payable	(6,500)	17,500
Accrued income taxes	2,000	2,000
Accrued expenses	15,200	(200)
Net cash flow from operating activities	200,920	157,450
Net cash flow from investing activities:		
Purchase of property and equipment	(69,000)	(50,300)
Purchase of investments	(13,000)	(69,000)
Net cash flow from investing activities	(82,000)	(119,300)
Net cash flow from financing activities:		
Dividends paid	(114,420)	(62,650)
Proceeds from long-term debt	21,500	49,000
Payment of long-term debt	(25,000)	(21,500)
Net cash flow from financing activities	(117,920)	(35,150)
Net increase in cash	1,000	3,000
Cash – beginning of year	17,000	18,000
Cash – end of year	$ 18,000	$ 21,000

The investing activities of a hotel company generally include both the sale and purchase of investments and property and equipment. The Mayfair had limited investing activities during 19X1 and 19X2 as it did not sell any investments or property and equipment. It did make purchases in each year, including $119,300 during 19X2.

The financing activities section of this statement reflects receipt and disbursements of funds related to long-term debt and equity financing. The net cash outflow for the Mayfair was $35,150 for 19X2.

The change in cash for the period as shown on the statement of cash flows of $3,000 for 19X2 for the Mayfair Hotel is the difference between cash at the beginning of 19X2 ($18,000) and the end of 19X2 ($21,000), as reflected on the balance sheets of the Mayfair Hotel.

Analysis of financial statements

The financial statements contain considerable information. However, to reduce them to a few meaningful numbers, ratios are used. Ratios are simply a comparison of two numbers to yield a result. For example, the division of current assets by current liabilities results in a ratio called the current ratio.

Financial ratios are generally classified into five categories as follows:

- Liquidity.
- Solvency.
- Activity.
- Profitability.
- Operating.

Each class of ratios allows the analyst to determine the 'success' in some way of the hotel. Liquidity ratios measure a hotel's ability to pay its bills as they become due and the most commonly calculated liquidity ratio is the current ratio, mentioned above.

The solvency ratios measure the hotel's ability to pay its bills in the long run. This class of ratios includes ratios based on balance sheet numbers, such as the debt–equity ratio and ratios based on the income statement such as the fixed-charge coverage ratio. These ratios will be explained later.

The activity ratios measure management's use of the hotel's assets. Two common activity ratios are the paid occupancy percentage and property and equipment turnover. Paid occupancy compares the number of rooms sold for the period to the number of rooms available. It is not a financial ratio; however, it is calculated on a daily basis by most hoteliers as an indicator of room sales success. The property and equipment turnover ratio compares revenue of the hotel from the income statement, to the property and equipment of the hotel as shown on the balance sheet.

The profitability ratios, most meaningful to owners, show the hotel company's ability to generate profits. Since this is one of the major objectives of most hotels these ratios are generally the most frequently calculated for owners. Profitability ratios to be discussed in greater detail in this chapter include profit margin, earnings per share and return on owners' equity.

The final class of ratios are the operating ratios, which reflect the results of operations. These measures of success are used most frequently by management and include the average daily rate (ADR), cost of labour percentage, cost of food percentage and operating efficiency ratio. A combination of the paid occupancy percentage and the ADR is revpar (see section on operating ratios, below). All these operating ratios will be discussed and their calculation illustrated in this chapter.

Perceptions of US lodging industry general managers and financial executives have been measured regarding the usefulness of financial ratios (Schmidgall, 1988, 1989). Members of each group through a mail survey were asked to reflect their perceptions of various users regarding the usefulness of ratios. The users included general managers, corporate (office) executives, owners and bankers. The overall results were as follows:

Both GMs and financial executives perceive the following:

- GMs find operating and activity ratios more useful than other user groups.
- Owners find profitability ratios more useful than other users.
- Corporate executives find liquidity ratios more useful than other user groups.

In regard to solvency ratios, the perceptions of GMs and financial executives differed. Financial executives believe bankers find this group of ratios most useful, while GMs perceive that owners find solvency ratios more useful than other groups.

Another way to view the results of this research is which class of ratios is perceived as most useful to each of the four user groups. The two separate research surveys of GMs and lodging financial executives yielded the same results, as follows:

- GMs find operating ratios to be the most useful class of ratios.
- Corporate executives place the most importance on profitability ratios.
- Bankers find solvency ratios to be the most useful class of ratios.
- Owners find profitability ratios to be most useful.

The most useful ratios from each class of ratios as perceived by these respondents will be briefly described, including the formula for each and the ratio will be calculated using information for the hypothetical Mayfair Hotel.

Liquidity ratios

The current ratio measures the ability of a hotel company to pay its bills in the short term and is determined by dividing current assets by current liabilities.

Both numbers come from the balance sheet, thus this ratio reflects the hotel's ability to pay its bills at a point in time.

For the Mayfair Hotel the current ratio of 19X2 was 1.28:1. This ratio should be compared to ratios for prior periods and also to the hotel's plan. The current ratio for 19X1 was 1.15:1; thus, the current ratio has increased, which suggests that the Mayfair has greater liquidity at the end of 19X2 than 19X1.

Another liquidity ratio of note is the operating cash flows to current liabilities ratio. The operating cash flow is shown on the statement of cash flows. This liquidity ratio may be preferred to the current ratio since it uses figures covering a period of time and includes a cash flow number. Bills are paid as they come due with cash rather than simply current assets, which is used in the current ratio. For the Mayfair Hotel this ratio is 77.5 per cent for 19X2 and 106.5 per cent for 19X1. The ratio is determined by using an average for current liabilities. The change reflects a reduced ability in 19X2 to pay bills as they become due compared to 19X1. This result contradicts the change suggested by the current ratio. Even so, the ratio for both years is relatively high so users should have little concern regarding Mayfair's liquidity.

Solvency ratios

A major solvency ratio is the debt–equity ratio. This ratio is computed by simply dividing total liabilities by total owners' equity. Both figures come from the balance sheet so, like the current ratio, this ratio is determined at a point in time. This ratio reflects the capital structure of the firm by revealing the ratio of debt to owners' equity. In essence, it shows the amount of debt for each dollar of equity.

For the Mayfair Hotel, the debt–equity ratio was 1.27:1 for 19X2 compared to 1.34:1 for 19X1. This reflects a decrease in debt relative to equity and suggests the Mayfair is slightly less risky as an investment.

A second solvency ratio which users of financial statements find useful is the fixed-charge coverage ratio. This ratio is a measure of solvency from the income statement perspective. The fixed-charge coverage ratio is computed by dividing earnings before interest, depreciation and lease expense (lease expense is often referred to simply as rent in the income statement) by the sum of interest and lease expenses. It reveals the number of times interest and lease expenses could be paid by a hotel company. For the Mayfair Hotel the fixed-charge coverage ratio was 3.99 times for 19X2 and 4.12 times for 19X1. This difference reflects a slightly reduced ability of the Mayfair to pay its lease and interest expenses in 19X2 compared to 19X1. So from a balance sheet perspective, the Mayfair's solvency position as revealed by the debt–equity ratio is slightly improved in 19X2 over 19X1 and the reverse is the case from the income statement perspective.

Activity ratios

Two activity ratios are suggested for determining operating performance of a hotel. First, the paid occupancy percentage is determined by dividing the number of rooms sold by rooms available. This seems straightforward until one considers the number for the denominator of the ratio. Which rooms are available? Are out-of-order rooms, complimentary rooms and rooms under renovation considered to be available? Many hotel companies calculate this ratio differently from each other. Probably the most important consideration is that the approach used should be followed consistently and the user should compare the results to the standard calculated in the same way.

Figure 1.4   Mayfair Hotel - other information

Other information

	19X1	19X2
Rooms sold	20,500	21,000
Shares of common stock outstanding	55,000	55,000
Food covers	55,500	56,000

Figure 1.4 contains information in addition to the financial statements of the Mayfair Hotel. It is assumed that 80 rooms on the average were available each day for the Mayfair. Therefore, 29 200 rooms were available for sale during 19X1 and 19X2 based on 365 days in each year.

The paid occupancy percentages for the Mayfair for 19X2 and 19X1 were 71.92 and 70.2 per cent, respectively. The increase in 19X2 over 19X1 suggests better utilization of the hotel's guest rooms. However, a note of caution is sounded as paid occupancy percentage only reflects rooms sold. Management should obtain a reasonable rate and still control expenses for the hotel to be successful!

The property and equipment turnover ratio compares the revenue generated by the hotel to the average amount of property and equipment of the hotel. Generally, the higher the turnover, the better the utilization of the property and equipment. The average is calculated simply by adding the beginning and ending amounts of property and equipment, net of depreciation, and dividing by two. For the Mayfair Hotel, the property and equipment turnovers were 1.22 times for both 19X2 and 19X2. A variation of this ratio is to use average total assets. This measure determines management's ability to use all of the assets in generating revenues.

Profitability ratios

Profits are a major objective of virtually all hotel companies. However, the bottom line by itself is somewhat meaningless. Comparing it to related numbers results in more meaningful information. The three profitability ratios suggested are profit margin, earnings per share and return on owners' equity.

Profit margin is determined by dividing net income by total revenues. This ratio simply reflects the percentage of net income compared to revenue.

Revenues are crucial; however, the bottom line reflects management's ability also to control expenses. For the Mayfair Hotel the profit margin was 9.24 per cent in 19X2 and 9.19 per cent in 19X1. Thus, the profit margin increased slightly from 19X1 to 19X2.

Earnings per share (EPS) are determined by dividing net income by the average number of shares of common stock outstanding during the accounting period. If a hotel company has other types of capital stock, such as preferred stock, the net income figure must be adjusted to reflect dividend payments to preferred stockholders. In the illustration used throughout this chapter, we assume the Mayfair Hotel has issued only common stock and that the average number of shares outstanding during 19X1 and 19X2 equal 55,000, as shown in Figure 1.4. Therefore, the EPS was $2.27 and $2.17, for 19X2 and 19X1, respectively. This increase of $0.10 is welcomed both by management and especially by the owners. Owners may desire to compare the EPS to the market price of their stock to determine the ratio of the two. Certainly, to the extent increased earnings lead to increased dividends and/or increased market price of their stock, owners are pleased and management will appear to be satisfying the owners!

The final profitability ratio to be discussed is the return on owners' equity (ROE). This ratio uses net income from the income statement and owners' equity from the balance sheet. Since a flow figure is used from the income statement, the average of owners' equity must be used and, like the average for property and equipment, it is determined simply by summing the beginning and ending of the appropriate account(s) (in this case the balances of owners' equity) and dividing the sum by two.

For the Mayfair Hotel, the ROE for 19X2 and 19X1 was 25.70 per cent and 26.39 per cent, respectively. This reflects a minor decrease, but both ratios are relatively high. A note of caution needs to be sounded for this ratio. The ROE for a hotel company may be higher than what an individual investor would achieve by owning the stock of this company. This is the case when the market value of a share of stock at which the investor purchased the stock exceeds the book value of a share of stock as reflected on the books of the hotel company. Thus, the value of the ratio is tempered by this reality.

Operating ratios

Since Chapter 3 of this book is devoted to operational analysis, only five measures of hotel operations are briefly discussed and illustrated. The five ratios are the ADR, revpar, cost of labour percentage, cost of food percentage and the operating efficiency ratio.

The ADR simply reflects the average price a hotel room is sold for. Generally, a hotel determines the ADR across all types of guest rooms sold inclusive of singles, doubles, suites, and so on. The ADR is determined by dividing room revenue by the number of rooms sold.

The Mayfair Hotel's ADR for 19X2 and 19X1, based on the information in Figures 1.2 and 1.4, were $38.57 and $38.05, respectively. These results reflect an increase of $0.52 in the ADR. As with all ratios, especially operating ratios how does this compare to the plan? A $0.52 increase is excellent if only an amount somewhat below $0.52, such as $0.40 increase was planned; however, $0.52 is poor compared to a planned increase somewhat in excess of $0.52, such as $1.00.

A combination of the ADR and the paid occupancy percentage is revenue per available room or simply revpar. This single ratio overcomes the weaknesses of using the ADR and paid occupancy percentage individually. A hotel may have a high paid occupancy percentage by sacrificing rate or a high ADR by sacrificing occupancy. Revpar is determined either by multiplying the paid occupancy percentage by ADR or by dividing room revenues by the number of available rooms. The revpar for the Mayfair Hotel was $27.74 for 19X2 and $26.71 for 19X1. The increase in revpar was by $1.03 or 3.86 per cent of the revpar for 19X1.

Often the largest expense of a hotel company is payroll and related costs including payroll taxes and fringe benefits. Therefore, the ability to control labour is often key to managing successful hotel operations.

As a control technique, this ratio should not only be determined for the entire hotel but for each profit centre. The labour cost percentage is calculated for the operation as a whole by dividing the total labour costs by total revenues.

The Mayfair Hotel's cost of labour percentage for 19X1 and 19X2 is calculated for the rooms department only for illustration purposes. The rooms labour cost percentage was 17.9 per cent for 19X2 and 17.3 per cent for 19X1. Thus, the labour costs of this department have increased relative to room revenues. Management should also compare these results to the targeted room department labour costs, as reflected in the operating budget for each year.

The cost of food expense is often one of the major expenses of a food operation; therefore, management must exercise maximum care to control this expense. A common approach is to monitor the cost of food sold by comparing it to food revenue, resulting in the cost of food sold percentage.

The cost of food sold percentage for the Mayfair Hotel was 33.26 per cent in 19X2 and 33.02 per cent in 19X1, resulting in an increase of 0.24 percentage points. As with other operating ratios, the cost of food sold percentage must be compared with the budgeted figure. However, management must be careful not to overemphasize this ratio. Even though a low cost of food sold percentage is desirable, it should not be pursued to the extent of curbing gross profits from food operations.

Briefly, consider two extremes. Assume that a foodservice operator can sell spaghetti for $6.00 a meal with a related food cost of $2.00, resulting in a cost of food percentage of 33.3 per cent. Alternatively, consider that this same food service operator could sell steak with all the works for $15.00 and a related food costs of $7.50. The cost of food percentage for this entrée would be 50 per cent. If only one meal is sold, which is preferred? If all other costs are the same, the steak should be sold even though the cost of food percentage is 50 per cent for the steak compared to 33.3 per cent for spaghetti. Why then sell steak? Simply put, the steak provides gross profit (sales–cost of sales) of $7.50 compared to a gross profit of $4.00 for spaghetti![3]

Finally, the operating efficiency ratio should be computed as a measure of the overall performance of unit-level management. Earlier in the chapter, where the details of the income statement were presented, it was noted that expenses following 'income before fixed charges and management fees' were the primary responsibility of the board of directors as the expenses following this figure related to decisions of the board. All revenues and expenses above this number are considered to be hotel management's responsibility.

Therefore, the operating efficiency ratio is computed by dividing income before fixed charges and management fees by total revenue. The results suggest the percentage of each revenue dollar that is available to cover management fees, fixed charges, income taxes and to yield a profit.

For the Mayfair Hotel, the operating efficiency ratio was 30.73 per cent and 30.39 per cent for 19X2 and 19X1, respectively. The increase of 0.34 percentage points suggests that overall management has marginally improved the efficiency of the hotel.

Limitations

The ratios suggested to measure success of the hotel operation and to be used for control purposes have limited usefulness in themselves. They should always be compared to a standard. The ideal standard is the plan (budget) for the accounting period. Other comparisons may be made to previous periods and hotel industry averages. Care should be used when interpreting a comparison to hotel industry averages as the industry figures are simply averages, not standards or ideals.

The ratios are merely indicators and management when using ratios for control purposes must take corrective action to guide the hotel company to the desired result when the ratio differs from the standard.

The user of ratios must be careful when using ratios to compare the activities of two or more companies. Accounting procedures may differ between the companies resulting in different figures by themselves. In addition, the mix of activities of each operation may be different. For example, in the USA the operating activities of the Marriott Corporation differ dramatically from Hilton Hotels Corporation. Hilton relies to a large extent on casino operations while Marriott has no gaming operations. The difference in activities results in differences in resources and thus many ratios.

Finally, ratios are often computed using historical figures. These figures are based on generally accepted accounting principles (GAAP) which do not purport to show market values. Thus, the results depending on the differences between recorded values per GAAP and market values may be significant.

The key word when using ratios is caution. Use the ratios carefully to measure the success of the hotel company!

Summary

The overall objective of a hotel company is to satisfy the desires of its stakeholders. In order to meet these desires a firm must generate profits. The operating activities, the resources and claims against resources, and the cash flows of the hotel company are reflected in financial statements which serve as scoreboards to indicate how the hotel company is performing. These statements contain large amounts of financial information which are analysed to determine the extent of success. The comparison of related numbers yielding a single number is the essence of ratio analysis.

Figure 1.5 List of ratios

Current ratio	=	$\dfrac{\text{Current assets}}{\text{Current liabilities}}$
Operating cash flows to current liabilities	=	$\dfrac{\text{Operating cash flows}}{\text{Average current liabilities}}$
Debt-equity ratio	=	$\dfrac{\text{Total debt}}{\text{Owners' equity}}$
Fixed-charge coverage ratio	=	$\dfrac{\text{Earnings before interest, depreciation and lease expenses}}{\text{Interest and lease expenses}}$
Paid occupancy percentage	=	$\dfrac{\text{Rooms sold}}{\text{Rooms available}}$
Property and equipment turnover	=	$\dfrac{\text{Total revenues}}{\text{Average property and equipment}}$
Profit margin	=	$\dfrac{\text{Net income}}{\text{Total revenues}}$
Earnings per share	=	$\dfrac{\text{Net income}}{\text{Average common shares outstanding}}$
Return on owners' equity	=	$\dfrac{\text{Net income}}{\text{Average owners' equity}}$
Average daily rate (ADR)	=	$\dfrac{\text{Room revenues}}{\text{Number of rooms sold}}$
REVPAR	=	Paid occupancy percentage x ADR
Cost of labour percentage	=	$\dfrac{\text{Payroll and related costs}}{\text{Total revenue}}$
Cost of food sold percentage	=	$\dfrac{\text{Cost of food sold}}{\text{Food revenue}}$
Operating efficiency ratio	=	$\dfrac{\text{Income before fixed charges and management fees}}{\text{Total revenues}}$

Ratios may be classified into the five categories of liquidity, solvency, activity, profitability and operating. Different users of financial information favour various classes of ratios which relate to their desires. For example, the owners place the highest preference on profitability ratios.

The ratios discussed in this chapter are considered to be the most useful; however, there are numerous ratios which can be used to analyse financial statements of a hotel company. Each ratio explains a small part of a hotel company's performance and may be helpful to some user, yet realistically most users resort to a few key ratios to gain an overview of the hotel company's performance.

The hypothetical Mayfair Hotel has been used to illustrate ratio analysis. Its performance is shown in Figures 1.1–1.4. Figure 1.5 is a listing of the ratios discussed in this chapter.

Understanding financial statements is a challenge and the author offers this chapter only as a starting point on the road to the quest!

Endnotes

1   Generally accepted accounting principles are discussed in detail in most elementary accounting textbooks. For further discussion, consider, Schmidgall R. S. and Damitio, J. W. (1994) *Hospitality Industry Financial Accounting*. East Lansing, MI. Educational Institute of the American Hotel and Motel Association.
2   The income statement prepared for internal uses is based on the *Uniform System of Accounts for Small Hotels, Motels, and Motor Hotels* (1987), 4th edn, published by The Educational Institute of The American Hotel and Motel Association, East Lansing, MI.
3   This concept of emphasizing gross profit rather than food cost percentage is covered in detail by M.L. Kasavana and D. Smith (1990) in their book, *Menu Engineering* (revised edn) published by Hospitality Publications, Inc., Okemos, Michigan, USA.

References

Schmidgall, R. S. (1988), How useful are financial ratios? *The Bottom Line*, June/July, **3**(3):1988, 24–27.

Schmidgall, R. S. (1989) Financial ratios: perceptions of lodging industry general managers and financial executives, *FIU Hospitality Review*, Fall, **7**, 1–9.

2 Methods for predicting financial failure in the hotel industry

Debra J. Adams

Introduction

The accurate measurement and interpretation of business performance are vital for ensuring success in all forms of organization. It is essential for the manager to know what has happened, why it has happened and what can be done to improve future performance. In practice, the focus of performance measurement is often centred on the traditional approach, where easily quantifiable aspects of performance, such as the relationships between measurable quantities, are compared with previous performance, budgeted values or standard benchmarks. More recently, several service-oriented businesses have found that, in addition to the traditional accounting measures such as profitability and return on investment, a range of non-financial measures can provide valuable information about, for example, the level of competitive success of the business. Consequently, measures for intangible aspects such as quality levels and degrees of flexibility are often used alongside the more familiar measures. This package of measures provides the business manager with a set of reasonable tools for successfully controlling the business. The combined use of these measures is discussed in more detail later in the chapter.

It is not only those parties within the organization who are interested in assessing the current performance and future potential of a particular business. The annual report, published by companies to meet the requirements of the Companies Act, forms an important part of the information available to parties external to the company interested in an individual company's performance. These parties include shareholders, both actual and prospective, loan creditors, debenture holders and trade creditors. The published financial statements can be supported by other sources of information, for example, investment reports published by leading brokers, computerized databases such as MicroView Exstat (Extel Financial Ltd.) and intrafirm comparisons produced annually by consultants. The potential investor is likely to wish to know if the company is high risk and whether additional funds could be lent with reasonable safety and if an adequate or good return can be expected. Normally the investor wishes to avoid a company where funds are required simply to ensure survival.

In summary, the key issues from the potential investors' point of view are short-term liquidity and solvency, efficiency and profitability (discussed in Chapter 1), actual growth and future potential. The UK hospitality industry is currently dominated by the restructuring and realignment of its key players as those who have survived the recession reposition themselves in the re-emerging markets. Others have been less successful, with the factors which are often cited as the cause of failure in the industry being the very characteristics by which the industry is typified. In many sectors of the industry, in order to launch and maintain the business, considerable levels of investment are required, resulting in high fixed costs, such as maintenance, energy and depreciation, producing a high break-even point. The levels of profit to be made are often significant once the break-even point has been cleared, although marginal costs such as material and labour can escalate rapidly if left uncontrolled.

The 1980s were, for the most part, a boom time for hotel operators with rapid expansion resulting in a substantial increase in the number of rooms in the market place. This period of growth was fuelled by the need for the large chains to maintain competitive advantage and by the provision of a suitable environment for growth. This has been followed by a period of severe recession with rapidly falling customer volumes and room rates: many firms have been forced into consolidation, a process typified by organizational restructuring, sell-offs, the growth of the management contract and a review of balance sheet financing. At any time, but particularly in a period of recession, managers need to concentrate on monitoring activities carefully in order to identify those areas of the business which may be candidates for failure in the future.

This chapter investigates the research which has been carried out on performance measurement in hotels and leisure operations. Both financial and non-financial measures of performance will be considered in some detail, but essentially the chapter will focus on whether financial analysis, in particular combined ratio analysis, based on published company accounts, can be used to predict the likelihood of business demise or even failure.

Terms of reference

Before an analysis of the success of corporate appraisal techniques can take place, it is necessary to define what is meant by the term corporate failure. The definition of failure can be rather ambiguous; to some it means a situation known as technical insolvency, where a firm is unable to meet its maturing obligations such as long-term loans and other deferred liabilities. Others restrict the term to the condition where the total value of the firm's assets is smaller than its liabilities. However, a firm can be temporarily insolvent yet continue to operate for a limited period, during which time it may recover following further investment. Alternatively, business failure may be interpreted in the legal sense of bankruptcy or liquidation where the firm is forced to cease trading by its bankers or creditors. For the purposes of this chapter failure is interpreted as constituting severe financial difficulties which have become obvious through forced liquidation or suspension of stock market trading followed by a takeover or forced acquisition.

It is also important to consider how the effectiveness of any technique for predicting corporate demise can be measured. In order to be of practical and reliable value to the investor, the measure should be considered in terms of the accuracy of the method over a large sample and the size of the 'grey area' – the area in which both success and failure are likely. It is also important to consider the size of the lead time, that is, the time between predicting problems and failure actually occurring. Clearly, the longer the time prior to failure, the more useful the technique. Many analysts believe that the signs of possible failure can be detected fairly early, possibly up to four years before failure, and, if these indications are dealt with, disaster may be averted. This correcting action, however, creates problems for research in this area where it can only be possible to classify clear success and obvious failure. Despite these difficulties a multitude of studies have concluded that performance measurement, particularly that based on financial analysis, can correctly predict success or failure with considerable accuracy.

Non-financial measures of performance

There are a range of non-financial measures appropriate to service industries, both quantitative and qualitative, which may be used as part of a control process where actual results are compared to plans, budgets, standards and targets. In the last 50 years experts in management have attempted to identify performance criteria to cover all aspects of business performance. Drucker (1953) identified seven generic criteria set by organizations for each performance area and these should be supported by appropriate measures to monitor and control performance against objectives. More recently, Sink (1985) developed Drucker's framework and redefined his own set of performance criteria: profitability, effectiveness, productivity, efficiency, quality, delivery performance, innovation and flexibility. The work of Fitzgerald *et al.* (1991) has focused specifically on service firms classifying the operation along a continuum based on numbers of customers processed per day and the level of services received by those customers. The research is based on operations drawn from this classification and has produced six dimensions against which measurement of business performance can take place. The research also suggests that every service organization needs to develop its own set of performance measures to help gain and retain competitive advantage. The six dimensions are summarized in Table 2.1.

Table 2.1   Business performance criteria

Financial performance
Profitability
Liquidity
Capital structure
Market ratios

Competitiveness
Relative market share and position
Sales growth
Measures of the customer base

Resource utilization
Productivity (input : output)
Efficiency (resources planned : consumed)
Utilization (resources available : consumed)

Quality of service
Overall service indicators
Measures of the twelve determinants of service quality: reliability, responsiveness, aesthetics, cleanliness, comfort, friendliness, communication, courtesy, competence, access, availability, security

Innovation
Proportion of new to old products and services
New products and service sales levels

Flexibility
Product/service introduction flexibility
Product/service mix flexibility
Volume flexibility
Delivery flexibility

The extent to which this comprehensive range of measures may be used will depend on the nature of the service business. Fitzgerald *et al.* included in their research a review of the performance measures used in a major international middle-range hotel chain. The following guidelines have been adapted from their work to illustrate how a range of a measures may be used to assess performance in a quality hotel operation (Table 2.2).

Table 2.2 Business performance criteria for a hotel operation

Financial performance

Profit and loss account	Weekly/monthly report to management team. Costs and revenue broken down by department
Average spends	Accommodation, food, beverage
Budget variance analysis	Each month general managers have to submit with their profit and loss account explanations for the largest variances
Breakdown of pay-roll costs, days absence, overtime etc	Reported by each hotel every week
Working capital measures	Debtors, creditors, stock, cash holdings

Measures of competitiveness

Market share (number of rooms occupied out of total number of rooms available in the local market)	Weekly/monthly report to management team
Number and percentage of rooms occupied for each of the top six local competitors	Weekly/monthly report to management team.
Average room rates charged by top six local competitors	Weekly/monthly report to management team
Number of rooms sold by customer type	Weekly/monthly report to management team
Customer loyalty: number of repeat bookings	Data available from computerized reservations

Resource utilization

Percentage of rooms occupied out of total rooms available

Percentage of beds occupied out of total beds available

Food and beverage sales per staying guest

Table 2.2   *continued*

Service quality measures

Customer satisfaction with overall service levels	Guest questionnaires with data compiled into statistics
Likelihood of repeat custom	Guest questionnaires
Staff turnover by avoidable/unavoidable reasons for transfer	Monthly report to management committee
Number of training days per employee	
Complaints per 1000 customers	

Innovation measures

Average age of menus

Flexibility measures

Average time to respond to a customer's request	Relevant in various areas

---

These measures can be used successfully by the managers within the business to monitor performance, but interested parties outside the business are limited to the use of published data and the subsequent financial measures which can be calculated from these data.

Financial measures of performance

Financial techniques may be separated into two approaches, the most common being that of single ratio analysis, sometimes referred to as univariate analysis. This technique is based on the calculation of individual ratios using data from the trading accounts and the balance sheet. These ratios may then be used for comparison with previous trends, budget or with other similar operations. A second approach is a technique known as multidiscriminant analysis (MDA) or Z-scoring. This technique has attracted much attention in accounting circles in recent years. The methodology is based on a series of traditional ratios such as return on investment and working capital measures, and combines them to produce a single weighted statistic. This statistic may then be used within specific guidelines to assess the potential for success or failure for individual companies. The method was initially devised to overcome the key problem associated with single ratios where some ratios sometimes move in the opposite direction to all the others, thus making interpretation difficult. The usage of MDA models will be considered later in the chapter.

Univariate analysis

The traditional use of these ratios is by grouping the measures into four categories. These are profitability and operating relationships, debt and gearing, liquidity (control of cash and other working capital items) and shareholders investment ratios. The constituent ratios for each of these groupings are shown in more detail in Table 2.3. Each of these classifications will be considered in turn.

Table 2.3 Financial ratios for measuring performance

Profitability and operating ratios

Return on assets
Return on equity
Number of times interest earned
Net return on assets
Net profit to revenue

Debt and gearing ratios

Debt ratio - total debts in relation to total assets
Interest cover

Liquidity ratios

Current ratio
Acid test ratio
Accounts receivable/payable ratios
Stock turn
Working capital cycles

Shareholders' investment ratios

Return on shareholders' capital
Earnings per share
Price/earnings ratio
Dividend yield

Profitability

In theory a firm may continue to operate with poor profitability as long as shareholders are compensated with a high return for undertaking greater risk. In practice failure due to cash flow difficulties is more likely. However, research has proved that business failure can be linked to low or declining profits.

Gearing

A firm may be relatively liquid in the short term but be susceptible to risk from reliance on long-term debt. Studies have shown that the greater the use of gearing, the less flexible the firm may be when faced with sudden changes in profitability or market conditions, and that dependence on debt increases as the firm draws closer to failure.

Liquidity

The capacity of a business to meet its financial obligations as they become due is normally termed as liquidity. Studies using this group of ratios show that substantial differences exist between the ratios of failing and surviving companies. In particular, general studies in the USA have shown that the current ratio is a significant indicator of financial difficulties. Many of these standard ratios are used throughout many types of industry where benchmarks and guidelines for ratios are commonly cited. However, care should be taken as the resulting values can vary considerably from one industry to another. For example, a standard for the current ratio for the measurement of liquidity is often quoted as 1.5–1, that is, ensuring that current liabilities are covered at least 1.5 times by current assets. However, companies in the hospitality sector have survived with ratios which are considerably less than 1. The leisure sector in particular is typical, where sales are predominantly made for cash, stocks and cash holdings are kept at minimal levels and purchases are bought on credit. A set of ratios for selected hotel and leisure companies are shown in Figures 2.1 and 2.2.

Figure 2.1   Ratio performances of selected leisure companies

Company	Year							
	1986	1987	1988	1989	1990	1991	1992	1993
Return on equity (%)								
Allied Leisure		44.8	23.5	13.2	13.4	7.8	(4.4)	5.8
Edencorp Leisur				9.9				
European Leisure				10.0	6.2	7.9	(164.0)	0.7
First Leisure	15.8	12.5	13.7	16.1	9.4	9.5	9.1	10.1
Leading Leisure	12.8	9.2	17.0	13.2				
Stanley Leisure	27.2	25.8	8.5	6.2	7.1	6.3	6.4	6.1
Net profit margin (%)								
Allied Leisure				11.8	23.0	27.2	2.0	19.1
Edencorp Leisure								
European Leisure				19.2	29.0	15.3	(62.4)	11.9
First Leisure				32.0	34.8	32.7	32.6	29.4
Leading Leisure								
Stanley Leisure				5.4	7.0	5.9	5.7	5.3
Current ratio								
Allied Leisure		0.44	0.35	0.36	0.65	0.85	0.36	0.62
Edencorp Leisure				1.68				
European Leisure				0.49	0.73	1.05	0.22	0.11
First Leisure	0.31	0.31	0.43	0.24	0.45	0.46	0.48	0.48
Leading Leisure	0.81	1.00	0.94	0.38				
Stanley Leisure	0.67	0.66	0.42	0.40	0.59	0.70	0.66	0.47
Total debt/net assets (book) %								
Allied Leisure		77.0	77.6	55.1	45.1	27.4	36.7	26.5
Edencorp Leisure				24.5				
European Leisure				37.9	41.1	48.6	67.1	68.0
First Leisure	16.1	11.0	18.2	25.6	15.2	14.4	14.0	15.2
Leading Leisure	49.8	58.3	64.3	62.6				
Stanley Leisure	4.4	18.0	7.7	13.7	26.0	29.0	28.6	28.2

Source: MicroView Exstat (Extel Financial Ltd)

Figure 2.2 Ratio performances of selected hotel companies

Company	Year 1986	1987	1988	1989	1990	1991	1992	1993
Return on equity %								
Friendly Hotels Plc			6.4	6.8	7.2	4.3	3.3	3.3
Queens Moat Houses Plc	4.3	4.3	5.2	5.2	6.6	(5.8)		(269.3)
Regal Hotel Group		26.3	29.7	(14.3)	(195.5)	(116.2)	(164.8)	
Resort Hotels Plc		6.1	6.2	5.1	8.1	8.2	6.9	(317.4)
Net profit margin %								
Friendly Hotels Plc			18.5	22.0	24.2	17.7	13.8	
Queens Moat Houses Plc			24.4	24.3	30.0	10.5	(235.2)	
Regal Hotel Group				(13.7)	(167.4)	(97.5)	(17.4)	
Resort Hotels Plc				38.0	41.7	48.8	39.7	(470.9)
Current ratio								
Friendly Hotels Plc	0.31	0.58	0.49	0.39	0.44	0.43	0.51	
Queens Moat Houses Plc	0.81	1.44	1.28	1.64	0.84	1.56	0.43	
Regal Hotel Group		2.44	1.98	0.13	0.04	0.03	0.11	
Resort Hotels Plc		0.47	1.15	1.16	0.58	1.06	0.59	0.02
Total debt/net assets (book) %								
Friendly Hotels Plc	28.7	12.8	27.8	14.6	18.3	25.5	31.3	
Queens Moat Houses Plc	34.7	42.3	37.7	39.3	43.6	50.3	130.7	
Regal Hotel Group			53.8	145.0	108.4	107.6		
Resort Hotels Plc		34.5	23.3	21.8	30.2	31.5	44.4	128.0

Source: MicroView Exstat (Extel Financial Ltd)

Shareholders' investment ratios

These are normally calculated by investment brokers and financial advisers for a range of companies to highlight levels of performance and are not considered in detail in this chapter.

Univariate techniques for predicting failure

The calculation of a series of individual ratios, using data taken from the company accounts for performance measurement, was first used in the 1930s. The technique is now widely used as a monitoring device, but there are three serious problems associated with using ratios. The first is based on the fact that published accounts are historical and by the time the results have been published it may be too late to take evasive action. Second, the practice of 'creative accounting' often introduced by failing companies may also serve to render the process of ratio analysis useless where values in the accounts have been manipulated to mask poor results. Finally, there is the problem of interpretation. One ratio on its own is virtually useless. Instead, a group of ratios should be calculated to obtain the overall picture.

Much research has been carried out to establish if ratios are capable of predicting failure. Ratios focusing on cashflow are generally recognized as being important indicators of performance. Beaver (1968), in a general study,

determined that the ratio measuring cash flow to total debt correctly classified firms as failed or non-failed at least 76 per cent of the time, with the ratio
profit to capital employed being the next best indicator. In each of the cases
the predictions were for one to five years before failure. In a study specifically on restaurant failure in the USA, Olsen et al (1983) found the ratios
shown in Table 2.4 to be the best indicators of impending failure over the
time spans indicated.

Table 2.4   Ratios indicating impending failure

Ratio	Months prior
Current assets / current liabilities	5 –9 months
Working capital / total assets	6 – 9 months
Earnings before interest and taxes/ total assets	16 –18 months
Earnings before interest and taxes/ revenue	12 –18 months
Total assets / revenue	11 – 19 months
Working capital / revenue	7 – 11 months

From: Improving the prediction of restaurant failure through ratio analysis, *International Journal of Hospitality Management* 1983; **2**: 187-193.

To use single ratio analysis effectively as a monitoring device, a variety of
ratios should be calculated regularly, taking care to ensure that a standard
formula is always used with similar data from the trading accounts to ensure
comparability. The predictive power is derived by the process of comparison, where ratios are compared over time for the same business to establish
whether the situation is improving or declining and to compare ratios
between similar businesses to see whether the company in question is
performing better or worse than the average industry result. Intra-firm
comparison, although useful to potential investors, industry observers and
participants, does have several inherent dangers, the most significant being
the validity of the resulting averages calculated by leading industry consultants using a diverse sample of companies from the hospitality industry. The
details of the individual companies within the sample are withheld by the
consultants to protect the individual organizations but the observer is
unable to ensure that comparability is valid.

Multidiscriminant analysis

The volume of information provided from traditional ratio analysis methods
has led many writers and analysts to be critical of accounting ratios as a

sound monitoring device. It can be argued that traditional ratios do not work as they have failed to change and adapt with changes in the business environment, and, in reality, businesses have continued to fail despite the use of the technique as a monitoring device. Altman (1968) proposed that the prediction of corporate solvency or failure could be measured by a single value or Z-score. The Z-score model was refined by Altman and subsequent predictive models in use in the UK and USA are all based on the statistical technique of MDA. Generally, MDA models contain a number of predetermined ratios (five in Altman's version) each with its own weighting, such that the sum of the products of the individual ratios and individual weights yields a Z-score. Guidelines are then provided from research for the interpretation of the score. A number of models have been produced by different researchers following Altman's first publication. Altman has revised his model releasing a later Zeta model, but details for this are not available for the outside user. In the UK, Taffler's (1982) model is perhaps the best known but the full details for the model structure and coefficients are not publicly available.

Prediction models

Altman released his first model in 1968; this was derived from the statistical technique of discriminant analysis. The component parts of the formula are shown in Figure 2.3.

Altman's model:

$$Z = 1.2\ X1 + 1.4\ X2 + 3.3\ X3 + 0.6\ X4 + 1.0\ X5$$

where: $X1$ = working capital/total assets
$X2$ = retained earning since inception/total assets
$X3$ = earnings before taxes and interest/total assets
$X4$ = market value of equity/book value of debt
$X5$ = sales/total assets

Altman's revised model:

$$Z = 0.717\ X1 + 0.847\ X2 + 3.107\ X3 + 0.420\ X4 + 0.998\ X5$$

where: $X4$ = book value of equity/book value of debt

Figure 2.3   Z-score model developed by Altman

The model predicts that if a score is 1.8 or less, then failure is certain and, if it is 2.7 or above, then failure is highly unlikely. The two limits can be considered as an upper limit, where no failed companies are misclassified and a lower limit, where no ongoing companies are misclassified. Lying between these limits is what Altman describes as the zone of ignorance or the grey area where a small number of failed and a small number of ongoing companies are misclassified. Altman's own research using broadly US manufacturing companies found that the model correctly classified 95 per cent of the firms one year before failure. Using data from the two years prior to bankruptcy, the correct classification fell to a 72 per cent level of accuracy. Earlier data did not provide a reliable classification. Altman has revised his earlier model to take the book value rather than the market value of equity and this was used to recalculate a result with the same groups of companies used to develop the original model. Changing the ratio X4 to the book value of debt, produced a change in the weightings in the model, indicating that a small change to the specification of an individual ratio does produce substantial changes to the weights of the other ratios in the model. As a result, the cut-off point in the model was amended to 1.23 from 1.81.

Taffler's and Tisshaw's model (1977):

Z = 0.53 X1 + 0.13 X2 + 0.18 X3 + 0.16 X4

where: X1 = profit before taxation/current liabilities
         X2 = current assets/total liabilities, i.e. total debt
         X3 = current liabilities/total assets
         X4 = the no credit interval

The no-credit interval is defined as:

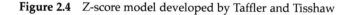

$$\frac{\text{Immediate assets} - \text{Current liabilities}}{\text{Operating costs} - \text{Depreciation}}$$

Figure 2.4   Z-score model developed by Taffler and Tisshaw

In the UK, Taffler and Tisshaw published a formula which was first identified in 1977 based on UK companies and the final model is shown in Figure 2.4. Much of the detail for this model remains undisclosed but in 1982, Taffler revealed that a score in excess of 0.2 and certainly 0.3 is characteristic of a company with good long-term survival prospects, whilst below 0.2 and certainly below 0.0, the company is likely to fail. However, because Taffler's model has not been published in full, only Altman's model will be used in this analysis.

Failure prediction in the UK hospitality industry

Two sectors of the UK hospitality industry have been chosen for analysis using Z-score techniques – the hotel sector and the leisure sector – with a small sample of medium to large companies drawn from each. Although nowadays many hotel groups regard themselves as being part of the leisure industry, for the purposes of this research hotel companies are defined as principally being involved in the provision of accommodation. Leisure industries are defined as being providers of a range of recreational activities and services such as sporting facilities, clubs, licensed and unlicensed eating facilities, theatres and concert halls. The principal activities of the companies chosen for study are shown in Tables 2.5 and 2.6.

Table 2.5 Principal trading activities of leisure companies analysed

Company name	Principal activities
Allied Leisure Plc	Unlicensed eating places; sporting facilities and sports players; night clubs and licensed clubs
Edencorp Leisure Plc	Theatres, concert halls etc; sporting facilities and sports players; other recreational services, unlicensed eating places
European Leisure Plc	Recreational services; public houses and bars; night clubs and licensed clubs; licensed eating places; sports goods, sporting facilities and sports players
First Leisure Corporation Plc	Holiday camps; other tourist or short stay accommodation; licensed eating places; other recreational services; sporting facilities and sports players; theatres, concert halls, etc; camping and caravan sites
Leading Leisure Plc	Licensed hotels; unlicensed hotels, building and construction; owning and dealing in real estate
Stanley Leisure Organisation Plc	Central office of mixed activity enterprises; betting, gambling; sporting facilities and sports players

The UK hotel sector has traditionally been dominated by several well-established companies, but more recently several new companies have emerged. The growth of the leisure sector has been more recent, with significant numbers of companies entering the sector in the last decade. During the growth years of the early and middle 1980s many hospitality operations thrived in a favourable economic environment, with high consumer demand and ample supplies of credit available for expansion. The hospitality

Table 2.6   Principal trading activities of hotel companies analysed

Company name	Principal activities
Friendly Hotels	Licensed hotels; licensed eating places; other tourist or short-stay accommodation.
Queens Moat Houses Plc	Licensed hotels; licensed eating places
Regal Hotel Group Plc	Licensed hotels; licensed eating places
Resort Hotels	Licensed hotels; licensed eating places; public houses and bars

industry as a whole has struggled through the late 1980s and early 1990s, witnessing considerable turbulence, with many companies struggling simply to survive. The ill fortune of a number of these companies has been widely reported in the financial press where in many cases the key features of the recession (high interest rates, increasing inflation, falling property values and rising unemployment) have been blamed as the cause of failure, along with the Gulf War in the early 1990s and the threat from terrorism. However, many authors believe the impending failure could have been foreseen earlier through an analysis of financial performance and this will now be considered in more detail.

Testing the model

In order to assess the effectiveness of the MDA model, financial data from a selection of companies have been gathered from computerized databases and published accounts. The data have then been analysed using spread-sheet models set up to calculate a Z-score based on the guidelines provided by Altman. A potential objection to this approach could be raised regarding the industry differences, that is, using UK company data in a USA model. It is considered that business and accounting practice is sufficiently complementary between the countries to minimize misinterpretation. In the application of the data to this model the following interpretations of the model have been made. For input into the 1968 model, market value of equity is considered as being equal to the book value of the reserves and ordinary shares from the balance sheet, as recommended by Altman in his early research. The book value of total debt is equal to the total of long- and short-term debt, whilst earnings before taxes and interest are equal to operating profit before other income. The results of the analysis are shown in Tables 2.7 and 2.8.

Table 2.7   Z-score performances of selected leisure companies

Company	Year							
	1986	1987	1988	1989	1990	1991	1992	1993
Model: Altman (original)								
Allied Leisure		1.62	1.01	1.23	1.44	1.77	0.95	1.622
Edencorp Leisure				1.55*				
European Leisure	5.34	(0.78)	4.11	1.46	1.00	1.25	(1.72)	(0.31)
First Leisure	2.21	2.87	2.69	2.36	3.48	3.36	3.5	3.3
Leading Leisure	1.10	0.79	1.06	0.96[†]				
Stanley Leisure	8.25	6.13	5.56	4.24	3.62	3.62	3.77	3.72
Model: Altman (revised)								
Allied Leisure		1.61	1.05	1.22	1.25	1.43	0.822	1.303
Edencorp Leisure			1.17*					
European Leisure	4.04	0.09	3.10	1.16	0.80	1.07	(1.2)	0.14
First Leisure	1.88	2.25	2.11	1.87	2.55	2.46	2.53	2.46
Leading Leisure	1.07	0.81	1.11	0.99				
Stanley Leisure	7.85	5.77	4.57	3.41	2.93	2.98	3.11	3.07

*Indicates the last year of accounting information available
[†]Trading suspended.

Table 2.8   Z-score performances of selected hotel companies

Company	Year							
	1986	1987	1988	1989	1990	1991	1992	1993
Model: Altman (original)								
Friendly Hotels Plc	1.19	3.67	1.58	2.27	2.28	1.6		1.39
Queens Moat Houses Plc	1.63	1.19	1.29	1.41	1.34	0.87	(3.4)	
Regal Hotel Group		3.17	2.51	0.23	(3.85)	(1.39)	(1.05)	
Resort Hotels Plc		1.62	2.56	1.85	1.44	1.51	0.33	(5.76)
Model: Altman (revised)								
Friendly Hotels Plc	0.98	2.7	1.25	1.74	1.76	1.22	1.08	
Queens Moat Houses Plc	1.25	0.92	0.99	1.08	1.04	0.63	(2.78)	
Regal Hotel Group		2.15	1.70	0.18	(2.85)	(0.9)	(0.57)	
Resort Hotels Plc		1.27	1.91	1.37	1.11	1.14	0.32	(4.57)

Background to the analysed companies

Allied Leisure

This company is one of the success stories of the 1980s. Established in 1982, the group achieved a stock exchange listing in 1991. During this period the company was very much at the peak of its success with extensive expansion plans, good trading results and shareholder confidence. Since that time the company has experienced some difficulty. Trading levels have fallen and the lack of shareholder confidence resulted in a plummeting share price. Finally in 1994 board-level changes resulted in a change of policy with many of the less profitable sites being offered for sale. However, with corporate restructuring and a new finance package, this company is optimistic about the future. The MDA results highlight 1992 as being a significantly poor year but the trend in the values is now upward.

Edencorp Leisure Plc (year of incorporation 1989, suspended from trading December 1989)

This company briefly traded in the late 1980's before being suspended. In the latter stages of its life the use of loan capital was substantially increased, raising the gearing of the company. Altman's model clearly indicates failure, but an analysis of the accounts for 1990 would provide more conclusive results.

European Leisure Plc (year of incorporation 1935)

This is a long-established company with a successful trading history. The early 1990s have been a very difficult period, with substantial losses recorded in 1991 and 1992. However, the company has managed to survive and is now focusing on capital restructuring in an attempt to convert debt to equity. The results provided by the analysis are not conclusive and the jump in values corresponds to changes in reserve levels in 1987 and poor profit performance in 1992.

First Leisure Corporation Plc (year of incorporation 1981)

This company had expanded rapidly during its life, achieving consistent sales and profit growth. Expansion has been funded from increases in both equity and long term loans. The market confidence continues to grow, with share prices increasing consistently each year, virtually without restraint. Altman provides very positive results for this company, with the Z-score increasing over the period considered.

Leading Leisure Plc (year of incorporation 1983, dealings in companies securities cancelled and receivers called December 1990)

This company expanded rapidly in the 1980s with the majority of funding coming from short-term loans. At the time of suspension the gearing was particularly weak and share prices at virtually zero. Altman provides clear failure predictions from as early as 1986.

Stanley Leisure Organization Plc (year of incorporation 1980)

This company expanded the asset base during the late 1980s with funding from a combination of equity and reserves. The market reports indicate confidence with share prices remaining buoyant and, although share prices showed a slow downturn in the early 1990s, this was probably due to lack of confidence in the industry as a whole rather than with this particular business. The company continues to report sales and profit growth and the Altman model provides an optimistic trend for this company.

Friendly Hotels Plc (year of incorporation 1977)

This company experienced substantial growth in sales and retained profits in the mid 1980s, sustaining a growth in earnings per share with market confidence peaking in 1987 and 1991, despite the fact that trading in the early part of 1991 was adversely affected by terrorism, adverse weather conditions and the Gulf War. At the start of 1992 the market share price was lower than 1988 levels, with a rapidly falling P/E (price/earnings) ratio. Both sets of Z-scores mirror this pattern, with a downturn in the values in 1988.

Queens Moat Houses Plc (year of incorporation 1946)

The trading in the shares for this company was suspended in March 1993 following difficulties in establishing the company's true financial position. Since that time substantial reorganization has taken place with several board-level changes and considerable attention paid to restructuring the balance sheet. The analysis provides a consistently low score for this company.

Regal Hotel Group Plc (year of incorporation 1920)

This group traded well until 1989 however poor trading in 1990–91 resulted in substantial falls in reserves, with the company's shares finally being suspended in May 1994 pending shareholders' approval for reorganization proposals. A strong score in 1987 swiftly drops into the failure band in more recent years.

Resort Hotels Plc (year of incorporation 1983)

Sales and retained profits grew consistently throughout the 1980s but the pattern of growth was interrupted in the early 1990s. Listings for the company's shares were suspended in July 1993 pending clarification of the company's financial position. Substantial asset revaluations in this year produced a substantial loss. The Z-score drops to mirror the company fortunes.

The value of the Z-score

Altman (1977) reports that classification accuracy for his subsequent Zeta model reaches 92.4 per cent of failed and 93 per cent of survivor companies. As a result he suggests that there are six courses of action available if a manager gets a poor Z-score:

1. Change the product or management personnel.
2. Sell off unprofitable equipment, operations or entire divisions.
3. Solicit a takeover from a healthy company.
4. Alter the financial structure (debt or equity).
5. Enter the process of a bankruptcy reorganization.
6. Enter liquidation.

However, the true classification accuracy of a predictive measure must depend on the capacity of the model to accurately predict success or failure and not to just to classify correctly the companies once they have already failed. The accuracy of the model from this perspective is not yet clear.

Problems in the usage of multidiscriminant models

Controversy has continually surrounded the use of the models and leading writers in the field of accounting continue to disagree on the effectiveness of the models as a means of predicting corporate failure. However, what is certain is that the models cannot in their present form be considered to be foolproof. In addition, the authors themselves have issued different and conflicting guidelines for the use of these models over the period since their initial release. The essential criticisms are that almost all models handle failing companies successfully but are less accurate in respect of surviving companies. Inaccuracies may be due to difficulty in establishing whether the model may be used to transcend industry groups, and particularly whether a model developed for the manufacturing industry may legitimately be used for service industries. Although there is no clear evidence to indicate the importance of industry type, it seems reasonable to assume that specific industries have specific requirements in terms of prediction models and that the ideal solution would be for each industry type to have its own model. Also, the methodology in developing the original model is complex and consequently a model cannot be easily altered in terms of constituents or cut-off points to meet different needs. For example, Altman's original model included a ratio based on the market value of equity and many researchers assumed, including Altman himself, that the book value could be substituted. This has since been shown to produce spurious results, and Altman has revised the model, as described earlier.

Conclusions

This chapter has reviewed a variety of performance measures and where possible has attempted to use the measures to assess company performance. Single ratio analysis continues to be the most widely used technique for monitoring company performance but many companies in the service sector are supplementing these with operational measures based on non-financial criteria. Finally, the process of MDA still requires substantial research in order to be able recommend Z-score analysis as a technique for predicting failure in the hospitality industry. This preliminary investigation, however, clearly suggests that Z-score analysis is an effective monitoring device, particularly when there is a dramatic change in the value from year to year. The next step must be to determine the effective lead time for the prediction of failure – the key to success if the model is to be used effectively by firms operating in international markets, where time is required to implement a strategic change in direction. The complexity involved in applying the models also poses a serious problem to the user as standardization of the definitions used in the model is necessary to ensure success and, consequently, the alternative approaches to items such as the revaluation of assets, the capitalization of interest and the misuse of extraordinary items can seriously undermine the effectiveness of the technique for monitoring performance. Therefore, current research indicates that the most effective use of the Z-score process is to develop models for specific industry types to take account of differing asset structures, financing needs and operating conditions.

References

Altman, E.I. (1968) Financial ratios, discriminant analysis and the prediction of corporate bankruptcy. *Journal of Finance* **23**; 589–609.

Altman, E.I., Haldeman, R.G. and Narayanan, P. (1977) Zeta analysis: A new model to identify bankruptcy risk of corporations. *Journal of Banking and Finance*, **1**; 29–54.

Beaver, W.H. (1968) Alternative Accounting Measures as Predictions of Failure. *Accounting Review*, **43**; 113–122.

Drucker, P. (1953) *The Practice of Management*, New York, Harper Brothers.

Fitzgerald, L., Johnston, R., Brignall, T. J., Silvestro, R. and Voss, C. (1991) *Performance Measurement in Service Businesses*, CIMA.

Olsen, M., Bellas, C., Kish, L.V. (1983) Improving the prediction of restaurant failure through ratio analysis. *International Journal Hospitality Management*, **2**; 187–193.

Sink, D.S. (1985) *Productivity Management: Planning Measurement and Evaluation, Control and Improvement*, J. Wiley.

Taffler, R. (1982) Forecasting company failure in the UK using discriminant analysis and financial ratio data. *Journal of the Royal Statistical Society*, **145** (Part 3); 342–358.

Taffler, R. and Tisshaw, H. (1977) Going, going, gone - four factors which predict? *Accountancy* 88; 50–54.

Data for analysis supplied by EXTEL Financial Ltd, Fitzroy House, 13–17 Epworth Street, London EC2A 4DL.

3 Operational analysis in hotels

Elisa S. Moncarz and Richard N. Kron

Overview of economic environment in the hospitality industry

The hotel industry has changed dramatically in the early 1990s. Affected by overbuilding, global competition, natural disasters, the impact of the Gulf War, under performance, lack of financing, a global recession and many other factors hindering economic growth, the hotel business (especially in the USA) has evolved from an industry often driven by ego and operated on tax breaks to one that has fully recognized that a hotel needs to concentrate on business strategies for survival and success. During the recent past, the US hotel industry has experienced some very positive and significant changes, emerging out of its prolonged decline in operating performance. During 1993, the increase in demand for accommodations exceeded the growth in supply and average room rates were nearly two percentage points higher than in 1992. This resulted in the reporting of the first positive results in over a decade. Based on data compiled by Smith Travel Research for the mid-year Hotel Report (1993), Randy Smith estimates total revenue in 1993 (for hotels with more than 20 rooms) at $61.3 billion and pre-tax income between US$ 3.0 billion and US$ 3.5 billion (Warmick, 1993). These were major accomplishments for an industry that suffered substantial losses in 1991 and was not expected to recover before 1995.

On a global perspective, the end of the Cold War has brought new opportunities for trade and tourism. The USA, Mexico and Canada are very optimistic that the North American Free Trade Agreement (NAFTA) will be a boom to their economies while the Caribbean and Central America are anxious about how the rest of the hemisphere may be affected (Quek and

Hopper 1993). Meanwhile, western Europe, the largest market for international travel in the world, is just emerging from the economic gloom. Statistics for selected international hotel performance in 1992 are presented in Table 3.1.

Table 3.1   Selected international hotel statistics

	Latin America	Caribbean	Europe	Africa	Middle East	Asia/ Pacific
Percentage of occupancy	66.1%	62.1%	63.0%	67.5%	60.6%	72.2%
Average daily room rate per occupied room (US$)	$79.37	$103.83	$120.28	$78.76	$95.72	$97.68
Income before fixed charges	26.3%	11.4%	28.4%	42.3%	38.1%	29.9%

From PKF International Consulting, USA (1993), with permission

Serious challenges confronting lodging operators

There are major problems facing hotel operators as well as significant opportunities brought about by a changing hospitality industry environment. Among them:

- The proliferation of economy hotels, which had been the fastest-growing segment of the industry, reflects not just the budget consciousness of consumers, but also the segmentation of the hotel market into many submarkets, ranging from very limited service hotels to luxury hotels.
- The number of employees for each 100-hotel rooms has decreased from 54 in 1988 to 50.5 in 1993 according to hospitality analyst Bjorn Hanson. This drop has enabled the break-even occupancy rate to fall to 64 per cent from 65.8 per cent in 1990 (McDowell, 1993).
- Analysts contend that the industry will continue to strengthen for several years, by which time hotel funds should again flow freely and new hotels will be under construction.
- The collapse of communism in Eastern Europe and the former Soviet Union has opened up investment opportunities worldwide. Furthermore, with the world moving towards a global economy, hotel development opportunities are available in many markets whose governments are actively seeking foreign investment.
- There has been steadily increasing competition in the lodging market not only from other hotels, but from transportation, entertainment and vacation ownership entities.

Declining performance factors

Certain factors affect the performance of hotels. They are mainly caused by incompetent management that lacks effective leadership.

An important factor is the lack of flexibility. The hotel industry on a global and market-by-market basis is changing on a daily basis. Newer products, changes in demand generators and modifications in guests' preferences require management to accept change as the only constant. Managers who cannot adapt to these changes generally are instrumental in causing a decline in financial performance.

Many problems also arise due to the lack of a business plan, including a well-thought-out strategic plan. This plan should clearly identify what are the hotel's strengths, weaknesses, opportunities and potential threats, thereby providing specific direction.

Increased competitive pressures

The franchise boom of the 1960s combined with the construction boom of the 1970s and 1980s created an oversupply of old and functionally obsolete hotels. With the industry shakeout of the late 1980s and the national and global recessions of the 1990s, lodging managers have been facing increased competition in all market segments. In such a climate, many hotels found themselves unable to compete since expansion and refurbishment of older rooms are key ingredients for success. This created a proliferation of reorganizations, restructurings and bankruptcies.

Fearful of losing their market share, lodging operators have been practising discounting of rooms in an effort to increase occupancies. However, since expenses have increased at the rate of inflation, this tactic did not result in increased profitability.

Due to the aforementioned competitive pressures and discounting practices, average daily room rates for US hotels have grown less than the annual rate of inflation during the five-year period ending in 1993. This has been a challenge for operators to look elsewhere to cover the increasing cost of operations, forcing them to make cuts in both personnel and services. Indeed, the inability of hotel operators to raise room rates remains a concern for industry analysts who have referred to it as 'the most pressing problem facing today's operators, comparable to the oversupply obstacle of the late 1980s' (Callahan, 1993).

Inadequate access to capital

Financing became scarce in the early 1990s as struggling hospitality firms desperately tried to restructure their balance sheets in order to recover from the excesses of the 1980s. Lending and capital markets looked negatively upon the hotel industry which had lost some of its lustre as hotel investments became very risky ventures. While debt financing for most projects became virtually non-existent, equity sources raised return on equity requirements further in response to perceived risks.

Under these very difficult conditions, most operators were unable to obtain financing for expansion, refurbishments and other major industry needs in the early 1990s. As conditions improve in the USA and global economies as well as in the hospitality industry, there should be more availability of financing sources. Nonetheless, future financing will only be done on the strengths of a firm's operating performance and cash flows in contrast to past financing, in which real estate values and tax breaks played a major role.

Early warning signs

Early signs that a hospitality firm might be headed for trouble rarely erupt overnight. Often by the time unhealthy trends are recognized, the underlying problems are too serious to solve easily, if at all. Conversely, if a problem is recognized early enough, a firm may still have time to take the necessary steps that will avert further declines in operating performance and cash flow. These steps might include cost-cutting, stronger operating and financial controls, renegotiating loans and/or organizational restructuring. Symptoms of potentially serious problems include:

- Steady rise in expenses
- Declining operating margins
- Management turnover
- Drop in sales and net income
- Consistent shortages of cash
- Increase in sales accompanied by decreases in net income

One classic warning sign is an increase in sales revenue not accompanied by a comparable increase in earnings. An increase in the number of customers served, for example, may not always lead to higher earnings if expenses are rising faster than sales. The inability to maximize revenues while simultaneously controlling costs is a sign of incompetent management in today's economic climate.

Another important early warning sign is the turnover of senior management and the attrition of middle management. The defection of middle and senior managers to other more stable, secure firms or industries, compounded by the shortage of both skilled and unskilled workers can have far-reaching implications for the firm and the industry as a whole. Indeed, a labour crisis is expected to continue to plague the industry for some time in the future, resulting in low morale and poor productivity.

Another key item to watch is sales dropping without corresponding reduction in expenses or with increased costs (especially cost of sales and other operating expenses) since there is a critical lag time before the company cuts costs or takes other actions to cope with the fact that operating margins are adversely affected.

It is also important to recognize that, even at the height of success, managers need to detect early warning signals and implement strategies to head them off. Recognizing developing problems early on gives the best chance for corrective actions.

Use of operational analysis

Faced with a changing economic environment, increasing costs and slowly rising room rates, hospitality managers have a pressing need to refocus attention on the use of operational analysis as a management tool to identify developing problems. Nonetheless, traditional operational analysis that merely monitors a company's progress is out of date in today's climate. New tools must be developed that spot incubating problems, taking into account the current hospitality industry environment. This will provide insights and lead the way to managerial corrective actions that are timely and could make the difference between a firm's success or failure.

Review of existing operational models

Most existing operational models have primarily dealt with revenue-enhancing methods or cost cutting measures in a broad sense. A review of literature disclosed that Dearden (1978) was a pioneer in developing a blueprint for profitability analysis of service industries starting with the most comprehensive definition of a segment of operations and moving downwards to the least comprehensive. Lesure (1983) contended that the basis of operational control in hotels was the comparison with a pre-established standard or goal. Brooks (1991) discovered that hints of trouble almost always became evident when industry business elements were broken out of the financial statement and examined separately. Quain (1992) emphasized revenue-enhancing techniques using profit analysis by segment (PABS). Moncarz and Kron (1993) developed an operational model geared to the improvement of operating performance of lodging firms in financial distress.

Developing model for today

In developing an appropriate model of operational analysis, management must sharpen its ability to identify the effects of current issues affecting the hospitality industry on the company's operating performance. By making a few simple changes in the way a company analyses its operating statement, lodging operators can focus on developing problems while recognizing the changing hospitality and global industry environment.

This operational model will serve as an excellent management tool for identifying problem areas, pointing out recommendations for improvement and monitoring appropriate courses of action.

Obtaining trends

The operational analysis of an entity's performance can be more meaningful if the results are compared with the results of competitors. When we interpret a set of figures it is important to have some point of reference or standard against which to assess current results. Indeed, monitoring operating performance against competition is vital in judging one's performance. Since size, occupancy, location, quality and facilities are just some criteria which might affect results of operations, care should be exercised in the selection of comparative industry averages.

Selected sources of specific lodging industry statistics compiled and published periodically follow:

- *The Host Report* – an annual publication (a mid-year report published until 1993) of Arthur Andersen with information assembled and compiled by Smith Travel Research. It includes operating statistics for the US Hotel Industry.
- *Trends in the Hotel Industry – USA Edition* – an annual publication (with quarterly supplements) of PKF Consulting. It includes operating statistics for the US hotel industry. (In addition, regional publications are also available periodically.)
- *International Hotel Trends* – an annual publication of PKF International Consulting, with operating and financial data on hotels based on voluntary contributions of 3,000 accommodations establishments worldwide.

In addition to the above industry sources the following is a list of American organizations that provide data on hotel statistics:

- Dun & Bradstreet, Inc. – it provides industry norms and key ratios using US Standard Industrial Classification (SIC) code numbers.

- Moody's Investor Services – Moody's manuals contain financial and operating ratios on industry companies.
- Robert Morris Associates Annual Statement Studies – it includes financial and operating ratios for approximately 300 lines of business on information obtained from member banks of Robert Morris Associates.
- Almanac of Business and Industrial Financial Ratios by Leo Troy – a compilation of corporate performance (both operating and financial statistics).
- Standard & Poors Corp. – Industry surveys of basic data on the hotel industry with financial comparisons of leading companies.

First signs of trouble on statements

The first indication of developing problems is generally found in the financial statements. Since financial statements give a comparison of current and historical performance, it will identify negative trends. As a result, lodging operators must acquire a good understanding on how components of the business affect profitability and operating performance by acquiring a very strong command of financial statements (especially operating statements). They must understand what goes into the financial statements, and most importantly, how to analyse these reports so that they are in a position to identify developing problems and take appropriate corrective action.

Emphasis on operating improvements

In today's uncertain economic environment, hospitality management has to place more emphasis on operating improvements than product development. At the same time, the erosion of profits that the industry suffered in the early 1990s accompanied by its inability to raise room rates significantly has focused more attention on making money on sales. Indeed, revenues might go up due to an increase in the number of customers but if expenses grow at a higher pace than revenues, the company will report lower profitability in spite of the increase in customer count. Failure to match each department revenue with its corresponding expenses might also lead to faulty management decisions.

Operational analysis will help hotel managers recognize and isolate problem areas. Once the problems are identified, further investigation is undertaken to identify the causes and potential solutions to the problems and the corresponding operating improvements that could make the difference between success and failure. Whatever the reason, prompt action becomes imperative.

Line-by-line analysis

Operating analysis will encompass the line-by-line comparison of all figures in order to determine if they differ from past performance and from industry averages. Each line item requires specific questions to identify causes of declining operating performance. The industry operating statement sample in Fig. 3.1 will be used as a point of reference to discuss major variables affecting the line-by-line analysis.

Number of rooms Occupancy percentage Average room rate				
	This year		Last year	
	Amount	Ratio (%)	Amount	Ratio (%)
Revenues Rooms Food Beverage Telephone Other operated departments Rentals/other income Total				
Departmental expenses Rooms Food and beverage Telephone Other operated departments Total				
Operated departmental income				
Undistributed operating expenses Administrative and general Marketing Property operation & maintenance Energy Other Total				
Income before fixed charges				
Fixed charges Management fees Rent/property taxes/insurance Interest Depreciation/amortization Total fixed charges				
Income before income taxes				

Figure 3.1   Sample operating statement

Rooms revenue

The rooms department is the key division in the hotel, usually making up a total of 50–75 per cent of the hotel revenues. Traditionally, rooms revenue was monitored by tracing occupancy percentages or average daily room rate. While both of these factors are important measures of managerial effectiveness, lodging operators are now placing more reliance in revpar (revenue per available room) as the best valuation tool for determining the actual revenue-generating capabilities of a property.

Is it better to get a high occupancy with a lower average daily room rate or vice versa? Management at a hotel should perform a revpar analysis to determine what is best. Revpar is calculated by multiplying the occupancy by the average daily room rate. For example, a hotel operating at a 60 per cent occupancy with a daily room rate of $70 has a Revpar of $42 ($70 x 60 per cent). This hotel is generating more rooms revenue than a hotel with a 70 per cent occupancy and a daily room rate of $50 which has a Revpar of $35 ($50 x 70 per cent).

Generally, the average daily rate and the occupancy are inversely related. As the average daily rate decreases (typically due to discounted packages), the occupancy percentage usually increases. Depending on the price-sensitivity of the market, a small decrease in rates may improve occupancy significantly. Conversely, if the market is not primarily driven by price, decreases in the rates charged for a guest room will only reduce revenues. Ideally, a hotel will decrease rates to increase occupancy only with specific markets for defined periods of time. This will allow a hotel to maximize revenues within those markets where price is not an issue and reduce it where it is.

How do room rates and facilities at a given property compare to those of the local competitors? Are the hotel rates strategically determined based on the location, quality and amenities within the property? The following should be addressed when considering the hotel's pricing structure:

- Age and physical condition of the subject facility.
- Visibility and accessibility.
- Location relative to demand generators.
- Hotel amenities.
- Quality of services.
- Market segments utilized.
- Quality of marketing efforts and reservation system.

Rooms departmental expenses

Rooms departmental expenses include the salaries, wages and benefits incurred by departmental staff and management as well as guest amenities, commissions to travel agents, reservations department, linen, dry cleaning, cleaning supplies and other related materials. The ability to control these areas can have a major effect on the profitability of the entire hotel.

How can a manager attempt to control the largest department of a hotel? Simply, training! Management must be trained to recognize efficiency, theft and lack of productivity. They must also have the ability to motivate the staff to perform at peak levels. At that point, the management team must be able to teach line employees to care about the success of the operation. How can this be accomplished? Are linens being used as rags? Is glassware being handled carefully to minimize breakage? Are room attendants being taught not to waste or steal room amenities and to handle hotel property as if it were their own? These are some examples of questions to be raised when analysing departmental expenses.

Food revenue

The sale of food products can be a significant profit centre or a devastating drain on the overall financial performance of a property. Attempts should be made to maximize revenues from hotel guests, guests from other hotels and the local market. What type of marketing is being utilized to encourage patronage? How effective is it? Do the management and staff understand the potential market or are they operating the department solely for their own personal gratification? Are the staff trained to hustle and, equally as important, to create an environment where the guests can have fun? Successful restaurateurs prepare menus for 'sales appeal' and a product with a great deal of visual appeal. Unsuccessful operators do not care about guest comments, suggestive selling of appetizers and desserts, in-guestroom merchandising or consistency of product or service.

Beverage revenue

The beverage department is generally the second most profitable depart- ment of a hotel after the rooms department but one of the most difficult to control. Products can be given away, items sold without money being properly recorded and deposited in a cash drawer or full bottles taken. In addition, bartenders not only prepare drinks for customers but also for servers from one or more restaurants and from cocktail servers in the lounge.

What procedures are in place to ensure all collected money is rung up? Do the staff suggest fun drinks or just approach a table with 'what would you like?' Do the guests plan to return again when they leave?

Food and beverage expenses

High food and beverage costs may be indicative of improper pricing, waste, theft or lack of inventory control. Indeed, food and beverage departments have extremely high operating costs stemming from the need to open seven days a week, frequently with around-the-clock room service as an amenity. As a result, many hotels are now leasing their food and beverage operations to outside entrepreneurs in order to remain competitive.

Telephone revenue

This account is credited with revenue generated from the use of the telephone equipment by guests, derived from local calls, long-distance calls, service charges and commissions received. Revenue per occupied room which is lower than industry averages may suggest a problem with the posting onto guest folios, an unreasonably high pricing structure which discourages usage, an unnecessarily low pricing structure or difficulty in placing calls. How easy is it for a guest to make a call?

Telephone expenses

The amount billed by the telephone companies through the switchboard and paid for should be included in this caption. In addition, salaries and wages, employee benefits, related printing and stationery and other departmental costs should be included. Higher than average expenses could again indicate revenues are not being posted for calls made, employee calls charged to this account, excessive staffing or overcharging by the telephone carrier.

Other operated departments

This classification includes departments operated by the hotel but not previously mentioned. It might include a beauty salon, health club, gift shop, newsstand and others. Revenue lower than industry average per occupied room could indicate that a valuable source of income is being lost due to a shortage of shops within the hotel. How well do the shops within the hotel cater to the needs of the guests and how many purchases occur off-premise?

Rentals and other income

Rentals and other income include the revenue earned from the rental of space for business purposes (e.g. office space, store space and lobby and showcase space) and income from commissions earned, income from electronic games, forfeited advanced deposits, service charges, interest income, income from vending machines and other miscellaneous sources. When shops or restaurants are leased instead of hotel-operated, this line item should be higher than average.

Administrative and general expenses

This area includes the salaries and wages of all administrative personnel not directly associated with a particular department, including accounting personnel and general manager's office, as well as other expenses including credit and collection charges, commission on credit charges, franchise fees and legal expenses. A higher than average administrative and general expense needs to be reviewed line by line to identify where a potential problem exists. Are the receivables turnaround excessive? Are legal expenses or payroll higher than average? Are all produced reports utilized or only added to a library?

Marketing

Marketing is a most crucial task for hospitality firms. Included in this classification are expenses associated with advertising (e.g. salaries of the sales staff, advertising expenses in newspapers, magazines, radio and television) as well as promotional efforts.

It is easy to spend on marketing a property but much more difficult to spend it wisely. While a marketing department should monitor all of its expenditures to ensure reasonable returns on investment, many hotels have no systems in place to monitor results. In analysing marketing costs, the manager should ask questions like: How effective and efficient is the department? How many room nights are the result of each effort?

It is important to recognize that even during difficult economic times advertising is crucial to prevent loss of market share. It is essential to target markets carefully and to look for new competitive edges. Companies that are already price leaders but lag in market share have a good opportunity during difficult times by expanding the advertising budget. A case in point is Motel 6 (the inexpensive no-frill motel company) which undertook a very successful radio campaign in the early 1990's, resulting in rises in occupancies to more than 80 per cent in spite of the difficulties that the industry was experiencing.

Property operation and maintenance

This classification includes expenses incurred in the ongoing maintenance of facilities such as salaries, wages and employee benefits, building materials, curtains and draperies, electrical and mechanical equipment, heating, ventilating and air-conditioning equipment, kitchen equipment, laundry equipment, elevators, engineering supplies and floor coverings.

Spending money judiciously in this department can make the difference between looking young, vibrant and competitive or old, dilapidated and cheap. Weather causes deterioration of the exterior of buildings and vegetation needs fertilizers, trimming or watering, regardless of how many rooms are occupied.

This is one area that frequently has problems because hotel operating management rarely has a complete understanding of its operation. Accordingly, operating managers either allow excessive spending or limit spending unwisely. It is important that upper management employs the most reputable chief engineer and learns as much as possible about this department.

Energy costs

Energy costs can easily be controlled but since energy consumption occurs throughout a facility, it can only be controlled by team effort. Some factors that cause high energy costs include poor energy management systems in the guest rooms, large air-conditioned atriums and non-existent energy awareness procedures as part of the employee training programmes. Some analytical questions might include: Do rooms attendants adjust thermostats to a comfortable but reasonable level while cleaning room? Are curtains partially drawn to reduce solar heat? Do rooms inspections include looking for leaks and are they repaired promptly? Is kitchen equipment turned off when not needed? Are air conditioning filters and evaporator fins cleaned regularly?

Fixed costs

Fixed costs are those which do not respond to changes in the volume of sales. Whatever the sales revenues, fixed costs are expected to remain constant. Examples include rent, management fees, interest expense and depreciation expense.

Most hotels and many other hospitality firms have a high proportion of fixed costs. High fixed costs mean high gross margins. This also means that small increases in sales revenue will result in a substantial rise in net earnings. Conversely, each decrease in total revenues will have a very substantial negative effect in profitability.

The combined effect of a high percentage of fixed costs and fluctuations in sales volume is to produce a condition of profit instability which is quite uncommon in many other industries. During the early 1990s, however, lodging operators facing declining revenues and increasing operating expenses were forced to analyse fixed costs for cost savings. As hotel values declined, for instance, a high percentage of hotels appealed against their property tax bills and in many instances they were successful in receiving reductions of 15–20 per cent in property taxes. Management fees are also down to 5–8 per cent of revenues due to the competition among hotel management companies. Accordingly, fixed costs are not always truly fixed in practice.

Case study

Introduction

The following case study will attempt to identify where management at a subject resort reacted properly and where delayed reaction resulted in not maximizing revenues, controlling expenses and therefore not optimizing earnings. Each line item will be reviewed and discussed for potential problems based upon variances from industry averages in an attempt to determine whether the variance occurred as a result of a wise business decision or ineffective management. Although only one hotel will be reviewed, the methods and procedures can be applied to any hotels, irrespective of price or market orientation.

A well-established, chain-affiliated resort hotel with approximately 400 guestrooms located in Cancun, Mexico was chosen as a model for this analysis. To evaluate the effectiveness of management at the subject hotel, statistical data for resort properties located in Cancun were utilized. This data, obtained from Tendencias en la Hotelería Mexicana (Pannell Kerr Forster, 1989, 1990, 1991, 1992, 1993), includes hotels with similar facilities, location and market orientation. All financial statistics are stated in US dollars.

Cancun market

Management of a resort facility must react quickly to external factors affecting its overall operating performance. To observe reaction times more clearly, the Cancun market was chosen due to the following factors. First, from 1988 to 1992, the available room supply increased from approximately 12,000 hotel rooms to nearly 20,000, or a compound annual growth of approximately 14 per cent. Second, in September 1988, the Yucatán

Peninsula including Cancun was struck by the devastating Hurricane Gilbert. This hurricane eroded many of the beautiful beaches in the area and also prompted much negative publicity, causing the cancelling of reservations and changing of travel plans. Lastly, AeroMexico, one of Mexico's major carriers, reduced flights as a cost-saving measure, greatly decreasing the number of seats flying in and out of Cancun International Airport.

Any one of the factors listed above could have a major affect on the overall profitability of a hotel. The combination of all of these factors requires effective management to reduce losses and regain and maintain occupancy and average daily room rates.

Subject resort

The subject resort, constructed in the early 1980s, is typical of many hotels in this resort destination. On a constructed beachfront overlooking the Caribbean Sea, amenities at this facility include swimming pools, private balconies, tennis courts, fitness centre, basketball and volleyball courts, and a children's playground. The visibility and accessibility of the property are also comparable to the other hotels in the sample which are located near demand generators such as the beach, shopping centres, nightlife and other attractions typically sought by resort guests and, therefore, neither element is a major factor in the subject hotel's financial performance. Comparing the subject hotel with similar hotels in the comparable sample will assist in identifying the effectiveness of the management in place at the subject facility. The discussion that follows the operating statement and resort averages presented in Figs 3.2 and 3.3 will consider the potential reasons that may have affected the operating performance of the subject hotel, while presenting suggestions on how to maximize revenues and control expenses within major departments.

The following discussion will consider the performance of the major departments of the subject resort and possible reasons for variances from industry averages.

Rooms department

Average daily room rate/occupancy percentage

The average room rate and occupancy percentage are the two most critical pieces of information relative to rooms revenue. The subject resort's goal, as should be with all hotels, is to maximize these two calculations, as this will result in maximum departmental revenues.

	1992 80% $87.74			1991 70% $79.30			1990 83% $74.42		
Year Occupancy percentage Average room rate	Ratio (%)	Per available room ($)	Per occupied room ($)	Ratio (%)	Per available room ($)	Per occupied room ($)	Ratio %	Per available room ($)	Per occupied room ($)
Revenues									
Rooms	66.7	25,458	87.74	64.2	20,125	79.30	65.0	22,449	74.42
Food	16.3	6,245	21.52	18.3	5,733	22.59	17.8	6,137	20.34
Beverage	6.1	2,327	8.02	6.5	2,024	7.97	5.7	1,984	6.58
Telephone	3.5	1,355	4.67	2.9	900	3.55	2.7	934	3.10
Other operated departments	4.5	1,736	5.98	4.5	1,416	5.58	4.5	1,556	5.16
Rentals/other income	2.9	1,108	3.82	3.7	1,170	4.61	4.3	1,502	4.98
Total	100.0	38,229	131.75	100.0	31,370	123.60	100.0	34,561	114.57
*Departmental expenses**									
Rooms	18.9	4,806	16.56	20.5	4,133	16.29	17.9	4,018	13.32
Food & beverage	78.5	6,726	23.18	79.4	6,161	24.27	78.6	6,379	21.15
Telephone	92.0	1,247	4.30	98.2	884	3.48	100.0	934	3.10
Other operated departments	62.0	1,076	3.71	129.3	2,314	7.21	127.7	1,987	6.59
Total	36.2	13,856	47.75	41.5	13,010	51.26	38.5	13,318	44.15
Operated departmental income	63.8	24,373	84.00	58.5	18,360	72.34	61.5	21,243	70.42
Undistributed operating expenses									
Administrative and general	9.8	3,735	12.87	12.4	3,897	15.35	11.3	3,892	12.90
Marketing	5.9	2,262	7.80	8.2	2,563	10.10	8.3	2,878	9.54
Property operation & maintenance	8.6	3,277	11.29	11.6	3,633	14.32	8.8	3,039	10.07
Energy	7.4	2,823	9.73	8.3	2,608	10.27	5.5	1,887	6.26
Total	31.6	12,096	41.69	40.5	12,701	50.04	33.8	11,696	38.77
Income before fixed charges	32.1	12,277	42.31	18.0	5,659	22.30	27.6	9,547	31.65

*Each departmental expense ratio is based on the department's revenue and does not add to the total departmental expense ratio

Figure 3.2 Subject resort operating statement, Cancun, Mexico

	1992 78% $82 $64			1991 71% $69 $49			1990 74% $65 $48		
Year Occupancy percentage Average room rate Revpar	Ratio (%)	Per available room ($)	Per occupied room ($)	Ratio (%)	Per available room ($)	Per occupied room ($)	Ratio %	Per available room ($)	Per occupied room ($)
Revenues									
Rooms	59.3	23,346	82.11	60.0	18,009	69.10	60.2	17,602	64.99
Food	22.3	8,870	30.88	20.9	6,272	24.07	22.0	6,435	23.76
Beverage	11.3	4,449	15.65	9.8	2,941	11.28	11.4	3,332	12.30
Telephone	3.0	1,181	4.15	2.6	781	3.00	2.2	643	2.37
Other operated departments	2.1	827	2.91	1.5	450	1.73	2.1	615	2.27
Rentals/other income	2.0	787	2.77	5.2	1,562	5.99	2.1	615	2.27
Total	100.0	39,370	138.46	100.0	30,015	115.17	100.0	29,242	107.97
Departmental expenses*									
Rooms	21.8	5,079	17.86	22.3	4,021	15.43	21.1	3,714	13.71
Food and beverage	68.8	9,094	31.99	70.7	6,512	24.99	68.9	6,727	24.84
Telephone	60.0	709	2.49	65.2	509	1.95	54.6	351	1.30
Other operated departments	61.9	512	1.80	167.1	751	2.88	61.6	379	1.40
Total	39.1	15,394	54.14	39.3	11,793	45.25	38.2	11,171	41.25
Operated departmental income	60.9	23,976	84.32	60.7	18,222	69.92	61.8	18,071	66.73
Undistributed operating expenses									
Administrative and general	12.1	4,764	16.75	15.2	4,562	17.51	13.3	3,888	14.36
Marketing	9.1	3,582	12.60	10.0	3,002	11.52	9.3	2,721	10.05
Property operation and maintenance	8.0	3,150	11.08	9.2	2,760	10.59	8.8	2,575	9.51
Energy	7.3	2,874	10.11	7.6	2,281	8.75	6.2	1,814	6.70
Total	36.5	14,370	50.54	42.0	12,607	48.37	37.6	10,997	40.60
Income before fixed charges	24.4	9,606	33.79	18.7	5,615	21.55	24.2	7,075	26.12

*Each departmental expense ratio is based on the department's revenue and does not add to the total departmental expense ratio

Figure 3.3 Industry averages, Cancun, Mexico

Table 3.2   Rate structure analysis

Resort	Number of rooms (rounded)	Rate range ($) (single/double)	Amenities offered
Subject	500	170/170	A,B,C,D,E
Competitor A	300	135/135	A,B,C,D,E
Competitor B	300	155/155	A,B,C,D,E
Competitor C	300	145/145	A,B,D,E
Competitor D	500	176/176	A,B,C,D,E
Competitor E	450	160/160	A,B,C,D,E
Competitor F	450	130/130	A,B,C,D,E

A = Swimming pool; B = access to golf course; C = tennis; D = beach; E = watersports nearby.

The subject hotel has attempted to optimize its average daily rate by critically evaluating its room rate structure and amenities offered as compared to its competitors. As outlined in the rate structure analysis shown in Table 3.2, the subject hotel's amenities are not unlike its competitors, but it has positioned its rack rates above most of the others. This is usually unwise in a price-sensitive market such as Cancun, but the strong chain-affiliation and the strength of its reservation system allow it to receive a rate premium.

Table 3.3   Revpar analysis

	1992	1991	1990
Subject resort			
Average daily rate	$88	$79	$74
Occupancy percentage	80%	70%	83%
Revpar	$70	$56	$61
Industry averages			
Average daily rate	$82	$69	$65
Occupancy percentage	78%	71%	74%
Revpar	$64	$49	$48

Higher average daily rates generally have an effect in reducing the overall occupancy percentage. As outlined in Table 3.3 the subject hotel has also been able to exceed the market in an occupancy comparison. Revpar, also included in Table 3.3, consistently increased during 1990 through 1992 and outperformed the market. What has this hotel needed to do to achieve such desirable results? Outrageous marketing expenditures, extravagant maintenance costs, burdensome labour expenses? Benefits usually come with some associated cost but the goal should be to spend less than the increased revenues and therefore generate additional profit. The remainder of the chapter will review these expenses.

Rooms departmental expenses

The subject room department, to be profitable, must control departmental expenses including payroll, room amenities, cleaning supplies, laundry expenses, etc. An analysis of these expenses, as outlined in Table 3.4, indicated that payroll expenses were significantly below industry averages. This was accomplished by strict adherence to labour productivity standards, good employee relations, which reduced employee turnover, and actual pay scales.

Through most of the analysed period, the subject hotel did, however, exceed industry averages on non-payroll-related departmental expenses. This area appeared to be the financial weakness of the department. Few

Table 3.4 Payroll expenses

Year	Per occupied room		Per available room	
	Subject	Industry averages	Subject	Industry averages
Payroll expenses				
1990	$6.36	$8.74	$1,918	$2,421
1991	7.75	8.48	1,966	2,132
1992	8.64	8.91	2,507	2,535
Non-payroll expenses				
1990	$6.96	$4.97	$2,100	$1,293
1991	8.54	6.95	2,167	1,889
1992	7.92	8.95	2,299	2,544

control procedures were in place to restrict employee pilferage and excessive guest usage. No analysis had been conducted to determine the 'reasonable' amount of shampoo, cream rinse, suntan lotion, and other complimentary kits placed in guest rooms. In addition, no analysis had been conducted to determine whether appropriate reservation expenses were charged to the subject resort from the corporate reservations system. Since there was an agreed-upon charge for each confirmed and guaranteed reservation, this could be a significant financial drain.

Food and beverage department

Until the recent past, hotel management frequently considered hotel food and beverage operations to be amenities to hotel operations and were not expected to add significantly to the hotel's overall financial performance. These attitudes have changed since the early 1980s and now food and beverage profit is often vital to the overall financial viability of a hotel.

Table 3.5   Food analysis

Year	Food revenue per occupied room		Food cost percentage	
	Subject	Industry averages	Subject	Industry averages
1990	$20.34	$23.76	37.2%	34.4%
1991	22.59	24.07	41.2	34.3
1992	21.52	30.88	42.0	30.7

Why is the subject's food and beverage department less successful than its competitors? The lower than average revenues 'per occupied room,' as outlined in Table 3.5, likely indicates that the product offering is not fully meeting the demands of the guests and therefore they eat out more frequently than guests at other hotels. Why is this? Is it the quality of product, pricing structure, type of menu or merely a lack of effective internal marketing? A review of this operation indicated that many hotel guests were unaware that the restaurants existed in the hotel. Poor overall design resulted in reduced visibility from the resort's public areas. Few signs indicated what was available and no cross-selling existed at the front desk during check-in. A little creativity and training could have increased revenues significantly.

Food department

Food cost as a percentage of revenues has historically been higher at the subject resort than the market. This may be the result of a conscious management decision to serve higher-quality food, sell menu items at a lower price to encourage higher volume or poor control procedures.

A study of food products served and pricing compared to competition indicated that the problem was not related to quality or pricing. A study of kitchen and purchasing operations clearly indicated that the problem existed with controls. Did they have a scale to weigh products purchased by the pound? Inventory products purchased by quantity? Alarmed kitchen exit doors to discourage employee theft? Procedures for competitive pricing? Written cooking procedures to reduce waste?

Each of the aforementioned points has a major effect on the profitability of the department and in each case the answer at the subject hotel was no. Part of an operational review is to question the management team about these types of procedures. In each case, the cause was a lack of training and understanding of how to implement controls and the overall benefit of each.

Beverage department

Beverage revenues and cost of sales were both below industry averages, as identified in Table 3.6. The lower cost of sales is a result of higher selling prices and the lower revenue is also a result of higher selling prices. In this price-sensitive market, the guests are looking for value – a concept not well-understood by the management of the subject resort.

Table 3.6 Beverage analysis

| Year | Beverage revenue per occupied room | | Beverage cost percentage | |
	Subject	Industry averages	Subject	Industry averages
1990	$6.58	$12.30	18.2%	19.1%
1991	7.97	11.28	17.7	19.0
1992	8.02	15.65	16.9	15.3

Telephone

Telephone revenue per occupied room is more a function of ease and convenience than need. The subject resort makes it easy for a guest to make domestic and international calls with direct-dial, printed phone instructions and multilingual operators. The analysis of telephone expenses, however, is more difficult. As seen in Table 3.7, the subject resort appears to have a departmental cost double the industry average. Although they properly charge marketing and administrative and general calls to their respective departments, this hotel charged the cost of leasing the equipment to the telephone department and not to fixed charges as listed in the *Uniform System of Accounts for Hotels* (Hotel Association of New York City, 1986).

Table 3.7 Telephone analysis

| Year | Revenue per occupied room | | Departmental cost | |
	Subject	Industry averages	Subject	Industry averages
1990	$3.10	$2.37	100.0%	54.6%
1991	3.55	3.00	98.2	65.2
1992	4.67	4.15	92.0	60.0

Undistributed operating expenses

Administrative and general

The administrative and general expenses for the subject resort run substantially below that of the industry (Table 3.8). Effective corporate management and support activities shifted some duties handling them more efficiently. The disadvantage experienced in this design was reaction time. Decision-making slower than that of its competitors sometimes caused the hotel to lose out on purchase discounts and certain group business.

Table 3.8   Administrative and general expenses per available room

Year	Subject	Industry averages
1990	$3,892	$3,888
1991	3,897	4,562
1992	3,735	4,764

Marketing

Effective corporate marketing and name recognition have allowed the subject resort to incur substantially lower marketing costs (Table 3.9). Each marketing effort was evaluated for potential return on investment and the effectiveness of the effort at the end of the promotion. In addition, cost savings were realized because each sales manager had specific, well-defined markets and goals.

Table 3.9   Total marketing expenses

	Per occupied room		Per available room	
Year	Subject	Industry averages	Subject	Industry averages
1990	$9.54	$10.05	$2,878	$2,721
1991	10.10	11.52	2,563	3,002
1992	7.80	12.60	2,262	3,582

Property operation and maintenance

A comparison of the cost of property operation and maintenance expenses to the industry average requires more analysis and adjustment than many other areas. The following affect the costs incurred:

- Age of facility and equipment.
- Number of hectares landscaped.
- Location (e.g., directly on ocean).
- Design of buildings.
- Types of amenities (e.g. number of food and beverage outlets, number of pools, etc.).
- Size, design and furniture of guest room.

As outlined in Table 3.10, the subject resort has incurred higher maintenance costs per available room than the industry average. The property, older than many in Cancun, requires equipment updates and a more complete preventive maintenance programme to bring costs more in line.

Table 3.10 Property operation and maintenance expenses per available room

Year	Subject	Industry averages
1990	$3,039	$2,575
1991	3,633	2,760
1992	3,277	3,150

Energy costs

Energy consumption must be reviewed on both a per available and per occupied room basis to obtain a complete understanding of the cost. As seen in Table 3.11, overall consumption increased each year on a 'per available room' basis due primarily to increases in kilowatt charges by the utility company. The 'per occupied room' expense, however, increased significantly in 1991 and then fell in 1992. The subject resort did not have any energy awareness programmes in place in 1991 when the major kilowatt increase took place and the room attendants frequently set room thermostats at 20° C or less. This, in conjunction with no sensors to turn off the air conditioner when the sliding glass door was open, caused excessive consumption. By the end of 1991, these problems were corrected and consumption dropped.

Table 3.11 Energy costs

Year	Per occupied room		Per available room	
	Subject	Industry averages	Subject	Industry averages
1990	$6.26	$6.70	$1,887	$1,814
1991	10.27	8.75	2,608	2,281
1992	9.73	10.11	2,823	2,874

Conclusion

As the hospitality industry continues to face an increasingly competitive environment, effective managers must utilize all available methods to maximize hotel earnings. A complete understanding of financial statements, knowing how to maximize revenues and control expenses and focusing on the appropriate questions to ask is imperative for timely solutions. Hospitality managers using operational analyses adapted to a changing hospitality environment will be more efficient managers and more effective leaders.

References

Brooks, G. (1991) Focus on Industry. *Journal of Accountancy*, 104–109.

Callahan, T. (1993) Making a case for higher room rates. In: *Trends in the Hotel Industry*. PKF Consulting, USA, p. 4.

Dearden, J. (1978) Cost advancing comes to the service industries. *Harvard Business Review* **78**; 132–140.

Hotel Association of New York City (1986) *Uniform System of Accounts for Hotels*, 8th ed. p. 99.

Lesure, J.D. (1983) Internal control in hotels. *Lodging*, **8**; 18–23.

McDowell, E. (1993) Hotel business wakes up. *New York Times*, 2 October, p. Y26.

Moncarz, E.S. and Kron, R.N. (1993) Operational analysis: a case study of two hotels in financial distress, *International Journal of Hospitality Management* **12**; 175–196.

Pannell Kerr Forster (1989, 1990, 1991, 1992, 1993) *Tendencias en la Hotelería Mexicana*. PKF Consulting.

PKF Consulting (1993) *Trends in the Hotel Industry – International Edition*, PKF Consulting, London pp. 7–8.

Quain, W.J. (1992). Analyzing sales-mix profitability. *Cornell Hotel and Restaurant Administration Quarterly* **33**; pp 57–62.

Quek, P. and Hopper, A.K.T. (1993) Tourism in a post-cold war economy. In: *Trends in the Hotel Industry – International Edition*. PKF Consulting, London, p 4.

Warmick, R. (1993) Operations problem solvers. *Lodging* 23.

4 Labour recruitment and turnover costs in hotels

Angela Maher

Introduction

The hotel industry is currently one of the fastest-growing and most competitive industries in the world. It is also becoming increasingly global, with many hotel companies operating on an international scale. In the UK, the hotel and catering industry is a major employer and, according to figures provided by Hotel and Catering Training Company (HCTC), the industry employed 2.4 million people in 1992 or 9.5 per cent of the workforce. Although hotels fared rather badly in the recession, they continue to be one of the largest employers in the commercial sectors of the industry, with some 289,200 employees (HCTC, 1994a). Furthermore, employment in hotels is expected to increase steadily to the end of the decade, reaching 317,000 jobs by the year 2000.

The labour-intensive nature of the industry means that the effective management of human resources is critically important. Human resources constitute a major element of total operating costs and the ability of management to control these costs is vital to long-term business success. Given the importance of human resources in the delivery of the service product and the high costs of labour it would seem appropriate to explore ways in which hotel organizations can, and do, measure the costs associated with the employment of people. The employment policies and practices of an organization will have a direct impact on labour costs, and management needs to ensure that human resource activities add value to the business.

Concern with measuring the economic worth of the human resource function is by no means a new phenomenon, but it is one that is receiving an increasing amount of attention in terms of practical applications. This surge in interest has been intensified by the current recessionary climate which has focused attention more acutely on the costs associated with human resource activities, and managers are increasingly being asked to justify their decisions in financial terms. This development has proven to be especially difficult for human resource managers as their activities are usually evaluated in behavioural or statistical terms rather than economic ones (Cascio, 1991).

The purpose of this chapter is to examine the extent to which hotel companies can, and do, account for human resource management in economic terms. The chapter will focus specifically on the financial costs of recruitment and labour turnover within organizations – two areas of particular concern to the hotel industry. The chapter is underpinned by findings from an ongoing research project investigating the concept of human resource value in UK hotels and it is divided into two main sections. Section One introduces the reader to the basic theoretical concepts of accounting for human resources and contains a brief review of the literature on human resource accounting (HRA). HRA is concerned with the value of people as organizational resources and encompasses several approaches to measuring and accounting for their cost and/or value. The principal impediments to the development of HRA are evaluated in this section as well as the reasons behind the renewal of interest in accounting for human resources.

The primary focus of Section Two concerns the practical aspects of measuring the costs of recruitment and labour turnover in hotels. Findings from survey research conducted by the author on the extent to which major hotel companies account for the costs associated with the employment of trainee managers are discussed in this section. The chapter concludes with some general comments on the importance of accounting for human resource management practices in the hotel industry.

SECTION ONE

Accounting for human resource management: theoretical issues

Management in the hospitality industry pays considerable lip service to the notion that the human resources of a hotel constitute a major organizational asset, and many are aware that it is the human element of the service product that provides the key to competitive advantage in the market place. However, one may question the extent to which these human resources are being managed with the same accountability, rationality and care as the plant, equipment and marketing resources of the organization, given the reputation of the industry for its poor personnel management practices.

Human resource activities are seldom subjected to the same rigorous financial evaluation as other areas of management and, within current accounting practice, investments in human resources are treated as expenses or costs of operation to be written off in the profit and loss account in the period in which they are incurred. This would seem to imply that, by accounting standards, human resources are treated in the same way as consumable materials with no value beyond the current accounting period (Dawson, 1989). However, one of the most important functions of management is the recruitment and retention of quality employees as it is a mechanism by which an organization can increase its stock of human capital. Therefore, resources devoted to recruitment and retention constitute a major organizational investment, one that is expected to provide returns well beyond the current accounting period.

The development of human resource accounting

This apparent imbalance in accounting practice has attracted the attention of academics from a variety of disciplines including economists, accountants and organizational psychologists and has led to the development of a field of research known HRA. According to Roslender (1992), HRA was one of the most researched areas in the accounting field in the late 1960s and throughout the 1970s. It was advanced as a means by which managers could improve their utilization of human resources through the use of various techniques and models designed to measure the economic value of the human side of the organization. HRA was envisaged as a way of providing managers with the information they needed to manage human resources more effectively and efficiently and for reporting the external value of human assets to external stakeholders. Many financial accounting-based models were developed for measuring the value of an organization's human resources and these ranged from fairly simple historical cost models to highly complex value-based models which employed more sophisticated mathematical techniques in their formulation. It is not within the scope of this chapter to present the models here and interested readers should consult Flamholtz (1985) for an excellent review of the development of HRA. However, given its apparent relevance for managers, it seems prudent to discuss the major reasons why HRA has made little progress in terms of empirical application.

Impediments to the development of HRA

The first impediment to the development of HRA concerns the debate surrounding humans as assets. There has been some controversy surrounding the exact definition of an asset, but it is generally accepted that certain conditions will be satisfied. First, an asset must possess future service potential (utility); second, it must be measurable in monetary terms and finally it must be subject to ownership or control. It is the third criterion of ownership that has caused most controversy as many people believe that humans cannot be owned by the organization. According to Ferguson and Berger (1985), even those who can accept the idea of the employee as an asset are left with the difficult task of assigning a realistic value to it. Thus the second basic objection is that human valuation is too difficult or subjective to measure. HRA models have been severely criticized on the grounds that no method is both objective and meaningful; those methods that are more objective are less meaningful and the reverse is also true. Even the most ardent supporters of HRA recognize the difficulties of conforming to the conventional accounting criteria of objectivity, reliability, timeliness and cost when measuring the value of human resources.

A further obstacle to the development of HRA has been the lack of cooperation and communication between human resource specialists and accountants. Dawson (1988) believes that neither profession has devoted much time to developing the necessary framework for making the personnel managers' arguments compatible and comparable with those of managers from other areas. Managers compete for the resources of the business on financial grounds and those variables that can be quantitatively measured tend to be emphasized in the decision-making process. As the activities of the personnel department are seldom subject to quantitative analysis, this would seem to indicate that there is a reluctance on both sides to develop meaningful ways to evaluate the effectiveness of the function.

HRA has also been criticized at a philosophical level. Concern has been expressed that, in attempting to account for their value, employees will become dehumanized and considered only in terms of their profitability. This seems a rather weak argument as the current accounting treatment of employees under conventional accounting systems (i.e. as consumable materials) is in itself dehumanizing. It seems ironic that this should be put forward as a criticism of HRA.

As can be seen, there have been various reasons proposed to explain why HRA failed to reach the potential envisaged for it by its advocates, but the most fundamental criticism lies at the conceptual level. This is articulated well by Roslender (1992), who argues that the problem lies with the emphasis placed on measuring the value of human resources for financial reporting purposes. This has proven difficult to operationalize as well as raising concerns about the defects inherent in conventional accounting systems concerning the valuation of assets generally (Armstrong, 1991). The limitations in these early HRA models meant they were perceived as having little practical utility, and interest in exploring this field declined in the early 1980s. Furthermore, the industrial climate at this time effectively focused attention on labour as a cost to be minimized, and elaborate methods of accounting for the value of human resources seemed to have limited relevance for management.

Accounting for human resource management in the 1990s

The need to develop meaningful ways of evaluating the contribution of the human resource function has become more pressing in the 1990s, and HRA has once again become the subject of an increasing amount of literary debate (Armstrong 1987, 1991; Dawson 1988, 1989; Cascio, 1991; Roslender 1992). This resurgence in interest can be attributed to a number of major factors. First, the transformation of many mature economies from industrial to high-tech service-based has highlighted the contribution of human resources in improving organizational productivity. Management are beginning to recognize the fact that it is people who add value to the product, and this is especially true in service industries where the human input is central to service quality. The second factor stems from the rediscovery of the neo-human relations philosophy of people management. This led to the emergence of what has become known as the *people initiative*, exemplified most vividly in the writings on corporate excellence by Peters and Waterman (1982). Evolving alongside this was the enormous amount of literature published on Japanese management practices and, more especially, human resource management which promotes the philosophy that people are a resource to be maximized rather than a cost to be minimized. Finally, the economic recession has forced organizations to rationalize their operations in an attempt to increase efficiency, and employers have been searching for ways to make more effective use of their employees. This has inevitably led to closer scrutiny of labour costs in order to evaluate the impact of personnel practices on the organization's bottom line.

Interest in accounting for human resource management has been analogous to the recognition of the intrinsic significance, role and value of employees as a major organizational resource. Thus, the central tenet of HRA holds true – that human resources constitute a major organizational investment, and further knowledge about the costs and benefits of different ways of managing people may help managers make more informed decisions in this area. Despite the criticisms outlined above, the HRA literature does offer some useful and practical advice concerning the measurement of human resource activities. Recent research in this area has focused on the use of HRA *expense models* to measure the economic consequences of employee behaviours (e.g. absenteeism, turnover, etc.) as opposed to *asset models* which assess the economic value of employees (Cascio, 1991). This may be seen as a way of circumventing many of the problems associated with the development of HRA as an aid to management decision-making, and this is the approach that underpins this chapter.

SECTION TWO

Accounting for human resource management: practical issues

The importance of accounting information in organizations

According to Hopwood (1972), 'accounting systems are often the most important formal sources of information in industrial organizations'. The information generated by such systems is intended to assist management in making decisions that are in accord with wider organizational goals. More importantly, accounting measures are frequently used as a basis for assessing managerial performance in their job. The dominance of accounting controls in UK organizations has raised concerns regarding the management of human resources (Armstrong, 1991), as performance in this area is usually evaluated in behavioural terms. Managers responsible for human resources may be tempted to adopt strategies which increase short-term profitability at the expense of longer term stability. For example, cutting investments in recruitment, training and development may result in short-term cost savings, but the effects of depleting the organization's stock of human capital could be devastating in the long-term. Another related point was highlighted in the previous section of this chapter and concerns the emphasis placed on quantitative, or financial, variables when making organizational decisions. If these variables are afforded more weight in the decision-making process, then it is reasonable to assume that those things which can be measured become more highly valued and gain in importance. Given that the functions of the human resource department are seldom subject to quantitative analysis, this would seem to indicate that they would be considered less important as a factor in organizational decision-making. This situation may have served to marginalize the human resource function in many organizations where personnel is assigned to a peripheral role in business decisions.

The myth that human resource activities cannot be evaluated in quantitative terms has been challenged by many authors. Cascio (1991) believes that 'all aspects of human resource management can be measured and quantified' in the same way as other operational functions. However, certain elements are more easily measured than others. The following sections explore recruitment and labour turnover issues in UK hotels and discuss the practical aspects of measuring the related costs.

Recruitment in the UK hotel industry

The recruitment of employees is a central function of the human resource management process and some would say it is *the* most important function. The ability of the organization to attract and recruit the right people for the right jobs at the right time is an essential prerequisite to long-term organizational survival. Unfortunately the hotel industry has acquired a rather poor reputation for being able to attract and retain quality staff. As stated in the introduction to this chapter, employment in the UK hotel industry is forecast to grow by approximately 28,000 jobs by the end of the decade. However, there are already signs that hotels are experiencing problems recruiting suitable staff. Although recruitment rates in the hospitality industry overall have halved since the 1979–80 level of 56 per cent (HCTC, 1994b), recruitment difficulties (in terms of 'hard-to-fill' vacancies) exist at rates well above the national average. Twenty-one per cent of establishments in the industry experienced difficulty in recruiting employees in 1993, compared with 13 per cent for both textiles and electronic engineering (Dale, 1994).

Difficulties in recruitment have been attributed, in part, to the poor personnel management practices seen as inherent in the UK hotel industry. Unstructured career paths, lack of access to training opportunities, long unsocial hours and poor pay and conditions have all been cited as problem areas. Other factors, external to the organization, have served to exacerbate these problems. The decline in the number of young people entering the labour market is likely to continue throughout the 1990s and, as the industry traditionally attracts a high proportion of young workers, this 'demographic timebomb' is likely to hit hotels particularly hard. Employers are increasingly being forced to look at alternative sources of labour in their recruitment drives and competition for skilled workers is becoming more intense. Equal opportunities legislation has also forced employers to re-evaluate their employment policies and, in particular, their use of 'word-of- mouth' recommendation as a popular and inexpensive way of recruiting employees. Such practices have been found to be discriminatory and can result in costly tribunal cases.

These pressures have meant that managers in hotel organizations have become increasingly cognizant of the need to place more emphasis on the recruitment process. Recognition of the importance of recruitment in the human resource management process has been underpinned by the increasing use of more sophisticated selection techniques, such as behavioural interviewing and the use of assessment centres. Psychological testing has also become a popular selection device, especially for management level employees. Understandably, the use of such procedures has led to escalating expenditure in this area and therefore an increasing need to maintain a firm control over such costs.

Measuring the costs of recruitment

Recruitment costs, as defined here, are those costs associated with identifying and attracting potential employees to the organization. The recruitment process can incur both direct and indirect costs: direct and indirect costs are terms used to indicate the degree to which certain costs can be directly attributable to the recruitment process. Direct recruitment costs may include expenditure in a number of areas, including advertising costs, employment agency fees, university/college recruiting costs, travel costs, costs of informational literature for applicants, etc. Direct recruitment costs should be relatively easy to identify from current accounting records as they involve cash expenditure on behalf of the organization. Indirect recruitment costs are less visible in most organizations and can include the costs of recruiting internally as well as the cost of time spent by different levels of personnel on recruitment activities. These activities may include writing job descriptions and person specifications, drawing up advertisements, dealing with queries about the job and sending information to interested parties, sifting applications, arranging interviews, etc.

Indirect recruitment costs are more difficult to ascertain, as time spent on recruitment activities is seldom monitored or recorded in organizations. However, this information can be collected fairly easily by asking the relevant people to detail the recruitment activities they undertake and the amount of time spent at each stage. This can be recorded every time they are involved in the recruitment of employees (through the use of a standard form designed for this purpose) or average times can be estimated for recruitment activities and standard costs established. Costs are calculated by multiplying the time spent on recruitment activities by the pay rates of the individuals involved. The standard costing approach may be more appropriate in situations where substantial levels of similar workers are recruited on a regular basis. However, it should be noted that these costs will need updating from time to time to take into account pay rises and changes in an organization's recruitment procedures.

Recruitment costs of management trainees in UK hotels

The actual expense incurred in the recruitment of employees will be dependent on the specific policies and procedures of a particular organization as well as the characteristics of the actual job itself. Evidence from a survey carried out in 1992 on the employment of trainee managers reveals that hotel companies in the UK tend to utilize multiple sources of recruitment rather than one particular source (Maher, 1993). Although this can add to overall recruitment costs, it may be an effective way of locating the most suitable applicants. It was also apparent from the survey data that a large percentage of employers recruit directly from educational establishments or use internal promotion as a means of filling trainee management positions. These methods of recruitment incur relatively modest direct costs compared with specialist employment agencies or advertising, though the indirect costs to the organization can be substantial.

The recruitment of management trainees usually takes place centrally in large hotel organizations and will involve direct input from senior human resource managers at head office. The cost of recruitment will therefore need to include the cost of time spent by these managers on recruitment activities. This cost can be significant given that the average salary of a personnel manager at this level is £27,033 per year (Touche Ross, 1993). These costs can increase substantially if a senior manager is involved in liaising with and visiting several educational establishments, as this can involve weeks of work. Administration costs associated with recruitment can also be high if a major amount of time is spent on processing application forms, sending out information about the post and arranging interviews for applicants.

Unfortunately, current information systems in hotels do not routinely measure the costs of personnel/management time spent on recruitment activities, and only two of the 37 companies responding to the survey attempted to measure this element of the recruitment process. Moreover, the survey evidence suggests that surprisingly little attention is paid to recruitment costs generally in hotel organizations. At unit level, for example, although there seemed to be considerable intervention by central management in the setting of recruitment budgets for individual hotels, the costs of recruiting trainee managers at this level could not be identified in almost two-thirds of responding organizations (in half of these, recruitment costs did not even appear as a separate item in the financial management reports of the units). Control over recruitment costs appears to be somewhat lax and the current reporting system operating in certain organizations demands no feedback from the units on how much was even spent on recruitment. Tracking expenditure in these organizations will involve changing present reporting systems and this may seem an unnecessary expense with the recent fall in recruitment activity. There is a danger that the recession has made employers somewhat complacent about the importance of recruitment in the human resource management process. This could lead to a short-term approach to resourcing and an indifferent attitude to measuring the effectiveness of recruitment.

The measurement of original recruitment costs is a fairly basic exercise for the most part (original costs are those related to the recruitment of employees for new positions within the organization). Data on original recruitment costs can be collected comparatively easily, if it is not currently available. It should be noted, however, that this model measures the costs associated with recruitment only. In practice, the isolation of recruitment from other human resource management activities is difficult because the majority of vacancies arise as a result of the movement of current employees through the organization. Recruitment is therefore closely linked to labour turnover, and the need to replace employees who have left the organization.

Labour turnover in the UK hotel industry

The latest figures provided by the HCTC (1994b) estimate a labour turnover rate in hotels of over 33 per cent per annum, or one-third of the total workforce. As with recruitment, employee turnover rates in this sector have declined dramatically over the past decade. Relative to other industries, however, catering and hospitality still had the highest turnover of employees in 1991–92.

Labour turnover is a topic that has received much attention from both academics and practitioners in the hotel industry. The vast majority of research in this area has concentrated on isolating the causes of labour turnover in an attempt to prescribe solutions for reducing the 'problem'. However, although all parties may agree that the hospitality industry has an extremely high level of employee turnover, there is a lack of consensus over whether this constitutes a problem for organizations.

There are those who argue that high levels of turnover are detrimental to the organization as they can adversely affect the quality of products and services and can induce dysfunctional behaviour amongst remaining employees. These writers place emphasis on managerial action as a means of alleviating high levels of employee turnover. Those who question this viewpoint believe that high turnover among employees is not only inevitable, but also desirable. They argue that employee mobility within the industry promotes workforce flexibility, allowing employees to acquire and develop new skills as they move through different organizations. The acquisition of transferable skills is thought to appeal to the entrepreneurial aspirations of hospitality employees and thus, turnover is actively encouraged in an attempt to create future managers for the industry. Labour turnover may also be used as a way of bringing new ideas into the workplace and preventing stagnation in creativity (see Wood, 1992 for a more detailed analysis of this debate). Clearly, whether labour turnover is good or bad remains an issue, but what does need to be recognized is that even low levels of turnover can be problematic if it occurs amongst valuable employees that the hotel wishes to retain.

Turnover rates tend to be much higher amongst operative level staff, yet the loss of employees in management positions can prove more costly to the organization. Management employees are seen as 'knowledge' workers in the industry and are therefore likely to attract higher levels of human capital investments. The loss of management employees can incur considerable financial cost in terms of investments that have been made in their recruitment, training and development. Furthermore, the industry is experiencing difficulties in replacing managers and this can add to the high costs of turnover. The industry is suffering a serious shortage of skilled managers and this situation has been aggravated by the tendency for departing managers to leave the industry altogether. The lack of opportunities for promotion and career development has been cited as one of the main causes of turnover among managers and more substantial levels of investment in this area will be required if attrition rates are to be curbed. Hotel organizations will also need to look further afield for suitable candidates and will find themselves having to compete on the same terms as industries which offer much more attractive benefit packages and career prospects.

Measuring the costs of labour turnover is an important first step to understanding its root causes, but it should not be seen as an end in itself. It is important to determine why employees are leaving and then concentrate on those aspects of turnover over which the organization has some control. The main reason for costing labour turnover is to use the information to improve managerial decision-making. Once turnover costs have been established, the benefits of investing in alternative human resource strategies designed to retain valuable workers can then be assessed.

Measuring the costs of labour turnover

Labour turnover refers to the movement of employees beyond organizational boundaries. Levels of labour turnover are relatively easy to calculate in terms of the number of incidents, but the actual costs of it to the organization are far more difficult to ascertain (Cascio, 1991). As with recruitment, labour turnover incurs both direct and indirect costs. However, because of its multifaceted nature, the indirect or 'hidden' costs of turnover can be difficult to measure. For example, it is widely acknowledged that labour turnover can adversely affect employee morale and this in turn can have a negative impact on productivity levels. The problem lies in determining the extent to which declining productivity levels are directly attributable to high labour turnover. Only when these costs can be determined accurately should they be included in cost calculations.

It should be noted that it is unusual for an organization to want to eliminate labour turnover completely as it may offer the opportunity of improving the business through the recruitment of better workers. It is important to establish exactly where turnover is occurring and to analyse its impact on productivity levels. Individual organizations have different labour requirements and will need to decide on the optimal levels of turnover for each job category in the organizational hierarchy. Once appropriate levels have been determined, the organization will then be in a position to evaluate whether turnover is potentially damaging its operations and consequently its bottom line.

The costing of labour turnover incorporates the notion of replacement costs, that is, all those costs associated with replacing an employee who has left the organization. The way these costs are computed will depend to a great extent on the current costing conventions in place in the organization. Consistency in the conventions adopted is essential throughout the costing exercise. In costing labour turnover it is useful to categorize the different stages of the employment process where costs are incurred. There are seven cost categories to consider:

1. Recruitment costs.
2. Selection costs.
3. Engagement costs.
4. Induction costs.
5. Formal training costs.
6. Informal training costs.
7. Separation costs.

The costs of recruitment were examined earlier and the remainder of this section will focus on the other six cost categories. Once the organization has attracted a pool of applicants the selection process can begin. Selection costs are those associated with deciding which candidates are suitable for employment in the organization. Direct costs of selection may include the costs of employment tests used and the costs of renting space for interviews or assessment centres. Indirect costs of selection would include the cost of time spent by current employees in selection activities, and this can be calculated employing the same technique as that for costing recruitment activities. Time spent interviewing candidates, administering employment tests and checking references should be costed, as should the time spent in meetings to decide who should be offered employment. It is usually the case that more candidates are interviewed than are required by the organization, but the costs associated with unsuccessful applicants form part of total selection costs and should also be included.

Engagement costs refer to the costs of actually appointing the new employee. Direct costs can be considerable if the organization pays the expenses of relocating replacement workers, although this practice is uncommon for hotel companies. Indirect costs would include the cost of time spent on administrative tasks associated with the new appointment (i.e. the creation of new personnel records). Induction costs are those costs associated with familiarizing new employees with the organization. Induction can be an expensive process, depending on the length and content of the particular programme, and direct costs may include the cost of providing replacement employees with staff handbooks, organizational policy literature, etc. Indirect costs will include the cost of time spent by current employees involved in the orientation process as well as the total wage costs of replacement employees, should they be unproductive during the induction period.

Training can take a number of different forms and can be broadly classed as 'formal' or 'informal'. Formal training usually takes place off the job and can be delivered by people from within the organization or by external experts. In either case, both direct and indirect costs will be incurred. The costs of training courses run externally should be relatively easy to estimate from current accounting records. Direct costs of training run by the organization itself may include the costs of training materials, costs of hiring equipment, and the costs of providing food and accommodation for both trainers and trainees. Indirect costs are comprised mainly of the trainees' wages for the period and the appropriate proportion of the trainer's salary that is related to training replacement employees.

Informal training, or training on the job, is a popular form of training in hotel organizations. The costs associated with this form of training are more difficult to measure as they are mostly indirect in nature. The replacement employee and informal trainer may be productive during the training period; however, the performance of both may be substantially lower than what is considered 'normal' for their particular jobs. To measure these costs accurately, the organization would need to establish standard productivity levels for each job category against which to measure the performance of trainers and trainees. This is a demanding exercise and may simply not be practical for certain service jobs where employee productivity is notoriously difficult to measure. Costs of informal training can be estimated by asking trainers to evaluate the extent to which their performance drops during the period of on-job training. For example, if they estimate a 50 per cent fall in their productivity levels during the period then the appropriate proportion of their wages (i.e. half) would be included in informal training costs. Trainers can also be asked to estimate the productivity levels achieved by trainees at different stages of their training. Trainees' performance levels may improve systematically over the training period and this should be taken into account when assessing the proportion of their wages to be attributed to the costs of on-job training. This may seem a rather crude method of assessing informal training costs, but it is a practicable alternative when more objective productivity measures are unavailable.

The final element of turnover costs is incurred during the separation period. Direct costs of separation may include payments made to workers who have been made redundant or, in the case of employees who leave voluntarily, the costs of employing temporary staff to cover the vacant position until a suitable replacement is engaged. Indirect costs of separation may include the cost of time spent in exit interviews and on administrative tasks associated with terminating the employment relationship. It is generally the case that, prior to separation, the leaving employee's performance declines and this should be costed whenever possible using the method described earlier in calculating on-job training costs.

Turnover costs of management trainees in UK hotels

The extent to which the costs of turnover can be measured will be dependent upon whether the organization currently computes the frequency of turnover among management trainees. Thirty-one of the thirty seven organizations responding to the author's survey claimed that it was possible to identify levels of turnover among this category of employee in their hotel units. Unfortunately, respondents did not specify whether turnover rates were measured and recorded in a formal way, only that it was 'possible' to identify the level. The accuracy with which turnover levels are measured could therefore be open to question. Indeed, findings of recent HCTC research reveal that, in a survey of over 2,000 UK employers in the hospitality industry, only 6 per cent of establishments had systems in place to measure labour turnover (HCTC, 1994b). If these latter statistics are to be believed, it would be reasonable to assume that the majority of hospitality employers in this country are, at present, unable to determine the financial impact of labour turnover in their organizations.

Almost one-quarter of survey respondents claimed to know the annual financial cost of turnover among management trainees. Once again, these responses must be treated with caution as regards the accuracy with which such costs are evaluated. As noted earlier, these organizations do not measure the cost of time spent by those employees involved in recruitment activities. Also, time spent at the selection and engagement stages is rarely accounted for in financial terms, even though it has been shown that costs in all these areas (i.e. recruitment, selection and engagement) can be substantial. Further analysis of the survey data revealed that only eight organizations in the sample were able to identify induction costs for management trainees, although almost all of these organizations operated formal induction programmes for this category of worker. Induction was rarely analysed in terms of its effectiveness in retaining valuable workers, and this may indicate that organizations are running costly programmes that accomplish little in inducing workers to stay.

The costs associated with training also seem to be afforded minimal attention in many organizations. Although survey respondents appeared to be aware of the significance of these costs with regard to management trainees, only one in four could identify training costs for such employees at unit level. Furthermore, it would seem that in the majority of cases these costs refer solely to the direct costs of formal training. The survey data revealed that a large percentage of trainee managers' instruction occurs informally on the job, yet only three of the responding organizations made any attempt to cost the time spent by employees on this form of training. Given these findings it can be assumed that the true costs of training are not known to most organizations, as informal training is seldom included in such calculations. The indirect nature of informal training costs means they remain hidden in the financial reports of hotel units, and there appears to be little incentive to evaluate the effectiveness of informal training. However, without this information it is impossible for the organization to compare the benefits of investing in different forms of training to achieve long term organizational success. Training on the job may seem inexpensive in the short term, but management trainees may be reluctant to remain in organizations that seem committed to investing only in basic skills development.

It would appear that the financial impact of turnover among management trainees has been significantly underestimated by respondents who profess to measure such costs. The information needed to measure turnover costs is simply not available in most organizations and the collection of appropriate data may seem too costly or complicated to justify. However, organizations will need to consider seriously how long they can remain competitive in an industry where employee turnover is estimated to cost in excess of £430 million per annum (HCTC, 1994b).

Conclusion

The hospitality literature is infused with management rhetoric about the value of human resources, and management pays considerable lip service to the notion that employees constitute a major organizational asset. However, one may question the extent to which these valuable resources are being managed with the same care and attention as other major resources of the business. Hotel and catering has the highest rate of labour turnover compared to other industries in the UK, and this is seen as symptomatic of the poor personnel management practices adopted by hospitality employers. However, labour turnover seems a matter of little concern to the majority of employers in the industry and this can only convey the message that, far from being seen as a valuable resource, employees are often viewed as an easily substitutable consumable.

The human resources of a hotel constitute a major organizational investment in terms of time and money, and effective and efficient use of these resources is vital to the long-term success of the business. Although the contribution and importance of human resources are often acknowledged abstractly (i.e. our people are our most important asset) the day-to-day decisions of line and top management often belie this sentiment. Human resource programmes are often the first to be targeted for budget cuts and managers have trouble justifying these programmes in subjective terms alone. Unfortunately, current accounting practice means that the costs of such programmes are often more visible and measurable than their benefits.

Insufficient attention has been paid to developing ways of evaluating the effectiveness of human resource strategies in economic terms, and there seems to be some reluctance in applying accounting methods in such an evaluation lest employees become dehumanized in the process. However, the dominance of management accounting controls in organizations is likely to prevail and managers who wish to invest in their human resources will find themselves under increasing pressure to present their arguments in financial terms.

Given its labour-intensive nature and dependence upon the quality of service, HRA would seem to be particularly pertinent to the hotel industry. Management in the industry are becoming increasingly aware of the need to make more effective and efficient use of the human resources available to them, and although HRA does not claim to solve all the problems, it is possible that certain HRA data may help management make more informed decisions regarding the human resources under their control.

References

Armstrong, P. (1987) The personnel profession in the age of management accountancy. *Personnel Review* **17**; 25–31.

Armstrong, P. (1991) Limits and possibilities for HRM in an age of management accountancy. In: Storey, J. (ed.) *New Perspectives on Human Resource Management.* Routledge, London, pp.154–166.

Cascio, W. F. (1991) *Costing Human Resources.* Kent: PWS.

Dale, I. (1994) Recent trends in skills shortages. *Employment Gazette* **102**(4); 123–126.

Dawson, C. (1988) The accounting approach to employee resourcing. *Management Decision* **26**; 31–35.

Dawson, C. (1989) The moving frontiers of personnel management: human resource management or human resource accounting. *Personnel Review*, **18**, No.3, pp. 3–12.

Ferguson, D. H. and Berger, F. (1985) Employees as assets: a fresh approach to human resources accounting. *The Cornell HRA Quarterly* **25**(4); 24–29.

Flamholtz, E. G. (1985) *Human Resource Accounting.* Jossey-Bass, San Francisco.

Hopwood, A. G. (1972) An empirical study of the role of accounting data in performance evaluation. *Journal of Accounting Research* **10**; 156–182.

HCTC (1994a) *Catering and Hospitality Industry – Key Facts and Figures.* HCTC, London.

HCTC (1994b) *Employment Flows in the Catering and Hospitality Industry.* HCTC, London.

Maher, A. (1993) Accounting for human resources in UK hotels: Some initial findings. Paper given at the Council for Hospitality Management Education Research Conference, Manchester Metropolitan University, April.

Peters, T. J. and Waterman, R. H. (1982). *In Search of Excellence: Lessons from America's Best Run Companies.* Harper & Row, New York.

Roslender, R. (1992) *Sociological Perspectives on Modern Accountancy.* Routledge, London.

Touche Ross and Co (1993) *Pay and Benefits in the Hospitality Industry,* Touche Ross, London.

Wood, R. C. (1992) *Working in Hotels and Catering.* Routledge, London.

Part II Financial Planning

5 Statistical cost estimation and prediction in hotels

Peter J. Harris

Introduction

An understanding of cost behaviour is relevant to managers as it provides an insight into the operating environment of an undertaking and in doing so assists in the decision-making process. For instance, it provides the basis on which to gain an impression of the cost structure and business orientation of an enterprise. Kotas (1973) drew attention to business orientation through the fact that low fixed-cost undertakings are product (cost)-oriented, whilst high fixed-cost undertakings are market (revenue)-oriented. Management should recognize the influence of cost structure on business orientation and approach decision-making accordingly. In addition, a knowledge of cost behaviour aids routine financial planning and control in an organization. Decisions concerning forecasting and budgeting, profit planning and pricing strategies are all partly influenced by the way costs react to the particular situation under consideration.

Whilst there are a number of subjective approaches to determining cost behaviour, such as observed by Harris (1992), the aim of this chapter is to explore a statistical analysis of costs associated with hotel undertakings. The content includes an illustration and explanation of the methods used, past and current research findings, and an evaluation of the technique and results in terms of hotel management decision-making.

Linear regression

Linear regression is a statistical technique for specifying the relationship between variables. The technique uses a formal model (equation) to measure the average amount of change in a dependent variable, e.g. cost, that is associated with change in one or more independent variables, e.g. volume of rooms occupied, covers sold, etc. Where only one independent variable is included in a model the technique is referred to as simple regression; where two or more independent variables are included, the technique is termed multiple regression.

Linear regression analysis uses a sample of past costs to estimate how the population of costs behave. The technique used is the method of least squares which determines the line of best fit for a given set of data. The least-squares line is so called because the sum of the squares of the vertical distances (residuals) from the regression line to the plots of the actual data points is less than it would be for any other line.

The least-squares line is represented by the following equation:

$$\hat{y} = a + bx$$

where $\hat{y}$ = estimated total cost (dependent variable); a = fixed cost (constant); b = average variable cost per unit of activity (slope coefficient); and x = measure of activity (independent variable).

The objective is to determine the a and b values in the regression equation and these are obtained by the simultaneous solution of two normal equations:

$$\Sigma y = na + b(\Sigma x)$$
$$\Sigma xy = a(\Sigma x) + b(\Sigma x^2)$$

where y = observed values (actual data points); n = number of observations in the sample; Σx = sum of the observations of the independent variable(s); Σy = sum of the observations of the dependent variable(s); Σx^2 = sum of the squares of the x observations; and Σxy = sum of the product of each pair of observations.

Simple linear regression illustration

The data in Table 5.1 relate to the restaurant department of an international hotel in terms of the monthly number of covers sold and direct payroll expense for a one-year period. However, prior to performing any computations it is essential to obtain a visual impression of the data by the use of a scattergraph, presented in Figure 5.1. Scrutiny of the data plot will indicate the degree of relationship which exists between the payroll cost and volume of covers sold. The scattergraph is a critical step in determining the cost behaviour pattern and should never be omitted. In Figure 5.1, the data plot indicates that a linear regression equation will provide a reasonable

Table 5.1 Restaurant data for statistical computations

Month	Covers sold x	Direct payroll £ y	x^2	xy	$\hat{y}$	$(y-\bar{y})^2$	$(y-\hat{y})^2$	$(x-\bar{x})^2$
1	22	88	484	1,936	84.439	462.25	12.667	51.366
2	7	56	49	392	46.892	110.25	82.961	61.356
3	20	80	400	1,600	79.433	182.25	0.321	26.698
4	8	40	64	320	49.395	702.25	88.264	46.690
5	19	84	361	1,596	76.390	306.25	49.986	17.364
6	10	52	100	520	54.401	210.25	5.766	23.358
7	12	68	144	816	59.408	2.25	73.829	8.026
8	19	64	361	1,216	76.930	6.25	167.183	17.364
9	13	60	169	780	61.911	42.25	3.651	3.360
10	17	76	289	1,292	71.924	90.25	16.617	4.696
11	15	56	225	840	66.917	110.25	119.185	0.028
12	16	74	256	1,184	69.420	56.25	20.973	1.362
Total	178	798	2,902	12,492	798.000	2,281.00	641.414	261.667
	Σx	Σy	Σx^2	Σxy	$\Sigma \hat{y}$	$\Sigma(y-\bar{y})^2$	$\Sigma(y-\hat{y})^2$	$\Sigma(x-\bar{x})^2$

$$\bar{x} = 14.833 \quad \bar{y} = 66.5$$

Note: The 'covers sold' column (x) and the 'direct payroll' column (y) represent thousands, but the zeros have been omitted in order to minimize the magnitude of the values computed in the remaining columns. However, the true values of the results are presented in the text.
   $\hat{y}$ is the predicted value (of y for each observed value of x) from the regression equation $\hat{y}$ = 29,369 + 2.50x. So, for example, $\hat{y}$ for month 2 is 29,369+2.50 (7,000) = 46,869 which agrees closely with the value stated above (46.892 or £46,892).

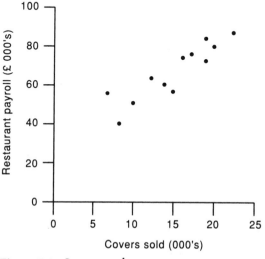

Figure 5.1 Scattergraph

representation of the relationship between restaurant payroll cost and covers sold. Matz and Usry (1980) point out that: 'In most analysis, a straight line is adequate because it is a reasonable approximation of cost behaviour within the relevant range'.

The computations can be performed on most programmable calculators which contain statistical functions. This is carried out by simply keying in the pairs of observations in the linear regression mode and displaying the totals through the appropriate function keys. Substitution of the data into the two equations provides the following:

$$798 = 12a + b178$$
$$12{,}492 = a178 + b2{,}902$$

The solution gives $a = 29{,}369$ and $b = 2.50$, but as an aid to computation the normal equations can be expressed as follows:

$$a = \frac{(\Sigma y)(\Sigma x^2) - (\Sigma x)(\Sigma xy)}{n(\Sigma x^2) - (\Sigma x)^2}$$

$$b = \frac{n(\Sigma xy) - (\Sigma x)(\Sigma y)}{n(\Sigma x^2) - (\Sigma x)^2}$$

The illustration now gives:

$$a = \frac{(798)(2{,}902) - (178)(12{,}492)}{(12)(2{,}902) - (31{,}684)} = 29{,}369$$

$$b = \frac{(12)(12{,}492) - (178)(798)}{(12)(2{,}902) - (31{,}684)} = 2.50$$

Entering the completed a and b values into the regression equation gives:

$$\hat{y} = 29{,}369 + 2.50x$$

Thus, $\hat{y}$ is the estimated total payroll cost for any number of covers sold within the relevant range, illustrated in Figure 5.2. If 15,000 covers are sold the estimated total payroll cost would be on average £29,369 + £2.50 (15,000) = £66,869.

Correlation

As illustrated above, the use of linear regression allows a line of best-fit equation to be computed, which may subsequently be used to predict the future level of payroll costs. However, having determined the equation the next step is to assess the goodness of fit of the line. This is achieved by the

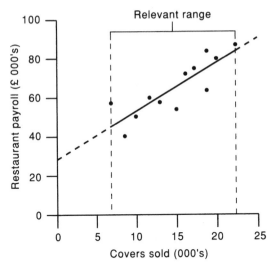

Figure 5.2 Regression line

use of the technique known as correlation analysis. The coefficient of determination, denoted by r^2, measures the extent to which the independent variable x (covers sold) accounts for the variability in the dependent variable y (payroll cost). It indicates, in percentage terms, how much of the total variation of the y values can be attributed to the relationship between the x and y variables and how much can be attributed to chance, as illustrated in Figure 5.3.

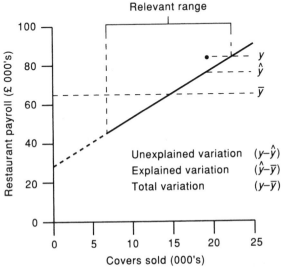

Figure 5.3 Measure of variation

The coefficient of determination (r^2) is expressed as follows:

$$r^2 = 1\,\frac{\Sigma(y-\hat{y})^2}{\Sigma(y-\bar{y})^2} = 1 - \frac{\text{Unexplained variance}}{\text{Total variance}}$$

Keying in the appropriate data from Table 5.1 shows that $\Sigma(y-\hat{y}) = 641.385$ and $\Sigma(y-\bar{y}) = 2,281$, therefore r^2 indicates the percentage of the variation in y (dependent variable) that can be explained by x (independent variable):

$$r^2 = 1 - \frac{641.414}{2,281} = 0.72 \text{ or } 72\%$$

Thus, it can be stated that 72 per cent of restaurant payroll cost is explained by the number of covers sold and 28 per cent can be attributed to chance variation and the effect of other variables not included in the regression equation.

The square root of 0.72 is called the coefficient of correlation (r):

$$r = \sqrt{1 - \frac{\Sigma(y-\hat{y})^2}{\Sigma(y-\bar{y})^2}} = \sqrt{1 - \frac{641.414}{2,281}} = 0.85$$

The coefficient of correlation (r) ranges in value from –1 (perfect negative correlation) to +1 (perfect positive correlation), while the coefficient of determination (r^2) ranges between zero and one. In the case of a perfect positive fit, the regression line will pass through every observed value of y. In such a case, the sum of the squares of the residuals from the regression line to the data points will be zero and both r and r^2 will equal one.

Standard error of the estimate

Having ascertained the degree of association between the x and y variables, the next step is to assess how accurate the regression line is as a basis for prediction. In essence, the object is to provide an indication of how close the predicted costs can be expected to come to the actual costs. The smaller the standard error of the estimate, the better the regression line fits the data. The standard error of the estimate for a population is estimated from a sample of past costs as follows:

$$S_e = \sqrt{\frac{\Sigma(y-\hat{y})}{n-2}}$$

where n is the sample size. The denominator, $n-2$, is called the degrees of freedom. One degree of freedom is lost for each value that has been calculated in the regression equation. In the illustration the intercept (a) and the slope coefficient (*b*) were estimated to establish the regression line, therefore two degrees of freedom are lost. The number of slope coefficients will be greater than one when multiple regression is employed.

Using the data in Table 5.1, the standard error of the estimate is:

$$S_e = \sqrt{\frac{641.385}{10}} = 8.009 \text{ or } £8,009$$

If the assumptions which underlie regression analysis are satisfied (e.g. normality, constant variance and independence of residuals – explained later), then the standard error of the estimate indicates the range of values of the dependent variable (payroll cost) within which there can be some degree of confidence that the true value lies. Thus, if 15,000 covers are sold then the estimate for payroll cost will be as follows:

$$\hat{y} = 29,369 + 2.50 \ (15,000) = 66,869$$

with a standard error of the estimate (probable range of error) of:

$$£66,869 \pm (£8,009)(1.0)$$

As approximately two-thirds of the data points in a normal distribution should fall within one standard error, it is possible to predict that 15,000 covers sold should incur an actual payroll cost of between £58,860 and £74,878, with approximately two chances out of three that the confidence interval will contain the true cost. This is due to the fact that 68 per cent (approximately two-thirds) of the data points in a normal distribution fall within a range of ± one standard error.

Statistical theory suggests that for linear regression analysis the data points are t-distributed around the regression line and that the distribution becomes normal as the number of observations reaches 30. In sampling terms, 30 or more observations are categorized as a large sample. The *t*-distribution is presented in Table 5.2.

If, for example, the above restaurant payroll cost estimate specified a 95 per cent confidence interval, the range of error would be:

$$£66,869 \pm (£8,009)(2.228)$$

Thus, it is possible for management to predict that 15,000 covers sold should attract a payroll cost of between £49,025 and £84,713, with approximately 95 chances out of 100 (19 out of 20) that the confidence interval will

Table 5.2   *t*-distribution table

df	$t_{.100}$	$t_{.050}$	$t_{.025}$	$t_{.010}$	$t_{.005}$
1	3.078	6.314	12.706	31.821	63.657
2	1.886	2.920	4.303	6.965	9.925
3	1.638	2.353	3.182	4.541	5.841
4	1.533	2.132	2.776	3.747	4.604
5	1.476	2.015	2.571	3.365	4.032
6	1.440	1.943	2.447	3.143	3.707
7	1.415	1.895	2.365	2.998	3.499
8	1.397	1.860	2.306	2.896	3.355
9	1.383	1.833	2.262	2.821	3.250
10	1.372	1.812	2.228	2.764	3.169
11	1.363	1.796	2.201	2.718	3.106
12	1.356	1.782	2.179	2.681	3.055
13	1.350	1.771	2.160	2.650	3.012
14	1.345	1.761	2.145	2.624	2.977
15	1.341	1.753	2.131	2.602	2.947
16	1.337	1.746	2.120	2.583	2.921
17	1.333	1.740	2.110	2.567	2.898
18	1.330	1.734	2.101	2.552	2.878
19	1.328	1.729	2.093	2.539	2.861
20	1.325	1.725	2.086	2.528	2.845
21	1.323	1.721	2.080	2.518	2.831
22	1.321	1.717	2.074	2.508	2.819
23	1.319	1.714	2.069	2.500	2.807
24	1.318	1.711	2.064	2.492	2.797
25	1.316	1.708	2.060	2.485	2.787
26	1.315	1.706	2.056	2.479	2.779
27	1.314	1.703	2.052	2.473	2.771
28	1.313	1.701	2.048	2.467	2.763
29	1.311	1.699	2.045	2.462	2.756
inf.	1.282	1.645	1.960	2.326	2.576

The *t*-value describes the sampling distribution of a deviation from a population value divided by the standard error. Probabilities indicated in the subordinate of *t* in the heading refer to the sum of the two-tailed areas under the curve that lie outside the points ± *t*. Degrees of freedom are listed in the first column (*df*).

For example, in the distribution of the means of sample size $n = 12$, $df = $n–2 = 12–2$ then $_{.05}$ of the area under the curve falls in the two tails of the curve outside the interval $t \pm 2.228$, which is taken from the $t_{.025}$ column of the table.

contain the actual cost. Note that the 2.228 standard errors, representing the 95 per cent confidence interval is obtained by referring to the *t*-table in Table 5.2. The illustration sample size is $n = 12$, degrees of freedom (*df*) = n–2 = 10. Therefore, 0.05 of the area under the curve falls in the tails of the curve outside the interval $t \pm 2.228$, which is taken from the $t_{.025}$ column of the table.

The standard error of the estimate at the 68 and 95 per cent confidence intervals for a small sample is illustrated in Figure 5.4.

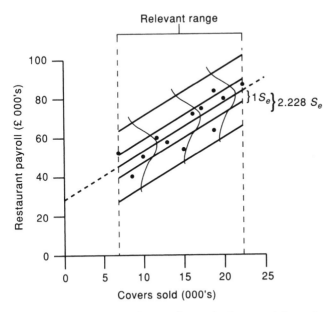

Figure 5.4   Regression line with standard error of the estimate

In principle, the standard error of the estimate is similar to the standard deviation in normal probability analysis, the difference being that, whereas the standard deviation measures the dispersion of data points around the mean, the standard error of the estimate measures the variability around the regression line.

Standard error of a prediction

As mentioned earlier, one of the reasons for engaging in cost analysis is to provide a basis for cost and profit projections. However, where an equation is employed in the prediction of costs for future periods, and thus uses data not incorporated in the initial equation, then it becomes necessary to introduce a correction factor to the standard error in respect of *each* prediction. This is termed the standard error of a predication (S_p), and arises due to the fact that with repeated sampling the estimated value of y will vary. Remember, that the estimated value of y for any given value of x is $\hat{y}$. With each new sample the estimates of the intercept and slope coefficients will vary to some extent. Therefore, each sample will produce a slightly different regression line and, thus, a different $\hat{y}$ value for a given value of x.

The standard error of a prediction is computed as follows:

$$S_p = S_e \sqrt{1 + \frac{1}{n} + \frac{(x_p - \bar{x})^2}{\Sigma(x - \bar{x})^2}}$$

from the formula it becomes apparent that the further the predicted value of x is from the mean of observed values of x, the larger the standard error will be. Thus, the further the covers sold prediction is from the mean of future covers sold, the wider the prediction interval, as illustrated in Figure 5.5.

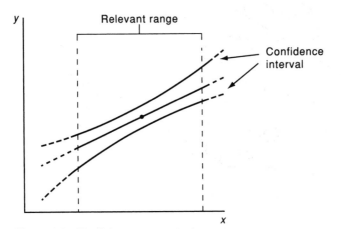

Figure 5.5 Confidence interval of a prediction

If 15,000 covers are predicted in a future period, and a 95 per cent confidence interval is specified, then the standard error of the prediction will be:

$$S_p = S_e \sqrt{1 + \frac{1}{12} + \frac{(15,000 - 14,833)^2}{(261.667)}}$$

$$= 8.009 \sqrt{1.083439915}$$

$$= 8.677 \text{ or } £8,677$$

$$\text{Hence } \hat{y} = £66,869 \pm (£8,677)(2.228)$$

$$= £66,869 \pm £19,332$$

It is therefore 95 per cent certain that if 15,000 covers are sold, the actual payroll cost will be between £47,537 and £86,201.

Standard error of the variable cost coefficient (b)

In addition to determining the accuracy of total cost estimates and predictions, it is important to assess the reliability of the *b* coefficient (variable cost). The standard error of the regression coefficient (S_b) is computed as follows:

$$S_b = \frac{S_e}{\sqrt{\Sigma(x-\bar{x})^2}}$$

Using the illustration data gives:

$$S_b = \frac{8.009}{\sqrt{261.667}} = £0.50$$

If in this instance a 90 per cent confidence interval is specified the range of error for the variable cost (*b*) will be:

$$£2.50 \pm (£0.50) \,(1.812) = £2.50 \pm £0.91$$

It is therefore 90 per cent certain that the true variable cost element of restaurant payroll lies within the range £1.59 to £3.41. Note that the standard error of 1.812 was obtained from the *t*-table in Table 5.2 by referring to row 10 and column $t_{.05}$.

Testing the variable cost coefficient (b)

Finally, having computed the standard error of the regression coefficient, it is possible to test if a significant explanatory relationship exists between the *y* and *x* variables. For example, the *b* coefficient suggests a change in the average variable cost of restaurant payroll for each additional cover sold. As the *b* coefficient of £2.50 is an estimate of the true variable payroll cost of population B, a particular sample may indicate a relationship by chance, even though none exists. If there is no relationship between *y* and *x*, the true slope of the regression line will be zero; in other words, *b* will be zero and restaurant payroll expense will be regarded as a fixed cost. The relationship can be tested by using the 'null hypothesis' (H_0) and the alternative hypothesis (H_1) expressed as follows:

$H_0 : B = 0$ (no relationship)

$H_1 : B \neq 0$ (payroll cost varies with covers sold)

To test the hypothesis it is necessary to compute how many standard errors *b* is away from B, and compare the computed *t*-value with the *t*-table.

Under the null hypothesis, H_0, the computed *t*-value is:

$$t\text{-value} = \frac{b-0}{S_b} = \frac{£2.50}{£0.50} = 5.0$$

therefore, *b* is 5.0 standard errors from zero. If a 95 per cent confidence interval is specified then reference to the *t*-table indicates a critical value of 2.228. Thus, as a deviation of more than approximately 2.00 standard errors is usually regarded as significant, it is very unlikely that a deviation as large as 5.0 standard errors could occur by chance. At the 95 per cent confidence level there are only five chances out of 100 that a significant relationship is indicated where none exists. Therefore the null hypothesis can be rejected and the alternative hypothesis accepted, i.e. that a significant relationship does exist between restaurant payroll costs and covers sold (assuming the assumptions mentioned later hold).

Evaluation of sample cost data

Clearly, the statistical analysis of data using regression and correlation techniques is a relatively mechanical process. In the restaurant illustration presented earlier, a calculator with statistical functions can be used for the computations, or alternatively the process may be carried out on a computer program which will automatically produce the scattergraph, regression equation, correlation analysis, standard errors and *t*-value.

Once the sample data have been processed the next step is to undertake an evaluation of the results to determine their validity for use in cost estimation and prediction decisions. For example, the illustration related covers sold to restaurant payroll expense, but other independent variables such as labour hours or sales revenue might have been selected for incorporation in the analysis. So the question arises as to how do managers and accountants choose between different cost functions? Horngren and Foster (1991) suggest there are four selection criteria required for the evaluation of cost functions and these are explained below.

Criterion 1: plausibility

The fundamental relationship between the independent variable (*x*) and the dependent variable (*y*) should be meaningful in terms of making operational sense. For instance, it is operationally plausible to relate payroll cost in a particular restaurant to the number of covers sold in the same restaurant, whereas it would not be meaningful to relate the payroll of one restaurant with covers sold in another establishment.

Criterion 2: goodness of fit

The independent variable selected should explain a considerable amount of the variation in the dependent variable. The coefficient of determination (r^2) is a particularly useful indicator of the goodness of fit as it measures the percentage variation in the dependent variable (cost) which is explained by the independent variable (covers sold). Generally, if the r^2 is around 0.40 or above, it is usually regarded as acceptable.

Criterion 3: significance of the independent variable

The *t*-value of a variable cost coefficient (*b*) measures the statistical significance of the relationship between the changes in the dependent variable against changes in the independent variable. In general, if there are 30 or more pairs of observations in the data sample and the *t*-value is at least 2.0, then a variable cost element can assume to be present in the cost population as a whole.

Criterion 4: specification analysis

Four underlying assumptions of regression analysis, referred to earlier, are required to be satisfied in order to make valid estimates and predictions from sample data about population relationships, as follows:

Linearity
This can be identified visually from a scattergraph and should reflect a general linear (straight line) trend in the data.

Constant variance
This relates to the scatter of data points around the regression line. The standard deviation and variance of the residuals should be constant for all values of x, which means that there is a uniform dispersion of points about the regression line, as illustrated in Figure 5.6. Where this is not so, the reliability of the slope coefficient (*b*) is reduced.

Normality
The distribution of data points about the regression line should approximately follow a normal curve, i.e. the residuals are normally distributed. This is, however, difficult to determine with small samples of data.

Independence
Residual values should be independent of one another. This means that the deviation of one data point about the regression line is unrelated to the deviation of any other data point. Where this is not so, then serial correlation

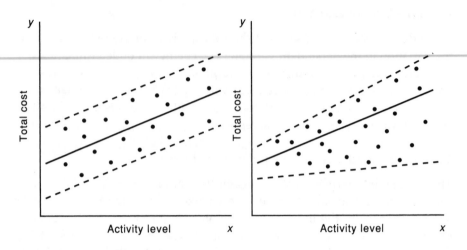

Figure 5.6   Constant and non-constant variance

is said to be present. One measure used to determine if serial correlation is present in sample data is the Durban-Watson statistic, which is incorporated in most computer programs. This condition can, however, be checked on a calculator by computing the correlation coefficient (*r*) of the cost residuals.

In cases where the linearity, constant variance, normality and independence assumptions are satisfied, then the regression coefficients and standard errors determined from a sample can be regarded as efficient, linear and unbiased estimates of the true population values.

Table 5.3   Restaurant illustration evaluation

Criterion	Cost function: payroll cost versus covers sold
Plausibility	Positive relationship between restaurant payroll and covers sold is operationally plausible.
Goodness of fit	$r^2 = 0.72$ indicates a strong degree of association between the variables.
Significance of the independent variable	t-value = 5.0 indicates a significant relationship
Specification analysis: Linearity	There appears to be a clear linear trend present in the data plot.
Constant variance of residuals	This appears to be satisfied, but is only based on 12 observations.
Normality of residuals	Difficult to draw a conclusion from 12 observations.
Independence of residuals	$r^2 = 0.18$, therefore serial correlation is deemed not to be present in the cost data.

Evaluation of restaurant illustration

Reference to Table 5.3 shows that the restaurant data sample generally satisfies the selection criteria. Experience shows that in many hotel restaurants, and indeed in stand-alone restaurants, the payroll cost is seen to change with the number of covers sold and is, therefore, a plausible operational relationship. This is confirmed in the illustration by a strong coefficient of determination and significant *t*-value. Furthermore, within the constraints of a small sample (less than 30 observations), the data appears to have satisfied the underlying assumptions of regression. However, whenever possible a large sample should be employed in the practical situation.

When using statistical cost analysis it is important to bear in mind that, as with many other techniques used in managerial accounting, ideal conditions and perfect results rarely occur. In dealing with cost relationships precision is often an illusion and, therefore, overcomplicating the method of analysis in order to achieve an impression of exactness offers little to the integrity of the decision-making process. What is essential in the application of regression and correlation analysis is that the user has a sound understanding of the assumptions and limitations which underlie the technique and so avoids decisions rooted in ignorance. Perhaps the single most important condition which should prevail when undertaking statistical cost analysis is that the cost data are drawn from financial records which closely adhere to the accrual accounting or matching principle.

Research in hotels – an example

Reference to Table 5.4 shows the partial results of two research projects presented by Harris (1984) and Green (1994). The studies were undertaken in single establishments in the same international hotel company, but in different locations. Both studies were conducted on a similar basis using

Table 5.4 Hotel department results comparison

Data period	1980–82 r^2	1990–92 r^2	1980–82 *t*-value	1990-92 *t*-value
Rooms department				
Rooms sold/payroll	0.18	0.66	2.7	8.1
Rooms sold/expenses	0.13	0.36	2.2	4.2
Restaurant department				
Covers sold/food cost	0.57	0.83	6.8	7.0
Covers sold/payroll	0.20	0.59	2.9	3.8
Covers sold/expenses	0.14	0.41	2.3	2.6

sample data drawn from a three-year period and analysed using simple linear regression. Whilst the results were obtained from two different economic periods the hotel organization continues to operate in the same market segments under broadly similar policies and practices, particularly in relation to the data collected.

Notwithstanding the differences in economic periods and site locations, although both establishments are sited in the south of England, the results are worthy of comparison. Both sets of data satisfied the plausibility and specification analysis criteria, but the most striking results occur in relation to the r^2 and t-values.

The r^2 and t-values obtained in the studies are consistent in terms of the relative magnitude of the values in each department, e.g. payroll comprises higher values than expenses in both departments for both studies, and food cost indicates the highest values in both studies. This is also consistent in relation to the gradation of accounting accuracy normally associated with food cost of sales, payroll and expenses. Also, in the majority of instances, Green's study indicates a significant improvement in r^2 and t-values compared to those of Harris. So why such an impressive change overall?

Knowledge of the organization suggests that, rather than economic or operating conditions being the key influences in the results, the changes may have occurred as a result of improvements in the accounting system. Harris's study revealed inconsistencies in the application of accrual accounting for direct departmental expenses, particularly with respect to payroll and expenses. However, in an effort to improve the accuracy of departmental profit measures, the organization introduced new procedures relating to cost allocation and the matching of monthly revenue and expenses. In order to substantiate the conclusion for the improvement in the cost functions, the analysis should be replicated in subsequent time periods. Nevertheless, this and other similar research does point to the growing likelihood that cost data relationships using regression and correlation analysis may provide a pragmatic basis on which to estimate and predict cost behaviour patterns.

Fixed-cost element

Discussion has centred on testing and evaluating the variable cost coefficient, but it is important to understand the role of the fixed-cost element in cost analysis. A business undertaking tends to operate within a particular band of activity (the relevant range). It is, therefore, inappropriate and often dangerous to make estimates beyond the range of the observed data.

Benston (1966) points out that it is tempting to interpret the constant term *a* as a fixed cost by extending the regression line back to zero activity. This presupposes a linear relationship which, as Figure 5.7 indicates, may not be a valid assumption.

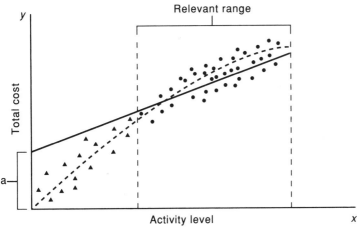

Figure 5.7   Fixed cost and the relevant range

The regression line was fitted from the equation $\hat{y} = a + bx$, where the dots are the observed values of the cost and activity. The line would provide an estimate of the fixed cost if the range of observation included the point where activity is zero. However, if additional cost and activity data observations were available they might show that the broken curve would be fitted and *a* would be zero. It therefore becomes apparent that *a* is not the cost that would necessarily be found if activity was at zero, but simply the value that is obtained as a result of the regression line computed from the available data. This helps to explain why the *t*-value of the fixed-cost element has not been computed for the restaurant illustration. Since the key objective is to estimate and predict how costs behave as activity changes over the relevant range, which is usually not at zero activity, the *t*-value of *a* is not normally relevant to the analysis.

Statistical cost analysis in decision-making

Statistical cost estimation and predication can aid management in a broad range of circumstances. As Horngren (1977) points out, 'A knowledge of how costs behave under a variety of influences is essential to intelligent predictions, decision making and performance evaluation'.

Planning decisions

Regression techniques can be helpful in profit-planning, budgeting and pricing decisions. The determination of regression equations for operating costs facilitates the use of cost-volume-profit analysis for profit planning purposes. For instance, the equations can be applied to the construction of flexible budgets which in turn can be used to assess the likely impact on profits of 'what if' questions relating to changes in budgeted volumes levels or revisions in pricing policy. Knowledge of the variable cost coefficient can also be of assistance in *ad hoc* pricing decisions, where the range of price discretion is required to be determined in order to submit competitive bids.

In addition to providing estimates of total costs and average variable costs per unit, regression enables the computation of the range of probable error through use of the standard error of the estimate and standard error of the variable-cost coefficient. The use of crude unqualified estimates as a basis for cost prediction is severely criticized. As Amey (1961) states: 'Much of their (accountants') apparent precision is found to be spurious; no self-respecting statistician would present an estimate without indicating the error to which it was thought to be subject'.

Control decisions

Regression analysis can also be useful in the area of cost control. The regression equations applied to construct the flexible budgets can be used to compare actual costs incurred at a specific level of activity with predicted costs at the same level. Here cost predictions for a fixed budget are flexed (adjusted) to the relevant level of activity achieved during a period. This facilitates the determination of cost variances for subsequent evaluation. However, significant cost variances between actual and flexible budgets may not prove to be the only signal to efficient or inefficient management of operations.

Cost standards that are developed from statistical analysis of historical data do not necessarily reflect efficient or optimal performance, but may actually indicate the level of cost behaviour that occurred in the past. The standards can be used to suggest whether current operations have improved or deteriorated from the past, but cannot in themselves point to suggest whether past activities represented an acceptable level of efficiency. In order to ascertain this, a detailed examination of the department in question would need to be carried out. As Kaplan (1982) points out:

High standard errors (or low r^2) are a result of large fluctuations in the cost centre. Thus, if the analyst, when modelling the cost behaviour in a cost centre, observes a poor fit to the historical data, he or she may conclude that the cost centre is not operating in a state of statistical control – that too many large fluctuations have occurred that cannot be explained by variations in the cost centre's activity levels.

In the event of such findings, operating procedures and working arrangements could be reviewed in an attempt to secure a reduction in the erratic cost behaviour patterns in the department. It becomes apparent, therefore, that cost investigations of a particular department can be prompted by either current or past results, i.e. changes in the mean of the actual data (cost observations which are more than two standard errors from the predicted figure), or by a configuration of historical cost data that is regarded as being too widely dispersed.

Business orientation

Finally, as mentioned at the outset, an understanding of cost behaviour can assist in gaining an impression of the business orientation of an undertaking. This is relevant to decision-making as a knowledge of whether a business is product-oriented or market-oriented can contribute to the formulation of management style and managerial emphasis in operating an enterprise. Product-oriented undertakings require a relatively more balanced approach to revenue and cost management than market-oriented undertakings which require a decidedly pronounced effort towards revenue generation. Whichever the case, a key element in the determination of business orientation is cost structure and that requires the identification of cost behaviour patterns.

In conclusion, statistical cost analysis is a useful alternative to the more subjective methods of analysing costs. With the widespread availability of programmable calculators and computer software packages statistical cost estimation and prediction can provide a powerful contribution to the decision-making process.

References

Amey, L.R. (1961) Professor of Accounting, University of Bristol. *Inaugural Lecture.*

Benston, G.J. (1966) Multiple regression analysis of cost behaviour. *The Accounting Review* **41**(4); 657–672.

Green, A. (1994) The Influence of Volume on Cost Analysis in the Hotel Industry. Unpublished dissertation, Oxford Brookes University.

Harris, P.J. (1984) A Study of Departmental Cost Behaviour in a Hotel Operation. Unpublished thesis, University of Strathclyde.

Harris, P. J. (1986) The application of regression and correlation techniques for cost planning and control decisions in the hotel industry. *International Journal of Hospitality Management* 5; 127–133.

Harris, P.J. (1992) Hospitality profit planning in the practical environment: integrating cost-volume-profit analysis with spreadsheet management. *International Journal of Contemporary Hospitality Management* 4(4); 24–32.

Horngren, C.T. (1977) *Cost Accounting, A Managerial Emphasis*, 4th edn., Prentice-Hall, Englewood Cliffs, NJ.

Horngren, C.T. and Foster, G. (1991) *Cost Accounting, A Managerial Emphasis*, 7th edn., Prentice-Hall Englewood Cliffs, NJ.

Kaplan, R.S. (1982) *Advanced Management Accounting*. New York: Prentice-Hall.

Kotas, R. (1973) Market orientation. *HCIMA Journal* 5–7.

Matz, A. and Usry, M.F. (1980) *Cost Accounting, Planning and Control*, 7th edn., South West Publishing, Cincinnati.

6 Risk assessment in capital investment

Geoff S. Parkinson

Introduction

That the hotel industry is capital-intensive is rarely challenged. Also, that the profits accruing from the operation of a hotel as a business result from the aggregation of millions of essentially minuscule transactions (compared to the investment made) is without doubt. The ability to generate the millions of transactions is dependent upon a myriad of non-specific and unquantifiable actions and reactions of management and the customer (the guest) – image, fashion, brand and brand loyalty, location, style, comparative price, friendliness, hospitality, critical acclaim, star rating, management style and management skill – all impact on and influence the ability to generate custom and so the level of profit. As a result, the hotel industry is recognized as high-risk by investors and operators alike. However, the assessment of investment risk appears to be little understood or at least rarely applied in the majority of investment decisions.

Traditionally, risk is addressed through a range of arithmetic techniques designed to determine an 'acceptable' level of investment. The arithmetic techniques are applied with varying levels of sophistication, but even the most sophisticated approaches only provide comfort that risk has been recognized; none of the traditional techniques attempts to quantify the risk itself.

The simplest form of risk assessment is no more than a comparison of one hotel with another. The investor assesses risk through a simple price comparison mechanism – the 100-room hotel next door was bought/sold for £10 million, which is £100,000 per room. The hotel, with 110 rooms, can be acquired for £10 million – £90,909 per room - it is therefore a good buy. Risk is being addressed on the basis of 'no greater risk'.

But this simple approach to investment takes no account of the business of the hotel and relies entirely on the assessment of risk adopted by the investor in the hotel next door whose motives for that investment at a price of £100,000 per room are unknown. This 'me too' approach to investment in the hotel industry has been at the root of the many disastrous investments in hotels made during the late 1980s and then lost through insolvency during the early 1990s.

Hotels are not simple properties, they are trading businesses and the risks associated with investments are the risks associated with the trading results. Rarely are they the risks associated with capital value movements between the time of purchase and sale.

This simple price comparison methodology can of course be modified through pay-back period, net present value, internal rate of return, return on capital employed and similar extended time period arithmetic calculations to reflect the time value of money and the earning potential of the business. In each instance the underlying assumptions are predicated on the investor's decision as to an acceptable rate of return and so the 'acceptable' level of investment.

Evaluation of traditional investment appraisal methodologies

Taking a range of these traditional investment appraisal methodologies in turn and assessing the strength and weakness of the underlying assumptions demonstrates how crude risk assessment applied to the hotel business tends to be.

Pay-back period

The required information is a series of projected annual earnings in the form of cash available for distribution to the risk-holding investor (the equity holder). These projections of earnings are then aggregated over the number of years required for the aggregated sum to equal the level of the initial investment – the number of years the distributable cash earnings take to repay the initial investment with any future distributed earnings representing reward for the risk undertaken. This assessment of risk is founded on the assumption that once the initial investment has been repaid then risk is removed and logically the quicker risk is removed the more desirable is the investment. In short, the rationale is that a pay-back period of five years is less risky than a payback period of 10 years, but hotels are known to be long-lived investments. Many of the most desired hotels have traded as such for decades. This methodology fails to take into account not only any value attributed to the continuing ownership of the business but also any risk inherent in the projection of earning over a period of time. The pay-back methodology seems at best a very modest approach to the assessment of the risk being undertaken and indeed is somewhat contradictory. In this method, if a short pay-back is perceived as lower risk than a long pay-back, then the assumption must be that a higher return offers less risk than a lower return – a 5 year pay-back offers a 20 per cent return, a 10-year pay-back, a 10 per cent return. This flies in the face of all other commercial logic which suggests that the relationship between risk and reward is contrary.

Net present value

This approach builds on the pay-back method by applying the return required by the investor to the cash earnings. It improves on the pay-back method by recognizing the time over which the investment is made. The investor decides that an average of X per cent return per annum is required. The decision on the level of the return required is based upon the return available from alternative uses of the cash to be invested.

This in itself requires some subjective judgement by the investor, which in effect prequantifies the risk to be associated with this investment. If the risk-free investment (usually a fixed-return government-backed investment) is y per cent, then in setting x per cent as the desired return, the investor is adding to that y per cent a quantification of the perceived risk. The difference between x per cent and y per cent is the reward the investor requires for the risk being taken. Typically, if a risk-free investment returns 8 per cent, then perhaps a further four or five percentage points will be added to the discount rate for a hotel-related investment. However, the decision as to whether the perceived risk is worth an additional four points or five points does impact the result significantly and that decision has little or no basis other than personal perception.

The method also takes account of the continuing value of the business or the value which can be applied to the business at the end of this investor's time frame, which the pay-back method fails to do. The terminal value becomes a part of the projected earnings. However, this terminal value is an equally subjective judgement - based upon either a simple multiple of final year projected earnings or similar unsophisticated 'guess', which in reality does little but compound the inherent subjectivity of the projected earnings. In this methodology, it is common for the terminal value when discounted to represent of the order of 40 per cent of the net present value. The decision then is being taken in a large part on the basis of the method utilized to calculate the terminal value.

The resultant decision-making process is however simple – if the net present value is positive, it is a 'sound' investment, meeting the criteria set; if it is negative then it does not meet the criteria.

Internal rate of return

Whilst this method seems to be the preferred approach to investment decision-making for the hotel sector, it is in reality no more than a slight change to the net present value methodology. In this approach the investor is required to predetermine the minimum rate of return required from the investment and compare that to the return produced by the projected earnings. Many texts explain the arithmetic methodology, but tend not to elaborate sufficiently on the total subjectivity of the residual, reversionary or terminal value applied to the final year of the cash flow to be discounted. The impact of the assumption on terminal value on the calculation as a whole is invariably significant.

Decision making in practice

For the investor, the decision-making is based upon whether the result obtained (the rate of return) is greater or less than that which is predetermined as 'acceptable' in the context of that risk. So, having explored the weakness of the bases under which current investment decisions are taken, what happens in practice?

It is recognized by most investors that the greatest weakness in the decision-making process and the arithmetic supporting that process lies in the projection of future earnings. To provide comfort to that recognition, most investors require the projection of earnings to be subjected to sensitivity testing.

Commonly, sensitivity testing relies upon the reduction of the best-guess projection by a factor of x per cent. In essence, the process is set to determine the resultant pay-back period or net present value or internal rate of return if the projected earnings fall short of expectation by x per cent. The decision then is whether or not the result produced is still acceptable in terms of risk. If the required return is 10 per cent, the best-guess projection indicates a return of 12 per cent and the sensitized projection indicates a return of 11 per cent, then all is well, but if the sensitized projection produces a return of 9 per cent, the decision is complicated. Having set the required return, which is then not met by the reduced earnings (sensitivity-tested by a reduction of x per cent), the investor is little wiser as to the robustness of the best-guess projection and so little wiser as to the level of risk being tested through sensitivity. In effect, through this methodology the investor is again predetermining the acceptable variance from the best guess and judging the investment on that criteria, but this is not assessing the risk of the investment itself.

Assessing the earnings risk

The recognition that the weakest point in the decision-making process is the projection of earnings is correct, but the assessment of the risk attached to that weakest point is really not addressed. The methodologies currently in use focus on the assessment of risk by flexing and assessing the level of the investment. In the pay-back method the investment is set on the basis that it will be repaid in the acceptable number of years. In the net present value and IRR methods the investment is set in the context of the required return. Risk is judged by subjectively extending or shortening the pay-back period or by increasing or reducing the required or acceptable (hurdle) rate of return.

What is missing in all of the currently used investment decision-making methodologies is the assessment of the risk attached to the achievement of the projected earnings. In all the techniques the earning potential of the hotel is accepted as being correct and achievable. Even when sensitivity testing is applied to the projected earnings, the focus of the test is the impact upon the return – not upon the achievability of the projections.

Theoretical approach

If an investor can assume, with some demonstrable certainty, that the projected earnings have, for example, a 95 per cent probability of occurring, then the investment can be taken with a 95 per cent probability of success. If the certainty of the projections is reduced to 65 per cent then the associated risk is measurable.

Investment is a gamble and in gaming the calculation of probability is a mathematical certainty given a sufficient (infinite) number of iterations. In hotel investment the portfolio theory is applied to increase the number of iterations and so theoretically increase the probability of overall aggregate success. For most investors the practicality of accumulating a sufficient portfolio to make this approach plausible is close to zero and for true success the portfolio needs to include investments which are countercyclical in trending and operations.

The alternative approach must therefore be to define risk in different terms. If risk is defined as the chance that the actual result will be worse than the projected result, we need then only to consider the downside – what is the probability of the projection not being achieved? Investors are rarely concerned with the possibility of the investment achieving greater than projected earnings.

The statistical data from which such calculations can be made are available. All the major UK-based consulting organizations have a database of historic trading results, and most of the major hotel operators have the historic results of their multiple operations, all of which can provide the information to compile the distribution of actual results. From the distribution of results, the likelihood of a specific combination of projected (expected) results occurring can then be measured.

If the process were that simple, then why does it not occur in practice? The answer seems to be twofold. First, it is not that simple. The multiple variations of factors influencing the trading performance of hotels are such that the construction of a perfectly matched set of distributed results is not simple and in practice is probably impossible to determine, as the factors themselves are not constant. And second, if it were to be possible, the cost of acquiring, analysing, codifying and applying the amount of data needed for scientific accuracy would probably outweigh the benefits which accrue.

Testing for reasonableness

However, the perfect theory can be modified into the realms of practicality by applying reasonableness tests to the projection of earnings. In most sets of accumulated data it is possible to rank the data rather than just average it, as is the common practice.

For most projections of potential operating results the process, and so the projected results, rely upon the simple mean of comparative actual results obtained through research of specific live operations. If the projected results

Table 6.1   Actual results

Hotel	Occupancy %	ADRR £	Yield	GOP %	GOP per room	No. rooms
A	86.0%	£90	£77.40	40%	£22,601	110
B	80.0%	£105	£84.00	35%	£21,462	150
C	75.0%	£110	£82.50	37%	£22,283	170
D	70.0%	£100	£70.00	38%	£19,418	180
E	69.0%	£95	£65.55	40%	£19,141	120
F	68.0%	£115	£78.20	35%	£19,980	130
G	65.0%	£120	£78.00	32%	£18,221	140
H	60.0%	£125	£75.00	39%	£21,353	160
I	55.0%	£130	£71.50	33%	£17,224	190
Projected results	70%	£115	£80.50	39%	£22,918	200

ADRR = Average daily room rate; GOP = gross operating profit are ranked against actual trading results, then at least the investor can assess where within a hierarchy these results sit and add a further factor to the decision-making process.

If from a set of actual results we can determine that the projected results lie within the upper quartile of the range, then the risk attaching to the non-achievement of that result must be greater than if the projected results were to lie within the lower quartile. From such a comparison with a set of actual results, the investor can also start to determine some 'real' sensitivity from the range of the set – the difference between minimum and maximum values. The greater the range of values, the greater the chance of inaccuracy in the projection and so the greater the risk.

The essence of successful investment decision-making is confidence that the projected results are indeed plausible and achievable. By way of demonstration, Table 6.1 sets out key indicators taken from the trading results achieved by a set of nine competitive hotels (A–I), together with those of the projected results of the investment contemplated.

Table 6.2   Ranked results

	Occupancy %		ADRR £		Yield		GOP %		GOP per room	
Maximum	A	86.0%	I	£130.00	B	£84.00	A	40%	A	£22,601	Maximum
	B	80.0%	H	£125.00	C	£82.50	E	40%	C	£22,283	
Upper quartile	C	75.0%	G	£120.00	F	£78.20	H	39%	B	£21,462	Upper quartile
	D	70.0%	F	£115.00	G	£78.00	D	38%	H	£21,353	
Median	E	69.0%	C	£110.00	A	£77.40	C	37%	F	£19,980	Median
	F	68.0%	B	£105.00	H	£75.00	B	35%	D	£19,418	
Lower quartile	G	65.0%	D	£100.00	I	£71.50	F	35%	E	£19,141	Lower quartile
	H	60.0%	E	£95.00	D	£70.00	I	33%	G	£18,221	
Minimum	I	55.0%	A	£90.00	E	£65.55	G	32%	I	£17,224	Minimum
Projected results		70.0%		£115		£80.50		39%		£22,918	

Comparison of the projected result to the actual results in the market produces an indication of the plausibility of the projection. For simplicity, Table 6.2 sets out the actual achieved results ranked in descending order of magnitude (with the property descriptor - A to I) adjacent to each indicator.

For this proposed investment, occupancy projected at 70 per cent falls within the range of the median and upper quartile. This is a plausible result, but over 50 per cent of the competitive hotels achieve a lower occupancy than this projection.

In terms of achieved average daily room rate (ADRR), the projected result again falls within the median to upper quartile range, which again seems plausible. However the ranking of occupancy is different to the ranking of ADRR and so the plausibility of the projection in terms of both indicators requires testing. This is achieved through the 'yield' – achieved rooms revenue per room available (rather than per room sold as is indicated by ADRR). The projected yield falls between the upper quartile and maximum values reported from the actual hotels. This places the projection well into the higher-risk area, with over 75 per cent of actual results falling below that projected.

However, revenue is not the only indicator. Gross operating profit (GOP) is the yardstick most commonly used for judging the profitability of a hotel. The projection at 39 per cent ranks at the level of the upper quartile in the range with 75 per cent of the reported results falling below that projected. When GOP is compared in terms of amount per room, the projection is higher than the maximum actual value reported. This indicates a very high risk attaching to the projection. Finally, in the ranking comparison, this property is planned as the largest in the competitive market at 200 rooms – again tending towards higher risk in terms of the plausibility of the trading performance.

On balance, using this assessment of risk – the plausibility/achievability of the projected earnings – this investment would have to be placed in the higher-risk category.

Reverting to the traditional investment approach to risk assessment, these projections produce a higher GOP per room than all the actual hotels. In the pay-back method, these projections will pay-back faster than the actual hotels – a faster pay-back indicates a lower risk. In terms of net present value the projection will produce a larger positive value than the actual hotels - the larger the positive value the lower the risk. In terms of IRR, the projection will produce a higher rate of return than the actual hotels – in comparative terms, the higher the return, the more preferred is the investment.

In each instance the projection produces a favourable investment decision if the investment approach to risk is determined through the traditional investment appraisal methodologies. If the plausibility of the projections is tested then the investment decision is somewhat less favourable.

It is fundamental to ensure that the earnings on which an investment decision is to be judged are reasonable and plausible. The sophistication of the arithmetic commonly used within the investment appraisal methods is totally dependent upon the earnings input.

Other factors to mitigate risk

What else can be utilized in the decision-making to mitigate the risk? Hotel projects are capital-intensive and long-lived. The terms on which investment is made need, therefore, to reflect these characteristics.

Capital-intensive projects do by definition require a mix of investment (between debt and equity) which is balanced. In general terms, simple arithmetic can demonstrate that the higher the proportion of fixed-term interest-bearing debt, the greater is the chance that the at-risk investment (equity) will be exposed to the failure of actual results to meet projected results.

For the equity investor the need is to balance the quantum of investment with the likelihood of the projected results being achieved. To do this, a number of features can be introduced into the overall investment to mitigate the risk in the short term. First, the terms of the debt can be balanced with rate of interest charged and the number of years over which repayment is required. For hotels, because of their capital-intensive nature, extending the number of years over which debt is repaid tends to provide equity with greater security than flexing the rate of interest to be paid. Second, it can be recognized that hotels are long-lived businesses, anticipating that at a future date the possibility of refinancing exists.

Typically, and in simplistic terms, a hotel will be funded as 30 per cent equity and 70 per cent debt. The debt will carry interest at, say, 10 per cent over a period of seven years. If the period of repayment can be extended to 10 years, the required cash flow to service repayment of the debt is reduced by 30 per cent. The risk attached to the equity investment is thereby reduced.

By reflecting the long-lived nature of the business with the structure of the investment, the risk attached to the equity investment can be further reduced. For example, if the 10-year debt is repaid 50 per cent in equal annual instalments and 50 per cent as a lump sum on the 10th anniversary, the risk to the equity investor is reduced by a further approximately 20 per cent by reducing the quantum of the required cash flow. The security offered to the debt finance is not compromised by such funding arrangements, but the impact of the risk to the equity investor (defined as the chance of the results being worse than projected) is mitigated.

7 Financial strategy formulation

Paul Fitz-John

A hotelier's story

A hotelier had been in business for two years. The profit and loss account showed losses of £35,000 in the first year and £15,000 in the second, but the hotelier was delighted! Why was this so? The hotel had been purchased for £250,000 and a contract had just been signed to sell it for £500,000!

This story is based on fact. The hotel had been bought cheaply as it was loss-making and had become profitable by the end of the second year. That alone was not enough for the hotelier to obtain twice the price paid for the hotel. There had also been a large upward movement in the property value of the hotel at the time – a 'profit' not shown in the profit and loss account.

Simply put, the net gain of £200,000 in two years represented a pre-tax return of 40 per cent per annum for each year when based on the original investment of £250,000. This would be an acceptable performance by most standards, but not when judged by the profit and loss account alone.

The investors' view

The hotelier's story demonstrates the attitude of entrepreneurs to investment and return. Returns do not have to come from operations alone and therefore the profit and loss account gives only a partial view of the returns available. What is more, the profit and loss account is prepared from a set of rules and conventions which are capable of different interpretations enabling different profit figures to be produced from the same situation. A cash investment was made in a project – in this case a hotel – with a view to obtaining more cash in the future from both operations and the eventual sale of the business, not necessarily with a view to providing a profit per the profit and loss account.

An investor in a public company does the same except that only part of the company is owned. A cash sum is expended on shares with the expectation of future cash flows in terms of dividends and sale of the shares. Return on capital or growth in earnings per share comes from the past. Even estimated for the future, they provide only a guide to future dividends and share price increases that give returns in that vital commodity – cash!

The amount and timing of the investment are important, but largely within the investor's control. The investor's skill is in the anticipation of the amount and timing of future cash returns. Profit figures can be polluted by creativity and can be difficult to apply for investment decision-making purposes. In the hotelier's story there was a capital gain of £250,000. Should this have been split equally between the two years or been taken entirely in year 2 when it was realized? Cash is much simpler to evaluate. In the hotelier's story the cash flows are shown in Table 7.1.

Table 7.1 Cash flows

Year 0	Purchase	(£250,000)
Year 1	Loss	(£35,000)*
Year 2	Loss	(£15,000)*
Year 2	Sale	£500,000

*The losses may need to be reduced for any non-cash flow expenses such as depreciation.

As long as the amount and timing of each cash flow are known, or can be estimated, and the time value of money assessed, the evaluation of a financial investment can be done using discounted cash flow techniques in the same way that these techniques are used for capital project evaluation within a business. The discount factor should cover the underlying cost of money with an addition for risk.

Although this chapter will not bring taxation into examples, it should be stressed that tax is a cash outflow and the amount and timing of tax payments, or receipts, should be included. Equally the discount factor should be assessed on an 'after-tax' basis.

Cash – the vital commodity

In certain circumstances profit and cash increases are equal. A market trader buying goods in the morning from a cash and carry, paying cash for a stall rent and other expenses, then selling all the goods for cash during the day, will have a cash increase exactly equal to profit. From time of purchase to time of sale the profit (adjusted for capital gains or losses) of a large hotel business will equal the cash increase plus any distributions of cash made in the meantime.

The difference between cash increases and profit is one of timing. As soon as a business acquires fixed assets or is involved with trade credit, profit and cash increases will not match until the business is sold. Management and investor reporting quite rightly demand performance information on a regular basis, before the business is sold. Profit rather than operational cash flow reporting has been easier to understand by operating managers and investors alike. This has lead to a concentration on performance measures such as 'return on capital' and 'increases in earnings per share' in spite of the sometimes misleading view these measures can give. Earnings per share have been, until the implementation of Financial Reporting Standard 3 (FRS 3), subject to the distortions of permitted creative accounting. Even post-FRS 3 investment advisers are seeking their own version of 'earnings per share' as a measure of profits on continuing activities. The success of this will be limited by lack of information or will rely on (unaudited) information supplied by the company.

From the investors' viewpoint 'return on capital' suffers both from the subjective decisions on depreciation rates and the conceptual problems of the technique itself. An example can explain the problem. A project to purchase equipment for £8,000, depreciated on a straight-line basis over four years with no residual value and producing an operational cash flow of £4,000 each year, is to be evaluated. The initial view could be that there is a net profit of £2,000 per annum (operational cash flow less £2,000 per annum depreciation) on an investment of £8,000 and hence a return on capital of 25 per cent per annum. But what is the effect in the accounts? This can be seen in Table 7.2 using the convention of comparing a year's profit with the year-end written-down value.

Table 7.2

	Net profit (£)	Written-down Value (£)	Return on capital (%)
Year 0		8,000	
Year 1	2,000	6,000	33.3
Year 2	2,000	4,000	50.0
Year 3	2,000	2,000	100.0
Year 4	2,000	0	∞

An improving return on capital employed is seen as the written-down value reduces, but what of year 5? If at the end of year 4 new equipment is bought on the same terms and with the same performance as the old, year 5 will be the same as year 1, a 33.3 per cent return on capital. If, however, the old equipment will suffice, not only will the infinite return continue but the reported profit will rise to £4,000 as there is no depreciation. This comparison is shown in Table 7.3.

Table 7.3

	Net profit (£)	Written-down value (£)	Return on capital (%)
New equipment			
Year 5	2,000	6,000	33.3
Old equipment			
Year 5	4,000	0	∞

Even if the old machine does not perform as well as the new and produces operational cash flows below £4,000, in 'return on capital' terms, *any* operational cash flows arising from the old equipment will produce an infinite return. This will always show as being better than *any* return on new equipment which has a written-down value. Thus investment in new equipment, although profitable in economic terms as judged by discounted cash flow techniques, is discouraged. 'Return on capital' provides misleading information for investment decisions.

This example is based on equipment purchases by managers within a business, but an investor can view a business as a collection of projects, albeit ones starting and ending at different times. Thus, the 'return on capital' for the business as a whole can be distorted in the same way that it is for individual projects within the business. It does not provide a reliable basis for investment decisions of any sort, even without further distortions caused by the effect of inflation.

As a concept, cash itself is easier to understand than profit, but from the investors' viewpoint cash reporting has been more difficult to understand than the profit and loss account. With FRS 1 cash reporting is improving, largely as a result of some spectacular company failures which clear cash reporting would have highlighted.

It is vital that managers and investors alike pay as much attention to cash management as to profit performance. Companies do not go out of business because their profit and loss account shows losses, they go out of business because they run out of cash. Several years of losses in a recession will not put a company out of business if it starts with a cash mountain or is able to raise cash by retrenchment or from shareholders (although it is more difficult to raise new funds from shareholders in these circumstances). Time is then available to reconstruct the business for a profitable, and cash-rich, future. Neither does a continual profit increase in boom times guarantee survival. A company concentrating on earnings per share growth, or even worse just growth, may simply run out of money to finance the expansion. The process is known as overtrading. Such a business will usually continue to operate but under new ownership, the original shareholders losing all or part of their investment and the senior managers losing their jobs.

The manager's view

Actual, or perceived, pressure from investors on senior management to produce short-term results in terms of increasing earnings per share can lead to cash management taking second place. Investors purchase shares in order to increase their wealth by way of dividends and realizable capital gains. In the long term managers have to provide them with this wealth increase through cash dividends and an increase in the (cash) value of the business.

Cash reporting and control are not enough. Cash control is essentially a short-term action to manage short-term flows. These are usually those associated with stock, debtors and creditors – the working capital elements. What is required is strategic cash management. This is concerned with the raising of long-term capital and its investment in new projects, essentially fixed assets or the purchase of existing businesses.

The life cycle

The strategic perspective is given in Figure 7.1. This shows a life cycle which, in the context of the hospitality industry, can be seen as a particular service or business. This life cycle plots business size in terms of sales against time and has four phases: innovation (or start-up), growth, maturity and decline. In profit terms there are losses during innovation, changing to profits as the move into the growth phase takes place. There would be little point opening a second or a third hotel if the first one could not be made profitable. Profits continue during maturity but revert to losses as decline sets in.

If in Figure 7.1 net cash flows are now added to the chart, the innovation phase incurs net cash outflows. As growth takes place, any cash from initial operating profits would be reinvested in growth. Thus cash from operating profits in the first hotel would be used to purchase the second and hence there is a net cash outflow in the growth phase. As growth declines, enter the maturity phase. The cash generated from profits now becomes a net cash inflow and can be retained for other purposes or distributed as a dividend. Although losses start to occur with the decline phase, a net cash inflow is maintained as the business size is reduced, perhaps by selling off some hotels, or if the business as a whole is sold.

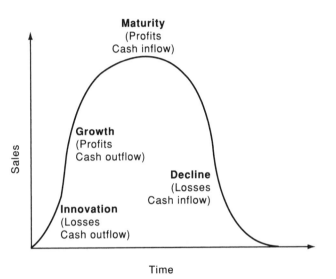

Figure 7.1   The life cycle

In terms of positive outcomes (profits or net cash inflows) or negative outcomes (losses or net cash outflows) the chart shows a match at innovation (both negative) and at maturity (both positive), but a mismatch during the growth and decline phases. This reflects the timing differences between profits and cash. At least during the decline phase the cash flow element is positive; the dangerous mismatch is during the growth phase especially in those businesses where profit holds sway and cash is left to take care of itself. Businesses expanding rapidly need cash to fund expansion and cannot rely on profits to do so – the classic overtrading problem.

Where on the chart should the business be? The maturity phase provides both profit and net cash inflows, however such a business faces eventual decline. The growth phase also provides profit but absorbs cash. A sensible approach is to combine businesses from each phase of the life cycle so that those in the maturity phase (often called 'cash cows') can fund those in the growth phase (the 'stars').

The skill of strategic managers is to know where their businesses and potential acquisitions are on the life cycle. Effective strategists would also be looking to sell a business towards the end of the maturity phase before decline sets in with its resultant losses. Not only are losses avoided, but the cash is received sooner and the amount obtained is likely to be larger. Clearly a supply of 'stars' is required. Some companies provide these via new start-ups. There are considerable risks in start-up situations and often cash outlays occur well before growth is possible. Other companies prefer these risks to be taken by entrepreneurs and buy-in smaller businesses when success seems to be assured just as the growth phase begins. Entrepreneurs may wish to sell at that time as they do not have the resources to fund the growth. Compared to start-ups, the buy-in route mitigates risk, even if it does not entirely eliminate it. It enables the cash outflow to be delayed, but the size of that outflow is almost certainly greatly increased.

Financial strategy formulation

The basics of financial strategy from a company viewpoint are very simple. An investment of cash should be made in projects which give a higher economic return than the cost of the funds provided to service those projects. A financial strategy must be formulated to affect and measure long-term economic benefits which ultimately maximize shareholders' wealth. A business can be seen as a collection of projects which is based on cash flow, adjusted for risk and timing, rather than on profits. The process is one of discounted cash flow. The assessment of risk throughout is vital. Once cash profits have been made there is the subsidiary dividend decision. How much should be retained to reinvest in the business and how much distributed as a dividend?

To develop these simple requirements, a strategy is needed. It can also be seen from the life cycle that there is a need to manage cash in a strategic way and not just on a short term control basis. A financial strategy cannot be developed by the finance function in isolation from the rest of the company. It must operate within, and form part of, a company's overall corporate strategy.

Corporate strategy is the result of a strategic management approach to long-range planning. This can be defined as a formalized approach, covering a period in excess of one year, conducted in a systematic way in order to direct and then control the use of resources towards required objectives. It covers a time period which is long enough to provide management with an opportunity to anticipate future problems, and thus have greater freedom to resolve them in an orderly way, before they become crises. There are many approaches to strategic management, one of which is presented by Johnson and Scholes (1993).

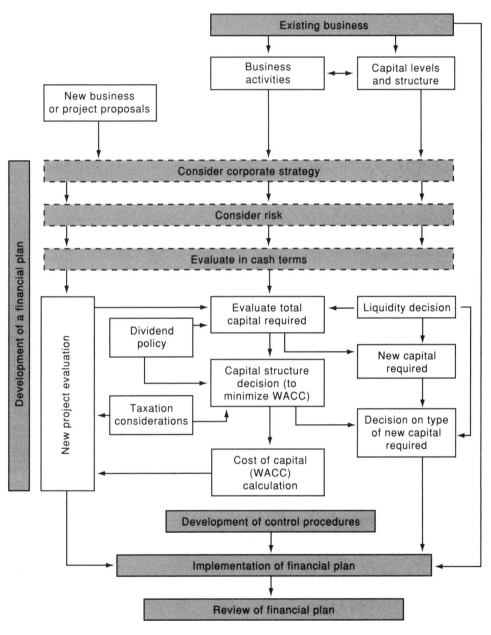

Figure 7.2   Financial strategy formulation model

A financial plan must be developed to incorporate the strategies set. This will be the collation of existing business projections with those for new businesses and projects which are approved. Figures are usually presented in the form of profit and loss accounts, balance sheets and, not least, cash flow statements. It is an iterative process in that a financial plan that does not show acceptable performance levels is likely to have inputs reviewed or to have the underlying strategies reconsidered. A financial strategy model is shown in Figure 7.2 and explained further in subsequent paragraphs.

Risk

All businesses incur business risks and these can be split into two types. Systematic risks are those that reflect risks in the economic environment generally, for example interest rates, inflation levels, and are not normally diversifiable. Specific risks are those associated with particular business projects and can be diversified by investment in a variety of different projects. Business risk is also reflected via the profit and loss account by the proportion of total costs which are fixed costs. When expressed as contribution margin divided by earnings before interest and tax (EBIT), it is known as operational gearing. Hotels, with high levels of fixed costs, are businesses which have high break-even points and require large contributions to cover the fixed costs; they have high levels of operational gearing.

Financial risk can only be added by borrowing. A business with no borrowing, i.e. no financial gearing or leverage, incurs no financial risk. A business is concerned with risk-taking in order to make potential returns and so must be concerned with the trade-off of risk against potential returns. The strategist is thus concerned with the total risk arising from both business risk and financial risk. For a given level of total risk, high levels of business risk should suggest low levels of financial risk. Thus hotels, with high levels of fixed costs in relation to total costs, have high levels of business risk and should be looking for low levels of borrowing, hence low levels of financial risk. Other businesses with low relative levels of fixed costs and business risk can consider taking on more borrowing. The addition of borrowing adds the fixed cost of interest to the operational fixed costs and thus increases the break-even point (see Figure 7.3).

Although the equity investor will consider the total risk of the business, a manager attempting to control this risk would do well to consider the operational (business) and financial aspects separately. The effects of financial gearing on the profit and loss account can then be seen.

Figure 7.4 shows the effect of borrowing in the 'good times' and the 'bad times'. In the good times, when the operational returns exceed the cost of borrowing, financial gearing improves the shareholders' return, per the profit and loss account. Unfortunately, in the bad times when the operational returns are below the cost of borrowing, financial gearing reduces the shareholders' return, per the profit and loss account. The break-even point is when the cost of borrowing equals the operational returns.

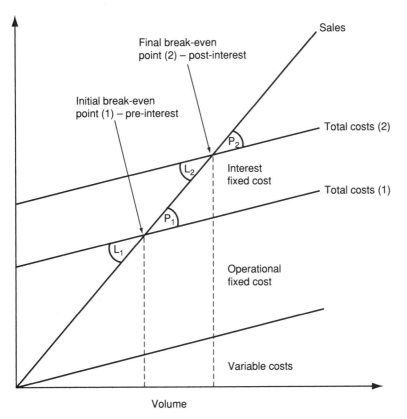

Figure 7.3 Break-even chart with gearing effect added. Position 1 is prior to a loan being taken out, producing loss L1 or profit P1, depending on volume. Position 2 is after loan interest becomes payable, producing revised loss (L2) or profit (P2) positions and a raised break-even point.

This profit and loss account viewpoint suggests that projects financed with borrowed funds only have to achieve a return greater than the interest on the borrowed funds to increase the shareholders' return. This may not be so if the financial risk added to the business increases the shareholders' expectations. It must also be remembered that financial gearing is concerned with long-term borrowing which cannot be turned off and on at will. Any changes of risk will affect several profit and loss account periods. Project returns should exceed the overall cost of capital to add value to the business. High levels of financial gearing appear attractive in boom times as

	The good times	The bad times
Given		
Return on operations	20%	4%
Gearing (constant)	40%	40%
Base	£000	£000
Shareholders' funds	600	600
Long-term loans	400	400
Total operating funds	1000	1000
Result	£000	£000
Return on operations	200	40
Less interest (10%)	40	40
Profit for shareholders	160	0
Return on shareholders' funds	27%	0%
Outcome for shareholders compared with return on operations	Gain	Lose

Figure 7.4   The gearing effect

shareholder returns in terms of earnings per share are increased. Greed at these times, epitomized by high levels of financial gearing, can prove disastrous in a recession. Low levels of financial gearing are safe, but in the long-term do not maximize the return to the shareholder. This is confirmed by analyses of financial gearing levels in relatively stable companies, which show that most companies have some long term borrowing but very few have high financial gearing levels. This suggests that there is an optimum financial gearing level above which the effect of a recession or a sudden increase in interest rates is deemed to outweigh the advantages to the shareholder in a boom. Levels lower than the optimum figure would be deemed to be safe, but not efficient in terms of increasing returns to the shareholder.

Optimum financial gearing levels

What then constitutes the optimum financial gearing level? To express this in figure terms first requires a definition. Financial gearing is variously referred to as gearing, leverage, debt to equity ratio. This latter expression does give one definition which can be used for calculation purposes. Another which is commonly used is based on 'long-term borrowing to total long-term funds used'. Further confusion occurs if overdrafts which are used permanently are included, although these are technically short-term borrowing repayable on demand.

	£000
Shareholders' capital invested	18
Retained profit	42
Total shareholders' funds	60
Long term loans	40
Total funds used	100
Loans/ total funds (40/100)	40%
Alternatively expressed as:	
Loans/shareholders' funds (40/60)	67%

Figure 7.5   Gearing definitions

The example in Figure 7.5 shows the main alternatives. In practice the debt to equity ratio may be used more often, but suffers from the disadvantage that it has no maximum figure for calculations, rather than judgements. Long-term debt, based on balance sheet values, has an effective maximum of 100 per cent. Anything over that would mean that the company was at least technically insolvent. Having a maximum helps when calculating the overall cost of capital, so in this chapter the definition used will ignore overdrafts and relate long-term debt to total funds used (the 40 per cent outcome in Figure 7.5). There is a strong argument that the gearing ratio should not be based on balance sheet values at all, which it is in Figure 7.5, as the balance sheet does not show the cash value of debt and equity in a company. For public companies at least, market values are easily available and should be used. This is far more difficult for non-quoted companies, although a valuation attempt could be made by reference to similar public companies. If the balance sheet has to be used, then realistic values for known assets, such as properties, could be substituted for the balance sheet values. This still leaves most balance sheets lacking values for intangibles such as brand values and goodwill.

The optimum financial gearing level will depend on the level of operational risk in the company. It might also depend on the level of security available to cover borrowing. A mortgage of 70 per cent would not be unusual, yet this is only a property-based financial gearing ratio. This would be high for financial gearing supported by non-property-based assets. In the UK financial gearing ratios of major companies have hovered around 20–27 per cent, although it is said that UK management is somewhat risk averse and an optimum figure should be higher, perhaps 35–40 per cent.

The establishment of an optimum financial gearing level within a company, whilst not fixed indefinitely, should be based on risk evaluations for at least the following few years. A company should not attempt to keep its actual ratio equal to its optimum at all times. To do so would mean obtaining debt and equity in the optimum proportions each year. Raising small quantities of debt, more so equity, is extremely expensive. It is far better to see an optimum financial gearing level as a mean around which annual levels fluctuate.

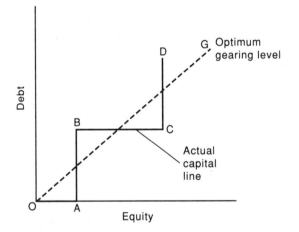

Figure 7.6 Use of optimum gearing for raising capital. Line OG is the planned optimum gearing line. Line OA is the initial equity capital raised (zero gearing). Line AB is the next amount of capital raised. This is debt and creates a capital structure at point B which is more highly geared than the optimum. Line BC is the third amount of capital raised. This is equity to reduce the gearing level and at point C creates a gearing level below the optimum. This process can then be repeated as often as required.

Figure 7.6 shows a graphical explanation of this stepped effect if a plot is taken of raising debt against raising equity. When the actual financial gearing level is below the optimum financial gearing level, the next amount of capital raised would be debt. This would push the actual financial gearing level above the optimum, which would later be reduced below optimum by raising equity. It must also be remembered that by retaining profits each year, the actual financial gearing level would drop even if new capital was not raised at all.

The cost of capital

This section will concentrate on the 'provision of funds at the cheapest cost' aspect of financial management. Although an important consideration, this phrase does not refer primarily to the cost of *raising* new funds, such as accountants' fees, underwriting commission, advertising costs, bank arrangement fees, etc. but with the cost of *servicing* those funds, interest, dividends etc. It is concerned with long-term funds for permanent use in the business rather than funds, for example a bank overdraft, intended to cover short-term, perhaps seasonal requirements. There are several approaches to the establishment of a cost of capital.

Capital asset pricing model (CAPM)

The CAPM is a method based on the addition of a risk premium to a risk-free return (usually the return on government bonds). The average risk premium is established by reference to the excess of historical stock market returns over historical risk-free rates. For a particular company, the average risk premium is varied by comparison of the company's risk (referred to as its Beta - 'ß') to the average risk of the stock market as a whole (where $ß = 1$). Companies with less than average risk have a ß value of less than 1 which is used to reduce the average risk premium for that particular company. Companies with greater than average risk have a ß value greater than 1 which is used to increase the average risk premium for that higher-risk company.

The simplified formula base for this is:

$$Er = Rf + ß(Rm - Rf)$$

where Er = expected market return (for use as cost of capital); Rf = risk free rate of return; Rm = average market rate of return; and $ß$ = risk factor for a particular, or similar, group of companies. Hence:

$$Rm - Rf = \text{average market risk premium}$$

Public company ß are published and calculated by reference to the company's returns over the previous five years compared with the average market returns over the same period. Average market returns are usually based on a suitable market index. Expected returns should incorporate an assessment of future risk, but ß calculations are calculated from past risk assessments. There are other questions raised by this method and reference to a detailed financial management text is recommended. Several suitable texts are given at the end of this chapter.

Weighted average cost of capital (WACC)

The WACC is based on the sources of funds for long-term use in a business. These fall into two main categories, those from debt and those from shareholders (equity). The equity funds can be further divided into the nominal value of shares and retained profits. The servicing cost of debt is the cost of interest after tax, as interest is a tax-allowable business expense. The payment of interest thus meets the expectations of the loan stockholders. In the case of traded debt such as loan stock the interest paid, after tax, would be related to the market rather than the nominal (balance sheet) value of the debt. Thus, the interest meets the expectations of the loan stockholders at the traded value of the loan stock.

With equities the situation is not so clear-cut. Unlike debt there is no cost that reduces the profit in the profit and loss account. There are several approaches to the establishment of a cost for equity.

In one approach it is argued that dividends, although an appropriation of profit after tax, are cash outflows and can perhaps be seen as a servicing cost of equities, at least in respect of share issues, but what of retained profits? Are they free of charge as no dividend is paid on them? There is an opportunity cost for retained profits. Had the shareholder received those retained profits as dividends they could have been invested elsewhere to earn a return. The shareholder expects the retention of those profits to earn a similar return for the same risk. If the company uses the retained profits wisely the value of the company should be increased, which should in turn raise the share price. The increase in the share price offers the shareholder a capital gain and thus, together with dividends, meets the shareholder's expectations. Shareholders expect dividends and capital gains. The servicing cost of equities to the company can be taken as dividend plus a level of retained profits sufficient to increase the share price. Taking both the dividend and retained profit together would be the 'after-tax profits'. Thus at a given share price shareholders expect the company to produce a certain level of profit. The provision of this level of after-tax profit thus becomes the 'cost' to the company of equity capital. The problem for the investor of interpreting what reported profits really are has been considered earlier. To this must be added the fact that shareholders are more concerned with future profits than historic profits.

Another approach is to regard a shareholder's expectations as the receipt of dividends into perpetuity. In practice it will be the receipt of dividends for a particular period plus the receipt from the sale of the share, but the sale value of the share at that time will itself be governed by the receipt of dividends into perpetuity thereafter. This is an entirely future cash returns basis of evaluation which is theoretically sound. Its practical difficulty is in the estimation of those future dividend levels. The dividend growth model provides a practical, if simplistic, approach to this problem. It is based on current dividend yields plus additional percentage points for dividend growth to account for the expected benefit of a capital gain on sale.

The formula base for this is:

$$K_e = d_1/p_0 + g$$

where Ke = cost of equity; d_1 = dividend *next* year (obtained from $d_0 * g$); p_0 = price *now*; and g = expected annual dividend growth rate.

The figure for the expected annual dividend growth rate (g) is critical in this formula, if a reliable cost is to be found. Clearly past dividend growth rates provide a guide, but extrapolation into the future is still a judgement.

Having established cost of debt and the cost of equity, a weighted average of the two should be taken. The weighting should reflect the market values and not the book values of each component. By using the market value, both the nominal value of shares and retained earnings are covered and in a way which better reflects their worth. If market values are not available, book values will have to suffice, providing they are adjusted to reflect, as near as possible, current values. The weighting should also reflect future rather than present or past gearing levels. The present position is acceptable if it is unlikely to change. The future gearing levels should be used because WACC will be used as a discount rate to evaluate capital investment projects.

WACC and optimum gearing levels

The calculation of WACC can help to explain why there is an optimum gearing level. There are differing views about the effect of financial gearing on cost of capital. What follows is the traditional view which appears to be confirmed in practice. Attempts have been made to produce mathematical models to prove otherwise, most notably by Modigliani and Miller (1958). Their model was based on a number of assumptions which did not hold true in practice, for example, the assumption that taxation did not exist. Later adjustments to the model to try to take account of these factors has brought the model closer to the traditional view. The traditional view is best expressed by way of a diagram, see Figure 7.7.

The diagram is constructed by plotting the cost of capital in percentage

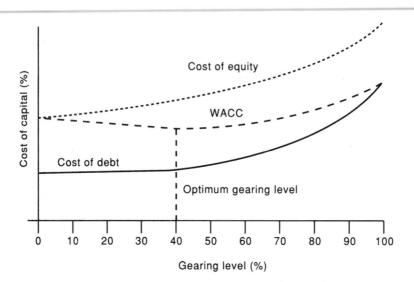

Figure 7.7   Weighted average cost of capital (WACC) – traditional view.

terms on the vertical axis against the financial gearing level on the horizontal axis. Financial gearing is defined by long-term borrowing as a percentage of all long-term capital used. This is done in order to give a theoretical maximum of 100 per cent, at which point all capital is borrowed and none provided by the shareholders.

If the debt line is viewed first, at zero gearing there is no actual cost to debt as no money has been borrowed, but as soon as small amounts are borrowed a percentage cost arises. As financial gearing levels increase, the percentage cost of debt remains stable until the lenders believe their risk increases as a result of reduced levels of security (debt as a proportion of security available increases) and there is a feeling that the business risk previously taken almost entirely by the shareholders is now being switched, in part, to the debt providers. Past this point the percentage cost of debt increases as the proportion of debt to total capital increases. In practice, financial gearing levels would not reach 100 per cent through increased money borrowing levels, as the lenders would simply refuse to provide more funds. The 100 per cent financial gearing level is sometimes reached or even exceeded as a result of losses and asset write-downs. The position of Queens Moat Houses plc in 1993 is a clear example of this. Exceeding 100 per cent makes a company at least technically insolvent, although it could continue with the backing of its creditors until a capital reconstruction can be arranged.

When the equity line is viewed, a similar trend to the debt line is seen, although the equity line shows equity to have a higher cost than debt throughout. Shareholders have higher expectations than debt holders as they take the greatest risk. In the event of a liquidation they are last in line to get their money back. Meeting the higher expectations of shareholders makes the cost of shareholders' capital greater than the cost of debt from the company's viewpoint. The debt cost is further reduced by the tax saving as interest is a tax-allowable expense. At low levels of financial gearing, the addition to the business risk already taken is perceived to be very small and the cost of equity as a percentage remains constant. As financial gearing increases past a certain point, equity holders perceive the financial risk to be increasing. What is more, the business risk of the now enlarged business is still being taken by the shareholders, although they now provide a smaller proportion of the company's total capital. The risks are larger and the shareholder expectations increase. Meeting these expectations further increases the cost of equity.

The WACC line can now been drawn between the debt and equity lines. Initially, with zero financial gearing WACC is equal to the cost of equity as debt does not have an actual cost. As financial gearing is introduced, WACC reduces as it moves towards the debt line. With equity costs, and in particular debt costs, increasing as financial gearing is increased, although the WACC line continues to get closer to the debt line, WACC as a percentage cost now increases and rises dramatically as financial gearing approaches 100 per cent.

Thus, as one aspect of financial strategy is to minimize cost of capital, it can now be seen that this does not just involve lowering the cost of debt, nor even lowering the cost of equity and the cost of debt, but also requires the optimum proportions of debt and equity to be held in order to minimize WACC.

The uses of cost of capital

The most obvious use for cost of capital is in capital investment appraisal, either as the discount factor (perhaps modified for specific project risk factors) in net present value calculations, or as a hurdle rate against which internal rates of return can be judged. It does, however, have other uses.

In the pricing of goods and services a figure for cost of capital on finance used should be included to ensure that the required profit level is in the expected price. The actual pricing may be a marketing function, but at least the marketing department will be aware of desired returns.

Cost of capital can also be used in management reporting where profit centres or investment centres exist. Merely allocating interest paid only charges centres for part of the capital used, even charging for all the capital used, based only on borrowing rates, ignores the extra risks taken by shareholders. Charging based on cost of capital ensures that all risks are covered. In doing this it should be noted that, in profit and loss account terms, a level of required profit is included in the charge.

Risk mitigation

Although investing in new hotels and other projects is the most risky part of financial management, obtaining funds has its risks, particularly when funds come from debt. This section will reflect on the risks in funds provision. The risk in funds provision comes mainly from the debtholders. In a public company shareholders can sell if they do not get a dividend and this could make the company more vulnerable to takeover. Takeovers tend to be more of a problem to the senior management than to the remaining shareholders, who may like to be enticed into selling by a bid. However, the providers of debt often sue when they do not get interest. If this happens they also sue for the return of the capital sum. Always having funds available to pay the interest on debt is of vital importance, but that does not always ensure that claims for the repayment of debt are avoided. Overdrafts are usually repayable on demand. Banks can and do call for overdrafts to be reduced or repaid immediately. This might reflect concern about the financial state of the company but could just reflect the bank's own need to reduce its outstanding loans.

Banks have an adage: 'Do not borrow short and lend long'. Banks do not always follow this rule. This is illustrated by the secondary banking crisis in the UK in the early 1970s and the problems with the USA Savings and Loan Institutions in the 1980s. Both were caused by borrowing short-term, often from small savers, then lending long-term to enterprises for property purchases. This should be a lesson to commercial companies, 'Do not borrow short and invest long'. The strategy should be to fund long-term investment in fixed assets with long-term funds, either by equity or long-term loans. Buying a hotel with an overdraft is dangerous!

Figure 7.8 shows a balance sheet presented in unusual format as an example of a company with fixed assets funded from long-term sources. Even that may not be sufficient. Some of the working capital needs may be semi-permanent.

Figure 7.9 shows a more prudent route whereby overdrafts are only used to fund seasonal requirements.

Funds	£000	Assets	£000
Shares	200	Fixed assets	1,000
Retained profit	400		
Shareholders's funds	600		
Debt (long-term)	400		
Long-term funds	1,000		1,000
Creditors (short-term)	50	Current assets	100
Bank overdraft (short-term)	50		
	1,100		1,100
Do not borrow short and invest long.			

Figure 7.8 Matching of funds to assets

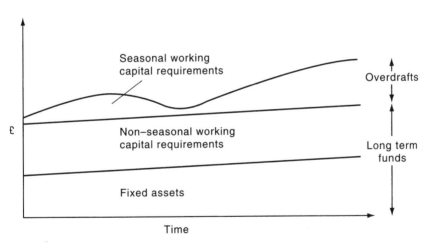

Figure 7.9 Prudent financing

Capital investment appraisal

Risk evaluation and control are important elements of capital investment appraisal. There will always be a business risk in such decisions but the specific risk element can be diversified by a spread of different projects or groups of projects. The main risk is that future net cash inflows will not be as high as expected. There is also some risk that the evaluation technique used may not be appropriate.

Return on capital is sometimes used. This is a profit-based technique but the example earlier in the chapter demonstrated the problems with it. Should the investment be based on the initial figure or the average book value? Should the profit be an average figure regardless of when it is made? Cash flow based techniques are much better.

The most widely used cash flow-based technique is pay-back. This technique is a cash flow technique and is simple to use, but it should be noted that it is a liquidity or safety technique. It is not based on profitability as it ignores all cash flows after the pay-back period. It also ignores the timing of cash flows within the pay-back period, although this can be overcome by using discounted cash flows. Pay-back is a useful initial technique, but should not be used as the final decision maker unless the need for liquidity outweighs the need for profitability.

The other techniques are all based on discounted cash flow incorporating the time value of money. Internal rate of return, net present value and profitability index are all discounted cash flow techniques.

Internal rate of return (IRR) produces a percentage answer enabling different projects to be easily compared. It can also be evaluated against the cost of capital, or hurdle rate. These advantages make it the most popular of the discounted cash flow techniques. However, it suffers from two problems. In certain circumstances with variable cash flows, more than one rate can be produced. It also assumes that surplus funds generated by the project can be reinvested at the IRR rate. This is unlikely if the IRR produced differs materially from the cost of capital.

Net present value (NPV) uses the cost of capital. Properly applied it is academically the best technique, enabling a decision to be made about a single project. However, when decisions are required between competing projects it does not easily enable projects to be ranked. If everything else is equal, the larger the initial investment the larger the NPV. If a certain sum is available for investment and the projects are of equal investment size, the larger the NPV, the better the project. It can also be used as a ranking mechanism for projects of unequal size if the funds not used by the smaller project will earn merely the cost of capital rate. In practice, often decisions are being made about several projects of varying size and potential returns, then NPV as such is not suitable as a ranking mechanism.

If project ranking is required, the best technique is the profitability index (PI), which, like NPV, uses the cost of capital and is thus academically sound. Unlike NPV, where the present value of cash outflows is subtracted from the present value of cash inflows to give a positive NPV for profitable projects, with PI the present value of cash inflows is divided by the present value of cash outflows to give an index number of 1.0 or above for profitable projects.

The higher the index number for a project in excess of 1.0, the more profitable the project. Some managers cannot relate to index numbers, hence the popularity of the flawed IRR technique which is expressed as a percentage. However, a variation of PI expressed as 'pence of NPV per pound invested' can overcome this problem. This can be seen in Table 7.4.

Table 7.4

	Project A £	Project B £
Net present value (NPV)		
Present value of cash inflows	1,100,000	150,000
Present value of cash outflows	1,000,000	100,000
Net present value of cash flows	100,000	50,000
Profitability index		
As an index number	1.1	1.5
NPV per pound invested	10p	50p

Table 7.4 shows the differing outcomes of NPV and PI. In this example, £1 million is available for investment. Project A is not very profitable, but is better than project B if no other project is available. Project B would be the choice if other similar projects can be done as well. If ten projects like project B were available, their combined NPV would exceed the NPV of project A alone.

Risk adjustment in capital investment appraisal calculations

The use of NPV or PI techniques requires a cost of capital. The weighted average cost of capital (WACC) represents the average risk for projects forming part of the current business. If the project being evaluated is considered more or less risky than the current business projects, the cost of capital can be adjusted accordingly. Another approach to risk adjustment is to use the WACC rate, but adjust net cash flows, taking a pessimistic view of higher-risk projects and an optimistic view of lower-risk projects.

All net cash flows must be 'after-tax' as the cost of capital is calculated on such a basis. The effect of inflation can also be critical. It must remembered that the cost of capital based on the money markets is a money rate, including an element for inflation, and not a real rate excluding inflation. It follows that future cash flows must also include a figure for likely inflation. Failure to adjust for inflation will not enable comparisons to be made on a like-for-like basis. There is a case for the removal of inflation from the cost of capital element and applying the result to unadjusted future cash flows;

however, cash flows do not all inflate at the same rate. Tariff inflation may differ from wage inflation. Both are likely to differ from the effect of taxation capital allowances which are based on the original capital spend and hence do not inflate at all. Incorporating inflation also enables post-completion comparisons of actual results to be made on a similar basis, although there is always the risk that inflation will not turn out to be as expected.

The main risk in capital investment appraisal is in the estimates of future cashflows, especially cash inflows. It should be remembered that the projection of a future cash flow is only one view and the evaluation of several views would be better. The best, most likely and worst outcomes approach is one that can be used. The use of a worst outcome may be important in a large project, if the best and most likely versions produce profitable outcomes, but the worst outcome would be likely to put the company into difficulties.

The use of probabilities, perhaps based on the views of different managers, can be useful. This can be extended to produce an expected value as a weighted average of all possible outcomes. The reduction of 'all possible' to a 'range of possible results' may be necessary for practical purposes. It should be noted that the expected value outcome is an average which may not itself be a possible outcome.

A sensitivity analysis can also give a view of risk. What is the effect of a change of ± 5 per cent, ± 10 per cent, etc on the cash inflows? A more sophisticated version of this is a form of break-even analysis applied to NPV calculations. Each element of the calculation is changed, one at a time, to produce a NPV = 0. Once one element has been changed, it reverts to its original figure, whilst another is changed. The aim is to produce the degree of change required for each element. This covers elements such as original investment cost, tariff, sales volume, labour cost, material cost, discount rate and length of the project. As an example, if the original cost was £50,000 and this investment was estimated to produce discounted cash inflows of £55,000 and hence a positive NPV of £5,000, then increasing the original investment cost by £5,000 to £55,000 would cause the project to break even. This would be a change, or sensitivity, in respect of the original investment cost of 10 per cent (£5,000 ÷ £50,000). Similar sensitivities are calculated for the other elements. The element with the lowest figure is the most critical. The factor with the smallest change which causes a potentially profitable project merely to break even is the factor whose estimate must be investigated most thoroughly.

Dividend decision

Once cash profits have been made there is the subsidiary dividend decision. How much should be retained to re-invest in the business and how much distributed as a dividend? A dividend is not just a sum of money, but is also seen by shareholders as a declaration of the directors' confidence in the future. It is a means of communicating that confidence. Dividends need to grow each year just to keep pace with inflation. However, increases do not have to be huge. In the good times the dividend rises do not have to match the rise in earnings per share. Paying high dividends when few requirements to fund new projects exist and paying virtually none when capital for new projects is required does not send a consistent signal to shareholders, even though it could otherwise be argued to be a sensible policy. Generally, companies in stable industries without growth prospects have been the high-dividend companies, whereas growth industries give low dividends, preferring to use retained earnings to fund growth.

It is far better to have a lower sustainable rise which can be continued during the more difficult times. Dividends do not have to be high. Typically, dividends are covered by profits two to three times, but companies tend to have a high-dividend or low-dividend policy. A high-dividend policy attracts shareholders looking for income, whereas a low-dividend policy attracts shareholders looking for capital gains. An existing policy will have attracted a certain type of shareholder; it is thus a very difficult policy to change. Any significant change will cause existing shareholders to sell and hence the share price to drop.

Although dividend policy could be said to be almost entirely within the domain of the finance director (certainly when compared to other financial policies), it is ironic that it is the policy area that is the most difficult to change.

Liquidity

Little has so far been said about liquidity as part of financial strategy formulation. It is a necessity that a company has a reasonable level of liquidity – so much so, that it is not even a strategic decision. If liquidity is strained it can, and should, be improved by raising long-term capital in excess of long-term needs.

Low levels of liquidity are efficient but dangerous. High levels of liquidity provide safety but are inefficient, hence a compromise between safety and efficiency is needed. Sometimes companies do use liquidity in a strategic way. Sitting on cash when a recession looms with high interest rates and low profitable business investment opportunities can be a good move. Other companies may invest unwisely and leave themselves open to takeover by a cash-rich predator just as the recession ends.

Summary

Whilst it is acknowledged that much of company reporting is in profit terms, the underlying success of a company depends on decisions about cash and the ability to handle risk. Decisions to obtain cash in such a way as to give the lowest cost of capital whilst investing that cash to give the best economic return holds the key. Financial strategies cannot be developed in isolation; they must form part of, and be in tune with, overall corporate strategy.

Financial strategies outline the way forward, but detailed financial plans, prepared with the aid of 'the art of the possible' provided by managers, indicate the likely outcome of both business and financial strategies. Should any outcome be unsatisfactory, the strategies need to be reviewed.

The aim of any strategy should be to increase shareholders' wealth. This is a long-term process which requires managers to 'think like an investor' (Barfield, 1994). The manager needs to think of increasing the cash value of the business, not just the short-term expedient of profit.

References

Barfield, R. (1994) Think like an investor. *Professional Manager*. March, 17-19.

Johnson, G. and Scholes, K. (1993) *Exploring Corporate Strategy*. London, Prentice Hall International (UK).

Modigliani, F. and Miller, M. (1958) The cost of capital, corporation finance and the theory of investment. *American Economic Review*.

Further Reading

Brealey, R.A. and Myers, S.C. (1991) *Principles of Corporate Finance*. New York, McGraw Hill.

Ellis, J. and Williams, D. (1993) *Corporate Strategy and Financial Analysis*. London, Pitman Publishing.

Lumby, S. (1994) *Investment Appraisal and Financial Decisions*. London, Chapman & Hall.

McLaney, E. J. (1994) *Business Finance for Decision Makers*. London, Pitman Publishing.

Pike, R. and Neale, B (1993). *Corporate Finance and Investment - Decisions and Strategy*. Hemel Hempstead, Prentice Hall.

8 The practice of management accounting in hotel groups

Paul Collier and Alan Gregory

Introduction

Hotel groups are an interesting context for studying management accounting practices[1] for two reasons. First, there is no accounting literature on management accounting and its contribution to the management of groups of hotels;[2] and second, the industry has a number of unusual characteristics which may influence the management accounting systems employed. For example, the industry is capital-intensive with a close link between profitability and asset values. Unlike factory plant and equipment, the assets may reasonably be expected to hold their value in the long-term and not be subject to obsolescence, provided adequate funds are devoted to maintenance, and that the earnings of the business are maintained.

Research objectives and approach

Research areas and objectives

The management of hotel groups may be anticipated to require the provision of information to assist with planning and control, and decision-making. The chapter commences with a brief review of the costing systems underlying management accounting information in the case study companies, before addressing the planning and control aspects which are taken to involve creating budgets and monitoring the performance of the group and individual hotels against these agreed targets. Decision-making situations for which management accounting might be necessary were limited to: information for price determination; information and techniques to assist with investment decisions; and the use of strategic management accounting in taking strategic decisions on marketing, finance and investment.

The approach adopted for addressing the research objectives was to undertake case study research.[3] The case studies documented the use of management accounting information in six hotel groups, and permitted the exploration and explanation of the uses of management accounting information.

The cases

The six case-study companies were chosen so as to provide a mix of sizes, patterns of ownership and spread of operations and include both UK and overseas-based companies. The main characteristics of the companies and a reference letter which will be used in the text to identify them are shown in Table 8.1.

Table 8.1   Profile of the case-study companies

Reference	Status	Size based on no. of hotels*	Spread
A	UK based limited company	Medium	UK
B	UK based plc	Large	International
C	Subsidiary of overseas company	Small	International
D	Subsidiary of overseas company	Large	UK
E	Subsidiary of UK plc	Medium	UK
F	Subsidiary of UK plc	Small	UK

*Small = up to 25 hotels; medium = 25–75 hotels; large = over 75 hotels.

The procedure followed in all cases was to send interviewees an *aide-mémoire* listing areas of interest and use this document as a base for the discussions. After the interview, a case study would be written up and a copy sent to the interviewee for agreement/amendment. The details of approaches to management accounting in this research are based on the agreed narratives.

Costing systems

General approach

The management accounting information for the case-study hotel groups followed a marginal cost approach, with the simplifying assumption that labour was fixed.[4] Contribution was identified at a departmental level, without much effort being applied in determining the variable costs for different departments. Typically, the contribution from rooms and leisure facilities was 100 per cent of revenue, while in the case of food and beverages it was revenue less the direct costs (materials) of food and beverages. From the gross contribution were deducted direct wages, usually analysed by department and direct expenses similarly analysed to arrive at the gross profit from operations. Other costs were offset to arrive at the net profit from operations (see Figure 8.2 for an example). The emphasis on departmental contribution was rationalized on the grounds that it assists with the aim of maximizing the yield from the facilities.

Activity-based costing

Despite the high fixed costs associated with the industry, none of the hotel groups interviewed used activity-based costing. Reasons for this included the integrated nature of the activities, the high margins and the market-based nature of pricing. On theoretical grounds, the absence of activity-based costing may be explained by the observations of Bromwich and Bhimani (1989) that decisions drive overhead costs and that most hotel costs derive from the decision to run a hotel of a certain capacity. As well as financial data, the management accounting systems in all the case studies also produced non-financial data. For example, the information system would include room occupancy percentage; average daily room rate and yield per available room.

Head office costs

There was general agreement that head office costs, covering areas as diverse as central reservation services, brochures, training, advice, marketing and personnel, should be charged to individual hotels to the extent that the costs are directly attributable to a hotel, such as television licences, stocktaking fees and credit card fees. This is consistent with the textbook position of charging divisions for a variety of central services where the consumption can be controlled even if the price cannot (Emmanuel *et al.* 1990) but not charging for general central overheads. As for these items the division can control neither consumption nor price and an 'incorrigible'[5] allocation method must be used. However, there were examples of percentage levies on budgeted sales for marketing and training expenditure.

Planning and control

Budgetary control

The keystone of the planning and control activities in the hotel groups was the budgetary control system, which was a major part of the day-to-day operations of the management accounting function. The budgeting process typically involved two inter-linked activities – the long-term budget, which covered from three to five years forward, and the annual budget covering 12 one-month or 13 four-week periods.

Long-term budgets

The long-term budgets were updated annually on a rolling basis within the annual budget cycle so that the first year of the long-term budget equated with the annual budget for the following year. The long-term budgets typically covered the balance sheet, profit and loss account and cash flow statement and was built up on a hotel-by-hotel basis. There was general agreement that certainly beyond two years forward the figures were very speculative, but it was still felt that the exercise was a worthwhile aid to forecasting and planning.

The preparation of the long-term budget usually involved forecasts at hotel level of key elements such as occupancy percentage and average room rate and the link between these and the contribution obtained from other activities. Figure 8.1 is representative of the practice among the cases.

The long-term budgets were essentially a strategic planning device, which allowed management to explore the impact of a range of strategies under a number of different scenarios. Strong emphasis was placed on identifying future funding requirements, and planning how the group through acquisitions, disposals and other activities could alter its shape to meet various corporate long-term objectives and the impact of these on financial performance and structure.

Annual budgets

Annual budget preparation broadly followed the textbook practices (see, for example, Edey, 1966 or Arnold and Hope, 1990). There were no pure examples of a top down or bottom-up approach to budget preparation. Nevertheless, among the six case studies there were examples of approaches

Hotel profit and loss account	Year 1	
	Qtr 1	Qtr 2 etc

Room revenue
Food revenue
Beverage revenue
Room hire revenue
Supplementary revenue

Total hotel turnover

Operating expenses – rooms
Operating expenses – food
Operating expenses – beverage
Operating expenses – room hire
Operating expenses – supplementary

Total operating expenses

Gross margin

Gross margin – % to total hotel turnover
Salaries and wages
Establishment costs
Sales and marketing costs
Overheads
Depreciation

Total indirect expenses

Net hotel profit

Net hotel profit – % to total hotel turnover
Cash sales
Credit card sales
Company account sales
Analysis of total hotel turnover
Salaries and wages – % to total hotel turnover

Figure 8.1 Any hotel – long-run budget

to preparing budgets which could be classified as top-down, iterative and bottom-up. However, the majority of cases followed an iterative process, which involved considerable interaction between head office management and the hotel. Typically, the process commenced with a bottom-up input from the hotels as each hotel was asked to provide for review by a head office details of its forecast occupancy percentages by class of business, average room rates by class of business, and a sales and marketing plan. The figures formed an initial budget for each hotel, which was scrutinized by head office member of finance staff who would often visit the hotel. Conflicts would be reported and highlighted for discussion at a meeting between the hotel general manager and senior head office personnel, at which a final hotel budget is produced. The hotel budgets are consolidated with head office budgets for administrative costs, marketing, training and personnel to produce a group budget.

At all the hotels, the budgets were prepared at a very detailed level over the main departments (rooms, food and beverage, communications, and other expenses) and the major overhead areas (administration and general, advertising and promotion, energy, and repairs and maintenance). Figure 8.2 gives a typical example of a budgeted profit and loss account for an individual hotel.

Among the case studies, only one set budgets principally as a forecast. This approach reflects the 'paternalistic' style of senior management and the close supervision of hotel general managers by senior management. Of the others, two hotels made the budget a clear target which general managers and head office management were expected to meet; while at the remainder the budgets were intended to reflect a realistic performance target.

Variances

In general, variances were only calculated on a line by line basis with the addition of percentages in some cases. Flexible budgets were not used and therefore volume variances were not calculated. The lack of budget flexing reflects the low marginal cost in all lines of business, the high fixed cost structure of the hotel industry, and a view that revenue was the priority. The finding is consistent with Fitzgerald *et al.* (1990) who stated that, although the flexing of budgets for the actual number of customers was desirable, the high fixed cost base means that there is little to be gained from flexing the budget.

Board-level budgetary information

At board level, the budgeted information was typically profits summarized at brand level with additional backing detail for individual hotels in large groups or merely the profits of each hotel in smaller groups. Comparison of the actuals on a period and cumulative basis being compared with the same items for last year and from the budget. Head office costs and financial charges are deducted from the profits to arrive at the group trading profit before tax. Figure 8.3 shows an example of the weekly group net profit summary used by one of the cases.

	Month 1	Month 2 etc
Sales		
Accommodation		
Other rooms and telephone		
Restaurants/food		
Bars		
Leisure club		
Golf		
Total sales		
Cost of sales		
Rooms and telephone		
Restaurants/food		
Bars		
Leisure club		
Golf		
Total gross profit		
Departmental employment costs		
Rooms and telephone		
Restaurants/food		
Bars		
Leisure club		
Golf		
Administrative and general		
Departmental expenses		
Rooms and telephone		
Restaurants/food		
Bars		
Leisure club		
Golf		
Total departmental contributions		
General overheads		
Laundry		
Legal costs and licences		
Printing, stationery and computers		
Sundries		
Promotional and advertising		
Repairs and renewals		
Utilities		
Depreciation		
Total general overheads		
Hotel profit		

Figure 8.2 Example of a budgeted operating statement

Group net profit summary
Individual hotels or the results of branded groups of hotels
Head office costs
Total trading profit

Administrative and general
Sales and marketing
Personnel
Audit
Other
Total administration charges
Financial charges
Group net trading profit

Figure 8.3 Management accounting information for the board.

Performance evaluation

Focus of performance evaluation

Performance evaluation within the cases was concerned with the evaluation of the general manager's performance. The decisions made by general managers tended to be at the 'programmed' end of the spectrum (for example, short-run tactical pricing and marketing).[6] In such circumstances it may be expected that budgetary controls feature strongly in the performance evaluation of hotel managers and, as was indicated earlier, this turned out to be the case. The theory of responsibility accounting would also suggest that there would be a direct relationship between the amount of autonomy a manager has and the extent to which he or she may be appraised on the basis of hotel profits.

Financial performance appraisal

All the case studies viewed individual hotels as stand-alone divisions, although some of our sample companies went further and measured profit at hotel departmental level. Financial performance measurement concentrated on budgeted versus actual profit. There were key differences between companies in the way that budgeted profit is arrived at with regard to whether the budget is a target or forecast, the degree of participation of managers in the budget-setting process, and the emphasis placed upon meeting the budget. These differences are summarized in Table 8.2. The 'budgeted profit' approach is at odds with the literature on the appraisal of the financial performance of divisions which favours the inclusion of some number reflecting the opportunity cost of capital employed. However, the position could be deemed to be consistent with the residual income measure which Tomkins (1973) points out is preferable given certain depreciation policies.[7] However, our case-study companies did not match the depreciation approach specified in the paper by Tomkins.

Table 8.2   Summary of budget preparation and bonus systems

Company	Preparation of budget	Target or forecast?	Bonus system?
A	Iterative	Target	Yes
B	Top-down	Target	Yes
C	Iterative	Forecast	No
D	Bottom-up	Forecast	No
E	Iterative	Forecast	Yes
F	Iterative	Forecast	Yes

Non-financial performance measures

Performance will also be evaluated by non-financial measures. Fitzgerald *et al.* (1990) classified hotels as 'service shop' businesses and suggested that such businesses need performance measures across five areas where performance cannot readily be measured in financial terms. The dimensions identified were competitiveness, quality of service, flexibility, resource utilization and innovation. Our sample companies tended to be active in measuring competitiveness, quality of service and resource utilization. In the hotel industry, resource utilization and *volume flexibility* were interlinked, as the basic room resource is fixed and the short-run objective is centred upon the maximization of room revenue. The other flexibility measures proposed by Fitzgerald *et al* are *specification flexibility*, the degree to which the service process can be adapted to meet individual customer needs, and *delivery speed flexibility*, which in a hotel would only apply to peripheral services such as check-in queuing, room service waiting time, and so on. These tended to be considered as aspects of service quality. Innovation was not measured as such, although the financial and non-financial results of innovations such as the addition of leisure facilities were measured.

All cases produced performance statistics associated with occupancy and capacity utilization. Room occupancy percentages and statistics reflecting average room revenue were common. Further statistical analysis included number of 'sleepers' (as opposed to rooms let) and average additional spending per guest. All of these statistics can be viewed as measures of resource utilization or volume flexibility (Fitzgerald *et al*, 1990). Further, all of the companies in our sample were well aware of the importance of quality and the majority, to greater or lesser extents, attempted to measure it using devices like guest questionnaires, visits by head office staff and 'mystery guests'.

Bonus systems

As is revealed by Table 8.2, two-thirds of our sample employed some form of bonus system, with rewards in all cases being based upon budgeted versus actual results. The dichotomy in employment of a bonus system was not linked to differences in the control system but their introduction was opposed because of negative experience of the effects of such bonuses. As one of these directors put it 'managers were more concerned with bonus maximization than the business of running their hotels'. In general the bonus schemes were based purely on budget versus actual figures with adjustments for any factors outside the control of the managers.

Decision-making

Pricing

Service complexity

Pricing in the hotel industry is a complex area as prices will be required for accommodation, both bedrooms and conference rooms; ancillary room services like telephone and video films; restaurant food and room service food; beverages; leisure facilities; and other items. Such price discrimination involves two main pricing strategies: segmented markets and service bundling.[8] In the cases, the following segmented lines of business, each with different prices or range of prices were typically present: rack rates[9] for private customers, although even for this customer group there are special offers and discounts; corporate business split between national (agreements negotiated by head office) and local (agreements negotiated by the hotel locally); and conference rates. Services were also bundled, as for example, in the case of the free use of leisure facilities for all guests or in full- or half-board terms and bargain breaks. According to Dorward (1987), the pricing strategies developed and pursued in such environments would centre on the development of distinct market segments and bundles where price skimming can be exercised in order to maximize revenue. This may explain moves towards the branding activities of various hotel groups.

Pricing policy

In all the case studies pricing policy was essentially market-driven along the lines suggested by pricing theory. Thus, pricing was a central part of marketing strategy, with management accounting currently making little contribution. In general, no cost information was provided by management accounting for either rack rates in individual hotels or promotion prices. These findings are consistent with those of Fitzgerald *et al* (1990), who observed that 'only professional services appear to use costs routinely for pricing decisions'.

The main source of variation between the case studies was in the degree of central control exercised over the pricing policy of individual hotels. Typically, promotional prices were determined centrally, following limited discussions with hotel general managers. General managers had a greater input into the determination of rack rates and discretion on discounts to customers from these rates. The greater consultation with the general managers reflects reliance on their expertise in local market conditions.

All the case-study interviewees stressed that the objective of pricing policy was to maximize revenue as direct costs, especially for letting rooms, are low and fixed costs high. The decisions are complicated by factors like the segmentation of the market and the bundling of services, and the existence of real opportunity costs if the hotel is full with discounted customers and full-rack-rate customers are turned away. All the accountancy functions concentrated on balancing the occupancy percentage with the average room rate in order to maximize revenue, while considering the knock-on effect of occupancy rate on additional income from telephone, food, beverage and other sources, and on staffing costs.

One company was installing a computerized yield management system, which was based on examples in the airline industry. The expert system worked by referencing past booking experience on a continuous basis. The system scans historic experience and advises management on the rate to quote on the basis that rates must fall, the nearer the current date gets to the actual date. For example, the system may advise that a booking two months out should get no discount to rack rate, while a booking one day before should receive a discount of 30 per cent. The approach is a price-skimming strategy where one price is charged in each time period but between price periods the price is progressively reduced as the price discriminator moves sequentially through segments of progressively increasing demand elasticity. The system assumes that the past is a reliable guide to the future, with the advice being given in the light of historic experience.

The findings on pricing decisions are at variance with the survey results obtained by Mills and Sweeting (1986). These researchers reported that full/absorption costing was widely used in both manufacturing and service companies in normal circumstances, and that market conditions were only an additional factor in determining prices. Further, the hotel accounting practitioners, by using marginal costs in decisions, avoid the criticisms of commentators like Bloom *et al.* (1984) to the effect that practitioners have a functional fixation with absorption costing.

Investment appraisal

Investment appraisal in the hotel industry has three unusual features. First, the investment decisions that are undertaken are relatively homogeneous; second, the investments have very long lives, with relatively little fall in value in real terms if they are well-maintained; and lastly, that strategic considerations predominate.

The homogeneity of hotel investments

Investment situations can be categorized as follows:

1. New builds (new hotels; extensions to existing hotels; or facility additions e.g. leisure clubs, gymnasia).
2. Acquisitions of existing hotels.
3. Disposals of existing hotels.
4. Equity stakes (new hotels, existing hotels or management contracts).
5. Refurbishment programmes.

Generally, the most simple cash flow patterns are exhibited by points 2 and 3, with the most complex arising under point 4 where care is necessary in defining the relevant cash flows.

The research found that every major investment appraisal process was in use, together with a few 'home-grown' techniques, which are derivatives of the four standard approaches (pay-back, accounting rate of return, internal rate of return, (IRR), and net present value. The practices employed by individual hotel companies are summarized in Table 8.3 and range from the very simple rules of thumb used by D ('the investment must cover its interest cost in the first year, and we take a two- to three-year view of the investment') to a complex analysis of IRR on total and equity investment in the case of C.

Explanatory or contingent factors which might explain the disparity in approaches between the cases when appraising homogeneous decisions are not readily apparent. However, further analysis of D reveals that, although it is now a part of a multinational conglomerate enterprise, until recently it was a hotel- and leisure-based company. In addition, the charismatic head of the hotel company remains in post and has considerable freedom of action; noting this, together with the fact that most investment decisions were made prior to the takeover of the company leads us to suggest that companies 'rooted' in the hotels and leisure sector tend to have dominant leadership styles associated with centralized control systems and simple 'rule of thumb' investment appraisal techniques. By contrast, those with parent companies located outside the hotel and leisure sector tended to make fuller use of DCF techniques.

Table 8.3   Summary of investment appraisal techniques

Case	Investment appraisal technique	IRR used?	Cost of capital*	Horizon valuation*
A	Profit pay-back	No	NA	NA
B	ARR/ Pay-back	Partly	Loan rate +	Cost + inflation
C	IRR	Yes	1.5 x loan rate	Cashflow multiple
D	Cover interest (year 1), profit (year 2)	No	NA	NA
E	ARR/ IRR	Yes	Business specification	Cost + inflation
F	IRR	Yes	Corporate WACC	Cost + inflation

* Companies using ARR or IRR only. IRR = Internal rate of return; ARR = accounting rate of return; WACC = weighted average cost of capital.

The diversity of techniques is well-illustrated by comparing case A and case C. At A, all capital investment projects are appraised on a pay-back basis, although this is not payback as usually defined. Pay-back is based on profit recovery (defined as cash flow less depreciation). There are no standard pay-back criteria and the profit pay-back period of the project is but one factor in the decision; however, as an indicator the maximum pay-back period allowable for extensions is 75 months. This pay-back calculation is based on the change in estimated future profits generated by the investment rather than changes in cash flows, in the hotel industry these may be close, since buildings in this company are depreciated at low rates.[10] The estimates of the parameters which will cause the change in profit are generated by the hotel, checked by management accountants for reasonableness, and entered into the planning model which estimates quarterly profits. The hotel does not fund the expenditure but depreciation is charged with rates of around 4 per cent for buildings and 10 per cent or more for refurbishments and these amounts are taken into account in the pay-back calculations. Profit changes are also looked at as a direct variable, as are changes in room occupancy rates.

The formal appraisal system at C was based around an IRR rule, although pay-back may be used for some minor refurbishment projects. Broadly, specific cash flows (including an inflation element) are forecast to five years after opening, by which time it is felt that the hotel should have reached maturity. The initial cash flows considered mirror the budget statements used by the company, and include assessment of room occupancy, average room rate, food, beverage and other sales, together with payroll and other cash expenses, yielding the controllable cash flows, from which are deducted management fees, property taxes and insurance, and capital expenditures[11] (typically set at a fixed percentage of turnover). The variables are considered at a site-specific level, and no generalized rules-of-thumb are employed. At a later stage, if the venture looks viable, consultants are employed to test the assumptions and conduct a feasibility study. Finally, when submission is made to the parent, additional figures for 'profit with the venture' and 'profit without' are presented. After a full divisional analysis has been carried out, around 10 per cent of projects make it to this stage of the process. Continuing or horizon value is factored in using a multiple of year five cash flow for the calculation of a five-year IRR.

The exercise is repeated for a 10-year horizon, with the same multiple being applied at that time. At this stage, the result is a return on the hotel investment. The return on the company's stake is then calculated by taking the appropriate share of cash profits, and adding on the management fee income (no head office fixed costs are considered in respect of the latter as it is felt that capacity exists to handle more of these contracts). An IRR is calculated on this stake, with a lower multiple of cash earnings being utilized, but with the assumption that the management contract is retained for the duration of the agreed term. Finally, the IRR on the equity stake is considered, for both the hotel as an entity and the company's stake, by deducting interest charges from the present cash flows, and utilizing the same 'continuing value' multiples used previously. The project hurdle rates are set by the parent company.

In the analysis, it appears that the return on the company's equity is the key indicator; a rule-of-thumb for an acceptable return is 1.5 times the current corporate borrowing rate, although this can be increased in the case of risky projects. The project has to achieve this return as a minimum, irrespective of its success in meeting the other benchmarks which are employed. These include the need for the hotel's IRR on equity to be at least equal to the current interest rate. The group regards it as important for the hotel partners to make a fair return, to avoid any reluctance to maintain and refurbish the hotel to the required standard. In this context, the management fee is negotiable, and can be altered to change the balance of return between partners and the company. Sensitivity analysis (± 5%) is also conducted as part of the appraisal process.

Exit values

Unlike many simple investment projects, such as the purchase of a piece of industrial machinery, a hotel does not usually have a finite life, at least in the medium term. This means that in evaluating an investment, consideration must be given to determining what may variously be described as the terminal, exit, horizon or continuing value of the hotel. To some extent, the problem is similar to that of valuing a company. A discounted cash flow approach to this problem consists of estimating the cash flows for a specific forecast period, typically until a steady-state scenario can reasonably be assumed and adding in the present value of the horizon or continuing value of the firm (Copeland, et al. 1990, Gregory, 1992). In all cases where IRR calculations are made for both new hotels (purchased or built) and for extensions, they are executed by including a terminal, horizon or exit value at the end of a specific cash flow forecast period. This ranges from five years in the case of B to 25 years in the case of E. In C two analyses are performed, one with an exit value after five years and one at 10 years, whilst in F the exit value is calculated at the end of 10 years. The most common approach, used by B, E and F, involved uplifting the purchase price or construction cost of the hotel by the rate of retail price index inflation, thus assuming constant asset prices in real terms.

Strategic issues

Strategic issues such as branding, location and package style (e.g. tour versus business hotel, star ratings, fitness and leisure facilities, etc.) were of fundamental importance. Indeed, all of our sample companies assigned more importance to these strategic areas than to the pure numerical analysis. However, the style of the strategic analysis differed in terms of formality and whether or not consultants were employed. In the most sophisticated case, the strategic analysis involved a complex scoring system based upon detailed customer mapping (both in the geographical and demographical senses) with back-up studies from local consultants. At the other end of the spectrum, two companies relied upon personal inputs (including site visits) by directors before acquisitions were analysed, and did not involve any use of consultants. As regards the initiation of new projects, for the most part 'new builds' were determined by reference to strategic considerations at a senior level within the hotel company. Expansions of existing hotels could either be initiated by the hotel manager, or by head office in consultation with the local manager. Refurbishments tended to be initiated at both levels, and often in response to a set time pattern.

Strategic management accounting

Defining strategic management accounting

The Chartered Institute of Management Accountants (1991) defined strategic management accounting as: 'The provision and analysis of management accounting data relating to business strategy: particularly the relative levels and trends in real costs and prices, volumes, market share, cash flow and the demands on a firm's total resources'. Bromwich (1990)[12] stressed that there is a need for accountants to consider the cost structure not only of their own firm but of all enterprises in the relevant market and of potential entrants, and that cost cannot be considered in isolation from demand factors. This aspect of strategic management accounting relies on the availability of relevant information. The hotel sector meets these requirements due to the open nature of the industry and the availability of price and some cost data.

Approaches adopted

Several of the interviewees described the industry as being fairly open, especially for the interchange of ideas on different approaches to solving common problems like automated booking systems, valuation practices and yield management systems. The common forum for such discussions is the British Association of Hotel Accountants (BAHA), which has over 1000 members, and a number of the interviewees, especially those who had spent the majority of their working life in the industry, were members.

The nature of the industry makes it difficult for companies to be secretive about such prices or costs. Rack rates and other standard terms are publicized and it is possible to pose as a customer to ascertain discounts off the published rates. While on the cost side, major components of costs may be determined with a degree of accuracy. For example, the valuation of hotels, site costs and building costs can be monitored and rateable values are publicly available.

As with strategic planning, major consultants specializing in the field offered services which were relevant to strategic management accounting. For example, Horwarth Consulting produces an annual survey of hotels from throughout the UK with detailed summaries that act as a basis for interfirm comparison. The 1992 *Statistical Report* was based on returns from 293 hotels and included data analysed across four regions (London, Provinces, Scotland and Wales) and across a variety of average room rates. The terminology used and accounts titles conformed to the *Uniform System of Accounts for Hotels*.

The reports covered:

- *Average room occupancy and rates* – average annual room occupancy; average number of guests per room; average daily room rate; and four categories based on average rate per guest night.
- *Market information* – guest analysis by country; percentage of repeat business; percentage of guests with advance reservations; and account settlement method.
- *Operational data* – percentage composition of sales split by rooms, food, beverage, and other; cost of sales data; gross operating profit; and employee statistics.
- *Revenue per guest night* – rooms; telephone and telex; minor operating departments; and rental and other income.
- *Payroll and other expenses* – both in terms of amount per available room and percentage of total revenue with a split across rooms, food and beverages, administrative and general, marketing, and property operations and maintenance.
- *Food and beverage statistics* – analysed by facility, percentage of total food sales, amount per seat, and per cover.
- *Departmental revenues and expenses* – in total and analysed by room across rooms, food, beverage, telephone, minor operated departments and rental and other income.

In this environment it is not surprising that in the majority of the cases studied, the accounting function monitored to some degree the cost structures and pricing policies of competitors. The exception was case study A, where there was no strategic management accounting within the accounting function, and competitor price review and market data assessment was the responsibility of the marketing function. In the case of F, although the accounting function took an interest in competitors' actions, no detailed studies were undertaken using published accounts, brokers' reports, analysts' reports or other data sources. However, the accounting function had an input into the development of strategic plans, including a formal SWOT analysis exercise,[13] which involved the gathering of extensive information about competitors. The exercise plotted the hotel group's competitive capabilities against business sector attractiveness. A range of business sectors was examined (for example, food, drink, accommodation and leisure) and the position of the company compared to competitors was determined using a range of measurable variables collected by in-house staff and external consultants. The exercise was deemed useful but deficient in one respect in that it did not take account of the relative costs of changing competitive position in the various business sectors. Again, the marketing function had responsibility for monitoring market conditions and the actions of competitors. The absence of any strategic management accounting in these cases is perhaps explained by special circumstances. In both cases, the groupings had only been recently formed and were focusing inwards on developing a market niche rather than being concerned with the actions of competitors.

In another two case studies, strategic management accounting was carried out irregularly by the accounting function. In case study D, although no formal analysis was made of competitors' cost structures, a keen interest was taken in competitors' actions. Further, the performance of the company against competitors was compared regularly at a return on sales level and information was gleaned from brokers' reports. However, in line with the less formalized control approach in this company, reliance was principally placed on senior management's experience in the hotel industry and the steps they take to keep in touch with their hotel general managers. The accounting function in case study E followed up their competitors' actions through an examination of published accounts, brokers' reports and analysts' reports.

The most wide-ranging exercises in strategic accounting were found in case studies B and C. Case study B regularly undertook *ad hoc* strategic management accounting exercises. The exercises focused on competitor performance and market data assessment. At one level, statistical information was obtained from the published accounts of major competitors and their performance compared with the company. In particular, performance was compared on a monthly basis with another group, which was felt to be the closest in business areas to the company. At another level, brokers' reports on the hotel and leisure sector were reviewed and, if deemed necessary individual companies were monitored through the use of specially commissioned consultancy reports. The company regularly tracks its performance against market surveys prepared by consultants specializing in the industry. In case study C, the assessment of position relative to competitors was undertaken through an examination of published accounts and the comparison of performance with other hotel chains in a similar class of business.

One common result of strategic management accounting activity was suspicion about the performance of Queens Moat House Plc, which was shown to be the clear market leader in the sector. Generally, the view was that the results were highly suspicious and 'too good to be true'. One case-study company was sufficiently interested to commission a consultants' report on the company to identify how it produced the results. However, none of the companies was able to understand fully the processes that had led to the apparently excellent results revealed in the published report and accounts, nor be alert to the subsequent financial difficulties that arose in 1993.

Conclusions

This chapter has provided an overview of the use of management accounting in six major hotel groups. The research shows that there is a tremendous diversity in the practice of management accounting within these homogeneous businesses. Major findings as discussed include the following:

Costing systems

Costing systems were based on marginal costs, with labour generally being treated as a fixed cost. Performance was measured at a departmental level, with variable costs only being attributed to a department when they were significant. Thus, the contribution on rooms was 100 per cent of revenue, and on food and beverages it was revenue less material costs. Overhead cost control reflected a separation of costs into controllable and uncontrollable costs categories and a focus on total wage costs. Despite the high overheads, there was no use of activity-based costing.

Budgetary control

As might be anticipated, considerable time and effort were expended in preparation of budgets, which would typically be fixed iteratively in order to balance the greater local knowledge of the hotel general manager with the better picture of general economic circumstances and group targets which was available to head office. In general, performance was based on performance against budget subject to meeting various service quality standards. However, there were considerable differences in the reward systems used, with a third of the cases having no bonus scheme for rewarding senior management.

Performance evaluation

As the literature suggests, performance appraisal systems are based upon budgeted results. The research showed that there is also considerable similarity in the financial and non-financial performance indicators used. However, there were real differences in the approach to reward systems. A clear dichotomy was found between those firms which have schemes based upon budget versus actual profits, and those which do not. Investigations suggest that the difference was based upon adverse past experience of bonus schemes. In those firms which do not pay bonuses, the budget is seen unambiguously as a forecast of cash and profit flow. Where bonuses are paid the budget is sometimes seen primarily as a target, in one case with provisions being made against non-achievement. There appear to be no obvious contingent factors which explain the differences in attitudes to bonus schemes, or in the use of budgets as targets within those firms that use such schemes.

Pricing

Pricing was a complex area given the bundled nature of the services provided and the distinct market segments in a hotel. Prices were found to be driven almost entirely by market forces and the management accounting input was limited to sensitivity analysis to explore the impact of different pricing structures.

Investment appraisal

The greatest variation in approach was in the area of investment appraisal. A variety of techniques and combinations of techniques were used. From our case studies, we noted that the more sophisticated analyses, both in terms of cash flow modelling and employment of DCF techniques, tended to be used by companies which were subsidiaries of non-hotel but non-conglomerate parent firms. In these firms the hotel activity was in some ways complementary to the main business, and the parent had a tradition of DCF analysis. It was also apparent that the least formal investment appraisal processes were found in firms managed in a 'hands-on' fashion by strong characters. By contrast, formal systems tended to be employed where the control systems were such that parent board approval was necessary to go ahead with the project. As well as formal techniques, standard rules of thumb such as 'build cost per room' for a given star-rating, and expected room yields were employed. Thus, overall the emphasis was on the processes followed in estimating the occupancy percentages and average room rate, and strategic fit rather than the techniques used.

Strategic management accounting

Strategic management accounting in some form was widely used in the monitoring by the accounting function of the cost structures and pricing policies of competitors. The importance of strategic management accounting reflects the open, relatively homogeneous nature of the industry, the ready availability of such data, and the high degree of competitiveness amongst the hotel groups in the market.

The results provide an interesting insight into the use of management accounting within the service sector.

Endnotes

1 This chapter is based on research which was funded by the Chartered Institute of Management Accountants.

2 However, there are a number of texts (see, for example, Everett, 1989; Thornfield, 1991; or Parkinson, 1993) which cover management accounting within a hotel in some detail.

3 The merits of the case study approach have been well-established by a number of authors (e.g. Diesing, 1972 or Mohr, 1985) and the technique has been applied in numerous accounting research projects (e.g. Kaplan, 1984 & 1986; Rickwood *et al.*, 1987; Davis *et al* 1991; and Holland, 1993).

4 In practice, it was recognized that labour was probably a semi-variable cost and that the fixed-cost assumption was a simplification.

5 The term incorrigible was used by Thomas (1974) to indicate that any method of allocation of such costs is unverifiable and irrefutable.

6 Emmanuel *et al.* (1990) classified decision-making situations into *programmed* decisions, where a reliable prediction of the decision outcome could be made; and *non-programmed* decisions, where there is no formal mechanism for predicting decision outcomes.

7 For a summary of these arguments, see Gregory (1988).

8 For a discussion of pricing in segmented markets and product bundling see Dorward (1987).

9 The published tariff – the term being derived from the price displayed in the rack.

10 In many firms, buildings are not depreciated at all. Queens Moat Houses had the most liberal policy in the industry, with not even fixtures and fittings being depreciated (although this policy has now been changed).

11 These replace the depreciation figure used to estimate profit in any management contract assessment, while, as the finance director observed, assuming steady capital expenditure on refurbishment, operating cash flows and profit are closely linked.

12 Bromwich (1990) defined strategic management accounting as: 'The provision and analysis of financial information on the firm's product markets and competitors' costs and cost structures and the monitoring of the enterprise's strategies and those of competitors in these markets over a number of periods'.

13 See Bhattacharya (1988) for a discussion of the role of the management accountant in SWOT analysis.

References

Arnold, J. and Hope, A. (1990) *Accounting for Management Decisions*, 2nd edn., London: Prentice Hall, pp. 275-295.

Bhattacharya, K. (1988), A management accountant's role in SWOT analysis. *Management Accounting*, **66**: 34–38.

Bloom, R., Elgers, P. and Murray, D. (1984) Functional fixation in product pricing: a comparison of individuals and groups. *Accounting, Organisations and Society*. **9**(1): 38–52.

Bromwich, M. (1990) The case for strategic management accounting: the role of accounting information for strategy in competitive markets, *Accounting Organizations and Society*, **15**: 27-46.

Bromwich, M. and Bhimani, A. (1989), *Management Accounting: Pathways to Progress*, London, CIMA, p. 4.

Chartered Institute of Management Accountants (1991), *Management Accounting: Official Terminology*. London: CIMA, p. 55.

Copeland, T.E., Koller, T. and Murrin, J. (1990) *Valuation: Measuring and Managing the Value of Companies*. New York, Wiley.

Davis, E.W., Coates, J., Collier, P. and Longden, S. (1991) *Currency Risk Management in Multinational Companies*, London: Prentice-Hall/ICAEW.

Diesing, P. (1972) *Patterns of Discovery in the Social Sciences*. London: Routledge, Kegan and Paul.

Dorward, N. (1987) *The Pricing Decision: Economic Theory and Business Practice*. London: Harper & Row, pp. 131–132.

Edey, H.C. (1966) *Business Budgets and Accounts*, 3rd edn., London: Hutchinson.

Emmanuel, C., Otley, D. and Merchant, K. (1990) *Accounting for Management Control*. London: Chapman Hall, p. 240.

Everett, M.D (1989) Managerial accounting systems: a decision-making tool. *Cornell Hotel and Restaurant Administration Quarterly*. **30**: 46–51.

Fitzgerald, L., Johnston, R., Brignall, S., Silvestro, R. and Voss, C. (1990) *Performance Measurement in Service Businesses*, London: CIMA, p. 21, 31.

Gregory, A. (1988) A review of divisional manager performance evaluation. *Management Accounting* **66**(1): 38–43.

Gregory, A. (1992) *Valuing Companies.* London, Woodhead Faulkner.

Holland, J. (1993), Bank-corporate relations: change issues in the international enterprise, *Accounting and Business Research* **23**; 273–283.

Kaplan, R.S. (1984) The case for case studies in management accounting research. Paper presented at the America Accounting Association Annual Conference.

Kaplan, R.S. (1986), The role for empirical research in management accounting. *Accounting, Organizations and Society* **11**: 142–155.

Mills, R.W. and Sweeting C. (1986) *Pricing Decisions in Practice: How are they made in UK service and Manufacturing Companies?* CIMA occasional paper. London CIMA.

Mohr, L.G. (1985) The reliability of the case study as a source of information. In: Coulam, R. and Smith, R. (eds) *Advances in Information Processing in Organizations,* vol. 2. London: JAI Press.

Parkinson, G. (1993) *Hotel Accounts and Their Audit.* London. Institute of Chartered Accountants in England and Wales.

Rickwood, C., Coates, J.B. and Stacy, R. (1987) Managed costs and the capture of information. *Accounting and Business Research* **17**: 319–326.

Thomas, A.L. (1974) The allocation problem: part two. In: *Studies in Accounting Research* no.9. Sarasota, American Accounting Association.

Thornfield, A. (1991) *Accounting in Hotels,* 3rd edn. London: CIMA.

Tomkins, C.R. (1973) Financial planning in divisionalised companies. *Accountancy Age,* London, Haymarket.

Part III Financial Information and Control

9 Identifying managers' information needs in hotel companies

Tracy A. Jones

Introduction

The aim of this chapter is to provide an understanding and evaluation of the critical success factors (CSFs) approach to identifying financial and other information needs for managers within the hospitality industry.

All managers are involved in decision-making. Decisions have to be made whenever choices exist. Whether the decision is routine or non-routine, to take action or no action, an informed decision can only take place after information concerning the choices available is considered and evaluated. It would be difficult for a manager at any level within an operation to perform his or her role effectively without receiving information to aid in making decisions.

What is information?

If information is important to managers, it is essential that a sound understanding of what is meant by information is understood. Management information can be defined as raw data that have been processed into a form which provides relevant and meaningful information that aids management in business decision-making.

Raw data ➔ Processed ➔ Information

Data are raw, isolated and unordered facts. Within hotels much data exists – every booking, guest history, invoice, docket, customer's bill can be considered as data. When processed, such data can provide information, such as average spend, future occupancy, total revenue, cost of sales, sales by customer type, day, week or month. The processing stage is important as it determines the information output, its content and presentation. Unless the information received is meaningful and relevant to the recipient, it cannot be classified as information.

If managers are to receive good-quality information which aids them in the decision-making process, certain aspects need to be addressed. Namely, the volume of information that is most useful; if the information is relevant to the situation; will the user understand the information? will the information arrive in time to be of use? the accuracy of the information, the completeness of the information and its frequency.

Volume of information

The use of computerized systems throughout many hotels has given rise to easy access to a vast volume of computer-generated management reports, many of which are built into the software package. Some systems can generate more than 100 different reports on various aspects of the business. It is essential, if quality information is to be gained, that regard is given to the volume of information an individual can deal with effectively. The computer may be able to produce a 20-page daily sales report, but that does not mean it is needed.

There is a danger of information overload when too great a volume of information is given. A one-page report containing key statistics may be of more use to some managers than 20 pages that they do not have the time to analyse on a daily basis.

Relevance of information

Information has to be relevant to the current situation. As the situation changes, so do the decisions that have to be made, therefore information must be reviewed to ensure it remains relevant to the current and the future, not the past.

User understanding of the information

As already stated, when defining information it has to be meaningful to the recipient (the manager using it). A financial report using technical terms unfamiliar to the manager is of little assistance. Assuming the manager has the financial knowledge to understand such a report is dangerous. Without understanding the information, a decision could be made without fully understanding the consequences.

Timeliness of information

This is essential – information that arrives after the decision has been made is of little use. Information should be available as needed, whether this be daily, weekly or monthly, and should not be out of date when received.

Accuracy of information

Is the information reliable? When producing information internally you can ensure that it can be monitored and controlled as to accuracy. It is more difficult to control the accuracy of information obtained from external, secondary data sources and this makes it difficult to rely on such information.

Completeness of information

It is essential that the information is as complete as possible. Information provides knowledge in order to make informed decisions. When information is partial, decisions are made with a degree of supposition.

Frequency of information

The frequency of information must relate to users' needs if it is to be of optimum assistance in decision-making. Information that is reported to a departmental manager daily may only be required by the hotel's general manager weekly, or by head office monthly.

Clearly, there are many considerations in gaining quality information that is of maximum benefit to individual managers. One key aspect is how the individual information needs of managers are identified.

Identifying the information needs of managers

In developing a management information system, it is the initial phase of identifying the information required that is most difficult. A simple solution is to ask the manager; 'what information do you need?' Responses to this question may not be useful for a number of reasons. First, individuals may only identify information they have used before and found useful, thus omitting potentially beneficial information of which they are unaware. Second, their response may be influenced by who asks the question. If an accountant asks the question, the response may be related purely to financial information, whereas to an operations manager the reply may be quite different. Finally, if the manager knows the question is being asked in order to set up a management information system, he or she may list all information on the basis that it may be needed in the future so should not be left out, irrespective of the need for such information.

Warner (1982) identified six starting points for designing a new management information system.

- What the current system allows the manager to have.
- What the accountant believes should be given.
- What a more senior manager considers appropriate.
- What the individual manager wants.
- What the individual manager needs.
- What the position, as opposed to the individual, needs.

Some of these will not give managers good-quality information for a number of reasons. In the short term, the system may restrict the frequency or type of information available. A short-term problem of this nature should not prevent the planning and development of an information system. If the current system is allowed to dictate the information managers receive, the quality and usefulness cannot be guaranteed.

In any commercial operation a substantial amount of management information is of a financial nature. This leads some companies to rely on accountants and financial controllers to design and provide all management reports. It is questionable whether this information will reflect the operational information needs of managers, or if it will lead to a bias that relates to the accountants' information needs.

Senior managers could be influenced by the information they would like to receive from subordinates, rather than viewing what subordinates require in order to complete their own management role effectively. They may consider their own needs if they were performing the subordinate's role rather than considering the subordinate's position directly.

It would be simple to give managers the information they want, but would this be effective? It must be questioned why an individual wants certain information. It may be that the information is simple and easy to deal with, and not that the information will aid in decision-making.

The actual needs of an individual manager must be an essential element in designing an effective management information system. Although the importance of this can be justified, it also has drawbacks. How do you identify managers' information needs realistically? As already stated, asking the individual concerned the direct question may not produce the correct answer, neither will leaving the decision to the assumption of others, such as superiors or accountants.

Finally, the information system could be based on the needs of the post, rather than those of the individual manager performing the role. The benefit of this is that the system does not have to change each time a new manager arrives. This basis does not focus on individual needs, therefore it ignores individual characteristics, such as experience and capability to make judgements from the information provided.

It can be seen that a compromise between the needs of the individual and the needs of the post would be a satisfactory solution. Although this solution has attributes, the problem of how to identify information needs, for either an individual, or a specific post, remains.

The critical success factors approach

One solution to this problem is to use the CSFs approach to identifying information needs. This approach was first developed by Rockart and his team in the late 1970s, whilst Rockart was director of the centre for systems research, Sloan School of Management. The approach focuses on individuals' current information needs and identified that information needs change with time and are different for each person. The approach received positive responses from executives in relation to the actual process and the resulting identification of information needs. The approach focuses on identifying individuals' work-related goals, CSFs and measures. From this the information requirements are gathered without need to ask individuals directly what their information needs are. The stages in the process are as shown in Figure 9.1.

Figure 9.1 Stages in the critical success factors approach

The approach Bullen and Rockart (1981) used identified an individual's goals – the specific objectives at which the manager was currently aiming. Once goals are established, the areas in which good performance is critical to achieving them are identified. These are the few key areas where things must go right in order to achieve the goals identified – the CSFs. It is logical that these critical areas are the ones that need monitoring the most, therefore they should be the areas for which managers need constant information. For each CSF it must be established how it can best be monitored, i.e. the measures that need to be taken in order to monitor progress.

The measures identified should form the basis for management information reports. Once it has been established what information is required the raw data required (database) and how the data are to be processed can be identified.

Business success should be measured in terms of meeting organizational goals and targets. The CSFs approach identifies the areas that must be right to achieve the goals; this is very different to providing information related to the goals in question without first considering the essential nature of some elements compared to others – the CSFs. Although much of the earlier research into this approach concentrated at the executive level, the team identified that this approach was useful at other levels of management.

When comparing the CSFs of individual managers they identified that certain CSFs were common across a whole industry, others were common to all managers in a specific company or managerial role, whilst others remained specific to an individual.

Throughout the 1980s the approach was used and debated by many within the USA. Some felt that managers would be incapable of identifying their goals and CSFs, thus giving incomplete answers when questioned. Managers should already be working to achieve goals. To obtain these, managers would need to identify the most important areas they have to control and monitor to achieve their goals. The CSFs approach is merely putting this into a framework in order to give managers appropriate management information.

A Primer on Critical Success Factors (Bullen and Rockart, 1981) provided detailed information for others wishing to use the technique. It gives guidance for individuals in terms of the process and how to conduct CSFs interviews effectively in order to produce optimum results. This publication is invaluable for those wishing to gain a working knowledge of the approach.

One concern was that two researchers using the method may not achieve similar results in relation to the same sample population. This was tested when two researchers both studied management information systems executives. They were unaware of each other's research; when they were compared by Munro (1983), it was found that, although the wording of certain CSFs was different, the CSFs were definitely comparable.

It is evident 'that a consensus exists to the need for focused information systems, the critical success factors approach is one method of achieving this that has been tried and tested over a number of years and even the sceptics of the approach have concluded it has value' (Jones, 1991).

The critical success factors approach in American hotel companies

Geller (1984) undertook a major study into the executive information needs of American hotel companies, using the CSFs approach. This culminated in an extensive publication that highlighted key statistics from his research. Three articles relating to specific aspects of his work followed: `Tracking the critical success factors for hotel companies' (Geller 1985a); `The current state of hotel information systems' (Geller 1985b); and `How to improve your information system' (Geller 1985c).

Geller's research focused on senior executives. These included chief executives, financial managers and operating managers at corporate and divisional level from twenty-seven companies. Seventy-four managers were involved in the study, which represents an average of fewer than three managers interviewed in each company.

Geller believed that two approaches could have been used for his research: to interview in-depth a small number of companies or, as he selected, to involve a greater number of companies, but not as deeply. He considered that 27 companies he included were representative of the American hotel industry. The sample included: organizations of various sizes; organizations in all stages of age and maturity; privately owned companies; and publicly owned companies.

Geller identified certain goals, CSFs and measures that were common across the whole industry, irrespective of the characteristics of individual firms or managers involved. The objective of Geller's research was to familiarize the hotel industry with the CSFs approach and to highlight its usefulness in executive information systems. The broad nature of his research helped to achieve the objective, but has led to some specific results being indecisive. With so many variables in different types of organizations and the small number of people interviewed in each organization, only general, industry-wide conclusions can be drawn as detailed information is limited.

He illustrated the effect of the stage in the company life cycle to show certain common CSFs for companies in each stage of the life cycle. The small number of organizations representing each life cycle stage in his research would make it difficult to draw conclusions for all new hotel companies in the USA, for example. Similarly, in comparing common CSFs of centralized and decentralized companies, it is difficult to place all companies into these two simple groups. Centralization and decentralization can be viewed as poles on a continuum, making it complex to place them into two distinctive groups in order to draw common goals, CSFs and measures.

Clearly, Geller's research was broad and highlighted the benefits of the technique in the hotel industry. At this time no other documented research, using the CSFs approach to identify management information needs, had been carried out within the industry and this added to the significance of Geller's research.

The CSFs approach to identifying information needs in UK hotel companies

Between 1988 and 1991 research was carried out using the CSFs approach within the UK (Jones, 1991). It aimed to evaluate the usefulness of the CSFs method within the UK hotel industry as a means of identifying managers' information needs.

It has been stated previously that CSFs vary with the industry, the company, the position held within the company and the individual. Isolating such variables in order to draw valid conclusions is onerous with such a mass of variables. Geller adopted the strategy of restricting his research to chief executives within companies. Restricting the position variable enabled him to draw conclusions relating to industry-wide and company-specific CSFs for chief executives. The research carried out by Jones, within the UK, was interested in differences within the management hierarchy, variables in CSFs due to an individual's managerial position. In order to allow CSFs due to the individual and the position to be reviewed in depth, a case-study approach was taken, restricting the research to one company.

The company used for the study is a large international hotel chain based in the UK. It was selected because it is a well-known, established company with many UK outlets and is large enough to have specialist managers at various levels within its hierarchy. Discussions took place with the senior vice president – corporate finance, financial controller and the UK operational accountant as to the nature of the research and to gain full head office support for the project. As the organization had recently taken over another hotel chain, they were keen for the research to draw comparisons between the two brand names and highlight any significant differences between the two in relation to management information needs.

Sample size and selection

The study involved 15 different establishments (two in the pilot study and 13 in the main study) varying in size, location and type of customer. All hotels were within England and Scotland. Due to the varying size of establishments, not all had the same management structure. For example, the smaller establishments only had a restaurant manager and no food and beverage manager, whilst larger establishments had several restaurant managers and a food and beverage manager. The main study involved 86 managers within the 13 establishments, which were broken down into eight key positions for data analysis. Further details of the managers involved in the main study are shown in Table 9.1.

Table 9.1   Summary of managers in the sample

Managerial position	Total
General managers	12
Deputy general managers*	4
Development managers*	1
Resident managers*	1
Executive assistant managers*	4
Financial controllers	10
Front office managers	11
Rooms division managers†	1
Head housekeepers	11
Food and beverage managers	6
Conference and banqueting managers	11
Restaurant managers	14
Total sample	86

* These positions were treated as equal in data analysis.
† For data analysis, this position is included with front office managers and head housekeepers.

The positions of deputy general manager, development manager, resident manager and executive assistant manager were grouped together for data analysis due to the similarities in their posts. Each of these managers reported directly to the general manager of the hotel concerned and administered the day-to-day operation of the hotel. Despite differing titles, the role was similar for all four positions.

Only one person in the sample held the title of rooms division manager. This position incorporated the functions covered by a front office manager and a head housekeeper in other establishments. For data analysis, the results pertaining to the rooms division manager were incorporated into the statistics for front office managers and those for head housekeepers.

The research was carried out by initial letter to all participants, detailing goals, CSFs and measures, with examples. This was sent two weeks before the interview in order to allow the managers time to consider their own goals, CSFs and measures. This was followed by an in-depth, structured interview at the establishment. Besides identifying information needs, using the CSFs approach, individuals were then asked about the information they currently received and their opinions concerning the current information system. The purpose of this was to identify where gaps existed in the current information system and the individual's perception of needs, as opposed to those identified using the CSFs approach.

Results of the study by Jones, within UK hotels

The CSFs approach is based on the individual and, by its nature, assumes that each individual will have distinct information needs. Despite the individual nature of information needs, certain common elements can usually be identified for individuals within the same managerial position, within a particular organization, or within the same industry.

The influence of managerial position

Although no two managers in the study had identical patterns of goals, CSFs and measures, several parallels were identified for managers in equal positions. The most frequently cited goals of general managers were:

- Achieving the profit required.
- Strengthen the management team.
- Operating to the standards laid down by the company.

When all of their goals are identified it can be seen that they relate to the operation as a whole. Due to the hierarchy existing within the establishments, the emphasis is on achieving the unit's goals through effective management at departmental level. The significance of departmental managers is shown in the general managers' CSFs for achieving their goals. The four most common CSFs all relate to the departmental managers and staff within the operation:

- Having a good management team.
- Having the right staff.
- Having a management that understands the objectives.
- Staff training.

The significance of their listed CSFs is that they are managing through department managers, therefore their own CSFs relate to developing the staff and general aspects of the overall product experience. The most frequently cited measures are also noteworthy:

- Customer feedback (complaints and compliments).
- Personal observation.
- Being on duty.
- Budget comparisons.
- Detailed financial information for all departments.

Due to the emphasis given to staff and product quality, judgemental, qualitative information is important in measuring the attainment of the hotel by the general manager. In addition, detailed financial information and comparisons are used; these are of a quantitative nature and provide general managers with a clear indication as to profits achieved. It is notable that little mention is given to controlling costs.

Deputy general managers and their equivalent view the operation as a whole with the emphasis on day-to-day management, leaving general managers time to consider strategic, long-term issues. Their most commonly cited goals, CSFs and measures identify this, as illustrated in Table 9.2.

Table 9.2 Deputy general managers and their equivalent, commonly cited.

Goals	CSFs	Measures
Efficient day-to day operation	Having the right staff	Personal observation
	A good management team	Being on duty
Achieving financial targets	Product quality	Budget comparison
Raising standards	Staff motivation	Communication meetings
		Staff feedback (positive and negative)

The stated goals give importance to general product development and product quality, whilst the CSFs show human resource to be an essential element. Although achieving financial targets is a goal, the CSFs give little consideration to finance; this is also reflected in the measures. The only common financial measure is budget comparison.

The role of the financial controller varied within the group considerably. Some hotels did not have a financial controller, certain controllers worked alone and provided financial services to meet head office needs only, whilst others headed a substantial department meeting head office and internal management needs for financial information. Despite these variations in responsibilities common patterns existed, as shown in Table 9.3.

Table 9.3   Financial controllers, frequently cited.

Goals	CSFs	Measures
Accurate month end accounts	Keeping paperwork up-to-date	Budget comparison
		Variance analysis
Providing head office with all information required	Accurate billing	
	Having the right staff	Detailed financial information for all departments
Providing internal management information	Maintaining stock levels	
	Management awareness of financial position	Internal audit/accurate paperwork
	Matching revenue to bills	Quality control spot checks
	Revenue control	
		Staff communication
	Staff training	

Most financial controllers had developed their own internal management information systems for the hotel and relied on this for financial information. The results of the companies' regular internal audits were used as a measure for assessing the accuracy of paperwork within the department.

All front office departments dealt with customers during their stay, but in the roles of advance bookings and sales, variations existed. Certain front office departments dealt with these aspects, whilst others had separate in-house marketing departments and booking offices. The organization employed area sales managers who were based at the largest hotel within the area. Some front office managers relied on their area sales manager, whilst others had very little contact at all. The individual nature of these departments was reflected in the fact that only one goal was commonly cited, as shown in Table 9.4.

The existing computerized reservation system could provide the information required for bookings. Staff evaluation could take place through staff training records and personal observation by the manager.

Despite the variations in size and standards of hotels, head housekeepers had similar goals. As a service department, with little degree of freedom, this was predicted, as presented in Table 9.5.

Table 9.4   Front office managers, commonly cited

Goals	CSFs	Measures
To maximize sales at the best prices	Staff training	Advance booking record
	Having the right staff	Personal observation
	Analysing bookings	Staff training records
	Monitoring bookings	Being on duty
		Customer feedback
		Daily statistical breakdown
		Weekly forecasts

Table 9.5   Head housekeepers, frequently cited

Goals	CSFs	Measures
Cleaning all rooms to the standard required	Staff attitude/approach	Quality control spot checks
	Having the right staff	
A smoothly running operation	Staff training	Personal observation
	Wage control	Revenue/wages ratio
Achieving high standards		Staff training records
		Stock control
Maintaining cost control		
Staff morale		

The nature of the measures reflects the fact that the housekeeping department is a cost centre, with the main cost being labour.

The hotels' food and beverage operations varied significantly, from a single restaurant to several restaurants, 24-hour room service and a banqueting department. Due to this, the role of food and beverage managers was diverse. Due to the size of the operations, some hotels employed a restaurant manager who reported directly to the general manager and saw no need to employ a food and beverage manager. Others employed a food and beverage manager, but no restaurant manager. In hotels with a substantial food and beverage operation, food and beverage managers could have numerous restaurant managers reporting to them. Generally, the orientation of food and beverage managers' goals was financial, whilst conference and banqueting managers' and restaurant managers' emphasis was on the product (Tables 9.6, 9.7 and 9.8).

Table 9.6   Food and beverage managers, frequently cited

Goals	CSFs	Measures
Achieving profit required	Having the right staff	Daily revenue reports
Achieving financial targets	Staff training	Personal observation
		Revenue/wages ratio
		Staff communication Staff feedback

The conference and banqueting manager's role related to procuring future business as many hotels employed a conference and banqueting co-ordinator to deal with the day-to-day operation. This situation is reflected in their stated goals.

Table 9.7   Conference and banqueting managers

Goals	CSFs	Measures
Fill all space	Guest satisfaction	Personal observation
Maximize sales at the best price	Product quality	Customer feedback
	Repeat business	Quality control spot checks
		Repeat business

It is notable in the CSFs and measures that little mention is made of the financial concerns of costs and profit. This is a possible indication of the way conference and banqueting trade is viewed in some establishments. In the smaller hotels, with no purpose-built facilities, conference and banqueting trade is used to fill otherwise unoccupied space in the hotel during sluggish periods. Due to this, it can be viewed as a peripheral earner of profits, as often the profits are hidden within general food and beverage and rooms' division statistics. This situation does not provide the conference and banqueting manager with a direct departmental profit motive.

Restaurant managers formed the largest management group in the sample. This was due to some large hotels having several restaurant managers. As all were involved in the day-to-day management of a single restaurant, significant commonalties existed in their goals, CSFs and measures, listed in Table 9.8.

Table 9.8 Restaurant managers, repeatedly cited

Goals	CSFs	Measures
Achieving financial targets	Staff training	Customer feedback
	Staff product awareness	Budget comparison
Providing a quality service	Achieving standards	Staff training records
Staff efficiency	Having the right staff	Personal observation
		Average spend
		Staff communication meetings
		Staff feedback
		Staff records

As can be seen, staff are paramount in achieving the goals of these managers. In a restaurant staff are selling the product and aiming to provide a quality service. Ninety-three per cent quoted staff training as a critical success factor in this department. The measures are balanced between quantitative and qualitative measures, stressing the importance of staff and financial information.

In reviewing the results as a whole, it was clear that managerial position does affect managers' information needs, but is not the only influence. Individuals performing the same role within the same company were seen to have many individual goals, CSFs and measures. This is important when designing an information system. It cannot be assumed that a standardized reporting system, giving the same information to all managers at a given level, is providing information that is meaningful and relevant to all managers in that position. The significance of the managerial position will be affected by the strength of other influences on an individual manager.

It becomes apparent that, when a managerial position is narrowly defined, such as head housekeeper or restaurant manager, the information requirements of individual managers within that position are more cohesive than for managers within broader, less defined positions, such as general manager.

The influence of factors, other than managerial position

The CSFs approach supposes that, although managerial position influences a manager's information needs, it is not the only stimulant that exists. The company, the industry, specific operational problems, the individual's expertise and personal goals also contribute to the total information package needed by an individual manager, if he or she is to be effective.

As stated earlier, the company had taken over another hotel organization. This had led to some rebranding and left the hotels in three distinct groups in relation to brand name and company of origin. The organization taken over kept its brand name; some hotels, with an international clientele, in the other company changed their brand name to that of the taken-over organizations; and others within this company were rebranded under a new brand. This meant that the hotels concerned had undergone major changes directly concerning their name changes. Customer perceptions and expectations of the hotel changed due to the alteration in brand name.

It was possible that the origins and branding of the hotels could be an influence on managers within the establishments. The influence of the changes and types of establishment on managers' information needs was analysed. It was established this had little significance on individuals' information needs. A manager's position had a substantial impact in comparison. When the sample was broken down into three groups due to their brand name and origin, there were no more commonalties than when the whole sample was viewed collectively. It was, however, noticed that when the sample was viewed in total there was an integrated element in their information needs. This would suggest either the company or the industry in general was an influence on the individual's information needs.

At the time the research was undertaken the two origins of the hotels had not been integrated in relation to operating systems. Computerized reservation, control and information systems were not compatible. The managerial structure at unit level was also disparate. This suggested that the principal goals, CSFs and measures stated across all types/groups of managers are more likely to be industry-inspired than company-influenced.

One hotel within the sample had various operational problems, distinct from the other establishments. These had been identified by the organization and consequently a new management team had been placed in the unit to address the problems. Members of the new management team had been present for less than three months and were fully aware that problems existed. This did influence their information needs. All their goals related to improving, implementing, developing, raising or strengthening the operation in some way. This pattern was not common in the other establishments and highlighted the specific economic situation at the unit concerned. Qualitative measures were prevalent throughout the sample as a whole, but due to the unit's problems – trading and profits being below targets – the commonest measures in this establishment were:

- Comparison to last year.
- Personal observation.
- Budget comparison.
- Revenue/wages ratio.

This might suggest that if an establishment is financially sound managers concentrate on qualitative, subjective measures as their primary concern is the interaction of their human resources and customers. However, when the unit is in financial difficulties a manager needs to turn to quantitative, financial reports to gain information.

The CSFs approach suggests that information needs are constantly changing, simultaneously with managers' goals within the operation. Once an operation experiencing financial problems recovers, the direction of the business will change in order for it to progress. This consequently will lead to new goals, CSFs and measures and new, different information needs.

Clearly, managers are influenced by many factors that have an effect on their individual needs for information. The degree of influence varies for specific factors and with time. A factor of major influence currently may be insignificant, compared to other factors in the future.

Evidently, whatever factors influence a manager, an individual manager's total information requirements are unique to that individual. Restaurant managers' information needs may be influenced by their position, but simultaneously they are being influenced by the individual hotel, the company, the economic climate, their personal agenda and experience.

Data collection using the critical success factors approach

As previously stated, data collection takes the form of an initial written explanation of the technique, followed by an in-depth, structured interview. The interview possesses potential hazards and, therefore, the skill and objectivity of the interviewer are critical. Goals, CSFs and measures need to be elicited from the manager. The interviewer should be sure that no details are omitted by the manager, whilst not leading the interviewee to give certain answers.

Qualitative data collection methods, such as structured interviews, are inherently vulnerable to the researcher's subjectivity. This is a potential problem not exclusively associated with the CSFs approach which can be overcome by careful selection of interviewers to ensure that they are unbiased and fully conversant with the CSFs approach.

Results using the CSFs approach compared to the existing information system

As the CSFs approach identifies managers' actual information needs, any difference between the identified measures and information currently received highlights imperfections in the current information system.

Table 9.9 Comparison of most common 'measures' and information currently received

CSFs approach, identified measures	Information currently received
Personal observation	Monthly profit and loss accounts, with statistics
Customer feedback (complaints and compliments)	Reports from CHAMPS computer system
Budget comparison	
Being on duty	Occupancy statistics
Staff training records	All financial information
Quality control spot checks	Function list
Staff feedback (positive and negative)	Department heads' meetings
	Staff communication meetings
	Weekly department statistics

Referring to Table 9.9, there are disconcerting discrepancies between the commonly cited measures identified and information currently received by managers. A single quantitative measure exists within those most commonly cited measures (a budget comparison); all other measures in the list are of a subjective, qualitative nature. In contrast, the majority of information currently received is of a financial or statistical nature. In the list shown the only current qualitative information is through management and staff communication meetings.

It would appear that the financial information needs of managers are generally being met by the current information system. A gap however is identified in the supply of non-financial information to managers. Staff were a critical success factor for the majority of managers within the sample; however, currently the primary information concerning staff is only obtained through communication meetings. The measures highlight the need for managers to assess staff training records and obtain feedback from both their staff and customers. The information currently received showed that this was not being carried out on a routine, consistent basis. It is significant that Geller (1984) identified personnel information systems as an area needing development from his research into chief executives' information needs within American hotels.

As a service industry, staff are of paramount importance; therefore, as shown, they need to be monitored closely by managers in a methodical manner. This essential element and gap in the information system was identified through the use of the CSFs approach, yet overlooked by the current information system. When asked for comments regarding the current information system, the managers did not identify this weakness, thus proving that asking the direct question of what information is required is not as effective at identifying information needs as using the CSFs approach.

Conclusions

The use of the CSFs approach is time-consuming as it is based on information gained from individual managers by interview. Benefits do however exist as it aids managers not only in identifying and gaining appropriate information, but also assists managers in considering a long-term view of the operation and ensures they are working towards specific goals and objectives.

Despite managers within the sample having goals generally, these were not written, or made clear to other managers in the operation. One restaurant was run by two restaurant managers who had different goals, but each was unaware of the other's goals. Thus, the CSFs approach aids managers in formally defining their goals, CSFs and measures in a structured manner along with forming the basis of a management reporting system.

The CSFs approach may require a greater initial investment in time, but the results make it worthwhile. By allowing managers to define their goals and CSFs in a structured way they will be able to perform their managerial functions more effectively. The personal involvement of managers in identifying information needs using the CSFs approach could also act as a motivating factor.

This approach clearly identifies needs, as opposed to wants, for information. It can therefore be concluded that it is a valuable approach to use in order to gain an effective management information system within the hierarchy of the hotel industry.

References

Bullen, C.V. and Rockart J.F. (1981) *A Primer on Critical Success Factors.* Working paper no. 69. Boston, MA. Centre for Information Systems, Sloan School of Management, MIT.

Geller, A.N. (1984) *Executives' Information Needs in Hotel Companies.* Peat, Marwick, Mitchell, USA.

Geller, A.N. (1985a) Tracking the critical success factors for hotel companies. *The Cornell HRA Quarterly* 76–81.

Geller, A.N. (1985b) The current state of hotel information systems. *The Cornell HRA Quarterly* 14–17.

Geller, A.N. (1985c) How to improve your information system. *The Cornell HRA Quarterly* 19–27.

Jones, T.A. (1991) Financial and operating information needs of managers in hotel companies. Unpublished thesis, Oxford Brookes University.

Munro, M.C. (1983) An opinion...comment on critical success factors. *MIS Quarterly* 67.

Warner, W.A. (1982) Management accounting and information. *Management Accounting* **60**: April 1982, pp. 28–30.

10 Management control in the hospitality industry: behavioural implications

Jacqueline Brander Brown

By their very nature, control systems are concerned with the regulation of human behaviour (Mullins, 1993).

Introduction

The modern hospitality organization is a complex entity. Its continuing existence – and, it is to be hoped, growth and success – will depend to a very considerable extent on the ability of the organization effectively to manage and control a number of significant variables. In particular, today's hospitality organizations face such variables as rapidly changing domestic and international environments, increasingly sophisticated technology, a widening variety of needs and demands of both customers and investors, differing locations and their associated cultures and languages as well as the variable degrees of skills and expertise of both current and potential employees.

If hospitality organizations are to achieve effective control in response to these, and other similarly important variables, management must seek to match the technical capabilities of their control system with the objectives and associated requirements of their organization. Of at least equal importance, however, is the need for management to be aware of and consider the significant human behavioural implications of their control systems – a factor that all too many management control systems appear to dangerously neglect.

The meaning of management control

The term management control has been interpreted in a variety of ways, by both practising managers as well as academic writers. For instance, the process of control has often been linked with ideas of domination, regulation, restriction and coordination while, from a more practical viewpoint, it is said to be concerned with the whole range of strategic and operational issues – both internal and external – that face most organizations.

However, a particularly useful and concise definition of the term which encompasses many of these notions is that provided by Flamholtz (1983), who describes the process of management control as being: 'any actions or activities taken to influence the probability that people will behave in ways which lead to the attainment of organizational objectives'.

One important implication of such a definition is that the exercise of control methods and techniques is not only in the hands of those employees holding managerial positions. Rather, it will involve every employee, as everyone in the organization is involved in activities aimed at achieving organizational objectives.

A second important implication is that effective management control systems will incorporate a wide variety of control methods and techniques. It is concerning to note then, that until recently approaches to management control have tended to focus almost exclusively on the use of accounting controls, and especially on the use of budgeting. Such narrow approaches can only ever give an incomplete picture. Instead, it is vital that accounting controls are seen as forming only part of a broader total system of management controls comprising such tools as standardized procedures and operating manuals, job descriptions, supervision and personnel appraisals, staff meetings and training courses, performance measures and reports.

Components of management control

A typical management control process within any business organization, as outlined in Figure 10.1, will normally comprise a number of important components.

Planning

The first stage in the control process is that of planning, which involves the clear specification of the organization's goals and objectives. For an organization in the hospitality industry, these goals and objectives may include such relevant areas as profitability and return on capital invested, occupancy levels and average spend rates, quality of service and customer satisfaction, staff morale and development. This is a vital first step in a management control system, as it is essential that both the organization's management and employees fully understand and appreciate what is being asked of them – and why.

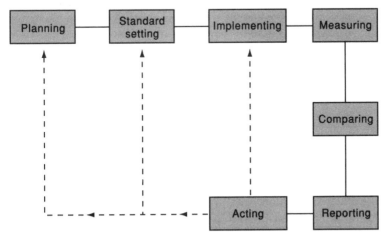

Figure 10.1 Components of control

Standard-setting

Following the determination of the organization's plans, the next stage in a system of management control is the setting of realistic standards of performance, which can be viewed as targets to be achieved. Typical standards used in the hospitality industry include profitability and liquidity targets, occupancy and usage percentages, indicators of customer acceptance and working capital management ratios. These standards can be utilized at a later stage in the control process in order to establish the degree of success of the organization in achieving its aims. It is worth noting though, that if such standards are to be useful it is vital that when they are determined they are specifically relevant to the organization's goals and objectives.

Implementing

With appropriate standards of performance in place, the organization's plans can then be implemented, using a range of control methods and techniques appropriate to the organization. Control tools often used in the hospitality industry include budgets, head of department meetings, briefing sessions, standardized procedure manuals, job descriptions, staff training and appraisals, quality programmes, guest comment cards, interdepartmental staff meetings, staff suggestion schemes and 'employee-of-the-month' awards.

Measuring

The next stage in the typical management control system is the measurement of the resulting actual performance of the organization. For such measurements to be worthwhile, however, it is important that they properly reflect the standard of performance achieved. An important implication of this is that a variety of measures must be utilized – accounting and non-accounting, quantifiable and non-quantifiable.

Comparing

The measures obtained relating to the organization's actual performance can then be compared with the standards set at an earlier stage in the control process, and the extent of any deviations – both positive and negative – assessed. A significant indirect result of this stage is that the degree to which the organization is moving toward the achievement of its goals and objectives can also be assessed.

Reporting

The results of the comparison stage should then be reported back, for instance by means of reports and review meetings, to those involved. Such feedback can assist in the confirmation and acceptance of deviations between the desired and actual performance achieved by the organization. More importantly, it should also assist with the identification of likely causes and implications of such deviations.

Acting

Using such feedback information, management can then decide whether they need to take any action – and, as appropriate, what action they need to take – in order to keep the organization moving towards the attainment of its goals and objectives. The choices facing management in this respect will involve actions either to improve actual performance or to modify the plans and standards set.

It should be noted, though, that even if an organization has all of these components in place in its control system, this would not be sufficient to ensure that the organization will achieve its objectives. For that to be the case a management control system will first need to reflect adequately the specific context in which the organization finds itself and second, to demonstrate a number of characteristics specifically associated with effective control. But before these important topics are considered, it may be useful at this stage to consider the evidence regarding the specific application of management control systems in the hospitality industry.

Management control in the hospitality industry

Evidence and opinions concerning management control in the hospitality industry are, to date, somewhat limited. Moreover, what evidence there is tends to be concentrated in two areas: budgetary control systems and the use of internal controls.

Budgetary control systems

According to the Chartered Institute of Management Accountants (1991), the process of budgetary control involves 'The establishment of budgets relating the responsibilities of executives to the requirements of a policy, and the continuous comparison of actual with budgeted results, either to secure by individual action the objectives of that policy or to provide a basis for its revision'. Although such a definition is very similar to the description given earlier of a management control system, it is worth emphasizing again that budgets are only one of a wide range of control tools available to management and that consequently the study of budgetary control can only ever give a partial view of an organization's overall approach to management control.

There is a considerable degree of consensus among managers in hospitality organizations and academic writers alike that the budgetary control process as applied in hospitality organizations is a very valuable control tool. An important underlying reason for this support, as indicated by Schmidgall (1990), is the perception that budgets can encourage managers to set positive targets for themselves and other employees. It is felt that such targets, when sensitively used, can provide a motivating influence, supporting the achievement of the organization's aims.

In addition, Schmidgall and Ninemeier (1987) have noted the utilization of increasingly sophisticated budgetary control systems in multiunit operations. In order for such systems to be applied effectively, a need for high levels of appropriately controlled information has been identified. Interestingly, though, Schmidgall and Ninemeier (1987) also established that simplified budgeting systems are felt to be more suitable for small or single-unit organizations or, as Rusth (1990) established, where perceptions of environmental uncertainty are high.

Significantly, the hospitality industry is recognizing that the budgetary control process should not be viewed solely as a technical process – for an example see O'Dea (1985). The need for hospitality organizations to consider the wide range of potential behavioural problems which can be associated with budgeting activities – for instance demotivation, information manipulation and conflict – is being increasingly accepted. Moreover, Umbreit and Eder (1987) have suggested that to be fully effective hospitality management control systems should not only provide quantifiable outcomes to be compared to standards set, but must also provide measures of such key dimensions of managerial behaviour as the ability to motivate and to communicate with employees.

Internal control systems

The term 'internal control system' has been comprehensively defined by the Audit Practices Committee (1980) as: 'The whole system of controls, financial or otherwise, established by the management in order to carry on the business of the enterprise in an orderly and efficient manner, ensure adherence to management's policies, safeguard the assets and secure as far as possible the completeness and accuracy of the records'. As such, internal controls tend to concentrate on the more day-to-day, operational aspects of an organization and, like budgets, represent only one of the range of control methods and techniques at management's disposal.

While it is for the organization's management to determine the nature of the internal controls to be applied, the need for strong internal controls in hospitality organizations is well-established, given that most hospitality operations will undertake, on a daily basis, a substantial volume of transactions – many of which will be for cash – usually involving a considerable number of staff.

Particularly typical examples of internal controls used by hospitality organizations include the following.

Records and documents

Given the volume of transactions normally undertaken by most hospitality organizations, it is vital that proper and effective records and documents are maintained. Typically such documentation will include guest registration cards, meal and bar dockets, authorizations for any allowances to be made, purchase invoices and approved timesheets. Additionally, in order to enhance their effectiveness such documents may, for instance, be sequentially numbered or in multipart form as appropriate.

Segregation of duties

The primary objective underlying the use of segregation of duties as an internal control is the prevention and detection of both errors and fraud. Given the particular nature of hospitality organizations, as already noted, it is especially important that no one member of staff can fully process and record a transaction. For instance, when purchasing food and beverage supplies, internal control can be established by ensuring that the actions involved in initiating requisitions, in authorizing orders, in receiving and storing goods and ultimately in executing payments are kept separate.

Physical

Organizations use physical controls to assist in the safekeeping of both their assets and their records. Common examples of physical controls used in hospitality organizations include keeping locks on cellars and storerooms, holding cash and important records and documents in fireproof safes and restricting access to computers by the means of passwords.

Personnel

Personnel are a vital factor in the quality of service provided by a hospitality organization. However, it is also essential for the proper functioning of the organization's internal control system that the personnel employed are motivated, competent and trustworthy. A significant implication of this for hospitality organizations is first, that both management and employees must be carefully selected and trained and second, they must be appropriately encouraged, supervised and rewarded for their efforts.

Organizational context

The idea that control system design should reflect the specific circumstances – that is, the context – in which the organization operates has been developing since the mid-1960s. This approach, generally known as the contingency approach, is based on the notion that there is no one management control system which can be applicable to all organizations in all circumstances.

Researchers such as Flamholtz, Hopwood, Merchant and Otley have identified a number of important contextual variables to which an organization's management control system should be 'matched'. A number of these variables are discussed below, while a simple contingent model showing the influence of such variables on a management control system – and ultimately on the attainment of the organization's objectives – is illustrated in Figure 10.2.

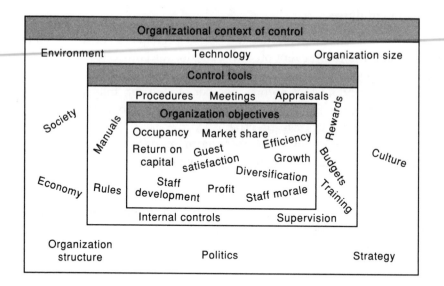

Figure 10.2 Contingencies and control

Environment

The environment within which organizations operate is likely to demonstrate such features as differing levels of risk and uncertainty, varying degrees of competition and changing political and social dynamics. With regard to the design of management control systems which can adequately cope with such features, it is worth noting the results of research by Otley (1978), which suggest that where an organization's environment can be categorized as being liberal, a rigid management control system appears most appropriate – whereas in a tough environment, a more flexible approach would be more effective. Comparable results were established by Rusth (1990) when considering hotel budgeting in a multinational environment.

Culture

Organizational culture comprises the pattern of values, beliefs and norms which are shared by the members of an organization, and which consequently tend to influence their ideas, behaviour and actions. Flamholtz (1983) has suggested that a failure by management to design control systems which are consistent with their organization's culture can lead to active resistance to the control system. Such resistance could then potentially result in the ultimate failure of the control system, and so seriously hinder the organization's progression towards its goals and objectives.

Size

The size of an organization is also an important factor to be considered in the design of effective control systems, especially as most organizations delegate more as they grow. Merchant (1981) established that in larger organizations an administrative approach to management control can be linked to better performance, while in smaller companies a more general, personal control system is likely to be more effective.

Structure

A number of typical types of organization structure have been identified by management theorists. Particularly well-established forms include that of centralization and decentralization, vertical (tall) and horizontal (flat) structures and functional and geographical groupings. Simple organization charts illustrating these forms are shown in Figure 10.3.

Research carried out by Hopwood (1972) and Otley (1978) concerning the impact of organization structures suggests that effective management control systems will particularly reflect the degrees of interdependence between responsibility centres, and that in particular, as interdependences increase, flexible management controls are likely to be more effective than more formal, rigid controls.

Technology

Technology has long been considered to have a major influence on the effectiveness of management control systems. Technological factors which managers should especially bear in mind when designing their management control systems are the volume and variety of activities carried out by the organization, the degrees of automation involved and the routineness of tasks. A significant conclusion reached from research carried out by Merchant (1984) in this respect is that there is a positive association between degrees of automation and the formality of the control system used – the more automated the organization, the more formal an effective management control system should be.

An important overall conclusion reached by Abernethy and Stoelwinder (1991) with regard to the possible impact of contingent variables is that the better the match between the management control system design and the contextual contingent variables, the more effectively an organization will perform.

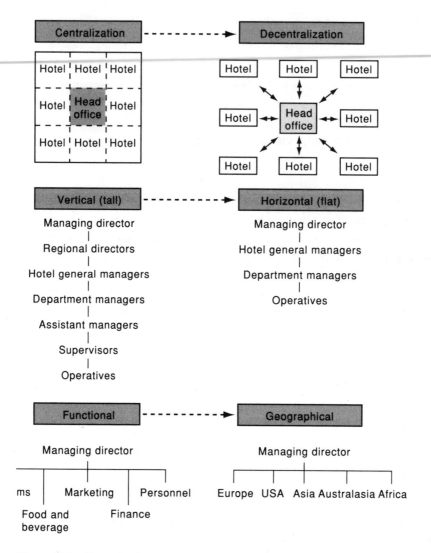

Figure 10.3   Organization structures

Characteristics of effective management control

However well-matched a control system is to its particular contingent variables, in order for a system of management control to attain even a basic level of effectiveness it will also need to demonstrate a number of other significant features. For instance, Otley and Berry (1980) state that for a management control system to be effective it must satisfy four necessary conditions, outlined below.

1. The organization's goals and objectives must be clearly identified: for without a clear aim, the process of control has no meaning.
2. The organization's performance must be measurable on a basis which is consistent with the goals and objectives identified, thus enabling a useful comparison to be made between desired and actual achievements.
3. A predictive model of those activities of the organization which are to be controlled must be established. This is needed to assist in the identification of the causes of deviations and in the assessment of proposed corrective actions.
4. There must be the capability of taking corrective action, such that the degree of deviation between desired performance and actual performance may be effectively reduced.

Furthermore, they suggested that if any of these conditions are not met then a management control system could be said to be out of control.

In addition to these required conditions, a number of other important features associated with effective management control systems have also been identified, as described below.

Understandable

If the organization's control system is to be fully effective it must be clearly understood by all employees involved with it. This has very serious implications, for instance, for the level of detail and technical sophistication of any reports utilized in the system.

Timely

For a management control system to be effective it is important that feedback reports are produced on a timely basis – indeed, it is considered desirable that indications of deviations should be reported even before they happen! Timeliness is vital if effective corrective action is to be taken.

Directed

Management control systems should concentrate on those activities vital to the success of the organization. Unnecessary controls can be both time-consuming and demotivating, as well as diverting attention from essential matters.

Flexible

Control system methods and techniques and resulting reports must maintain their relevance by adapting to changing circumstances. It is particularly important that they should not reflect the often-used response: 'but that's the way we've always done things'. Indeed, it is essential that management control methods and techniques are reviewed on a regular basis to ensure that they remain appropriate and relevant – and therefore, it is to be hoped, effective.

A common element has been identified which underlies all of these aspects of effective management control. That element is the human, or behavioural, element, for how management and employees perceive their part in the control process and how they are affected by it as humans will be the overriding determining factor in the success of any control system.

Behavioural aspects of management control

Behavioural scientists have for some time questioned whether the full impact of management control systems on human behaviour has been adequately determined, with regard to both their design and implementation. This concern is worthy of consideration and evaluation, especially as a wide variety of significant behavioural issues concerning the effective operation of management control systems have been identified. A number of these issues are discussed below, incorporating some practical examples to illustrate the issues raised.

Pressure

As has been noted already, management control systems are frequently utilized to evaluate actual performance against standards set. The very concrete and public nature of such a process has been identified, for example by Argyris (1953), as a significant source of pressure for both management and employees, leading to such reactions as tension, mistrust, suspicion, resentment and eventual resistance to the control process itself. Moreover, as management control systems often broadcast widely the deviations between actual and desired performance and as such publicity is often channelled first to the higher levels in the organization – rather than to those directly involved – and generally does not include any explanations or reasons for the deviations, the pressure felt by management and employees can be intense. Another common result of this intense pressure is that of friction, particularly between the management control staff – such as a head office accounts department – and those employees whose actions are being controlled.

A potentially damaging tactic often used by an organization's staff to reduce the effects of such unwanted pressure is the creation of cohesive, informal employee groups. As Argyris (1953) found, a significant reason underlying the formation of such groups is that employees believe they can both reduce tension and feel more secure if they combine and unite together against the perceived source of the pressure.

Example

The finance director of one hotel company sent a memo to each of the general managers of the company's some 20 hotels warning them that reports giving full details of all overspending by hotels by more than 5 per cent, on cost and expense budgets will be circulated to the board of directors, to all other general managers and all heads of departments in the group. It went on to say that these reports will replace the group's current practice of just informing the particular general manager concerned of such overspends. The memo also noted that any general manager exceeding, by any degree, their cost or expense budgets in two consecutive months: *'would have their management abilities seriously questioned'*.

Consider how the group's general managers might feel about this approach to control in their organization, and also how they might choose to respond.

Stultification

There is a degree of evidence that management control systems are often viewed by both management and employees as being a form of strait-jacket. Wallace (1966) considers that a significant implication of such a view being taken of control systems is that they are seen to provide little opportunity, or indeed encouragement of, the exercise of personal initiative, which may be linked to a seriously damaging effect on motivation.

Example

A manager responsible for personnel and training in a large international hotel and leisure group was proud of their thrifty approach to using their budgeted allocation of funds. At the end of one budget year they had a significant amount of surplus funds remaining and expected to be congratulated on this achievement. However, they were extremely surprised when the group's chief management accountant, speaking at the senior management team's annual budget review, described the surplus as being *'the result either of poor planning or incompetent management'*. Furthermore, when this manager then requested additional funds for the following year to support a new training initiative, the request was denied by the chief management accountant, who referred the manager to their *'apparent inability to make a full and effective use of the funds allocated to them in the previous year'*.

Consider how other thrifty managers responsible for expense budgets in this group might react.

Emphasis

Indications are that within the management control process both management and employees tend to emphasize their own areas of responsibility. A probable result of such a limited or concentrated outlook is that important interactions between departments – for instance, between front office and housekeeping – or between individual hotels and their head office may be neglected. Moreover, following on from this neglect, it is likely that dysfunctional and damaging decisions may be taken with regard to the organization as a whole.

Example

The purchasing manager for a UK-based hotel and leisure group has just agreed a contract with a large printing and stationery company, P&S Ltd., which will cover all of the group's operations. Using information provided by the group's management accountant, the purchasing manager has estimated that the contract could lead to total annual printing and stationery costs for the group being reduced by at least 20 per cent – a significant factor in the purchasing manager's decision. As a result of agreeing the contract, the purchasing manager has now sent a memo to all of the managers of the group's operations informing them that, with immediate effect, all their printing and stationery requirements will be handled by P&S Ltd. – indeed, a condition of the contract enabling P&S Ltd. to give such reasonable rates had been that they would receive all of the group's printing and stationery business. In addition, in order for the group's purchasing department to have sufficient time to deal properly with the group's printing and stationery needs, the memo also informs the managers that they must submit their orders to the purchasing manager quarterly in advance.

Consider how the managers might react to such a memo from head office, having particular regard to the restrictions it is likely to place on their decisions and on the degree of flexibility with which they can operate.

Non-participation

Another potentially demotivating aspect of some management control systems arises when there is a lack of participation in the system, especially, for instance, at the standard-setting stage. Such lack of participation has been found to underlie emotions associated with lack of involvement or of control without responsibility, which have been found to lead to active resistance to, or manipulation of, the control system. Common examples of such resistance and manipulation include the overstatement of expense forecasts and the understatement of revenue or occupancy estimates.

Example

Every autumn, the management team of a large city-centre hotel – part of a significant international group – are involved in a frantic few weeks of activity, resulting in the submission of the next year's budget to the head office financial control team for approval. The hotel's general manager invariably refers to the process as the silly season, while the hotel's financial controller has often been heard to wonder why the management team have to go through this fiasco every year as 'head office never take any notice' – a response to the fact that at the end of all their efforts, head office have always imposed a budget they have prepared for the hotel.

Consider what effect these managers' attitudes might have on other managers and employees in the hotel, and also what the likely effect on staff morale and commitment to the budget will be as a result of head office imposing their own budget.

If organizations do not sufficiently consider such potentially dysfunctional behavioural implications associated with the operation of management control systems, it is likely that they will use inappropriate management control methods and techniques. Moreover, this use of inappropriate controls may well result in intended improvements in the organization's performance not materializing. Indeed, it might even be suggested that, partly as a result of their behavioural impact, these inappropriate control methods and techniques may even be responsible for preventing the organization from achieving its objectives in the first instance! What then are the implications for management if they want to prevent such a state of affairs arising in their organization?

Implications for management

Given the probable significance of the behavioural aspects of management control, as already indicated, it is encouraging to note that a number of areas over which management may be able to exercise positive control in order to minimize any potentially dysfunctional behavioural effects have been identified, as follows

Targets

Researchers such as Hofstede (1968) have established that up to the point where a control target is perceived as not achievable – and therefore in all likelihood not acceptable to those whose activities are being controlled – the more demanding a target is, the better are the actual performance results which are achieved. Targets which are set too low tend to foster complacency among staff, while those that are too high can seriously damage staff morale and motivation. The optimum level is where a target is perceived by staff to be difficult, but potentially achievable. Indeed, Hofstede (1968) has suggested that the targets which motivate the best performance are unlikely to be reached in many circumstances.

Participation

When both managers and employees participate in the setting of standards and targets, research – including work done regarding the hospitality sector by Ferguson and Berger (1986) – has shown that not only do they tend to experience reduced levels of anxiety and frustration, but they are also likely to exhibit enhanced degrees of motivation, resulting in higher degrees of commitment to the control system. However, it must be recognized by both managers and employees in hospitality organizations that for participation to be effective and real requires consistent commitment and effort.

Feedback

Hofstede (1968) also found that feedback can enhance both employee aspirations and their level of job satisfaction, thus facilitating their acceptance of, and commitment to, management control targets. However, it has been suggested by Ferguson and Berger (1986) and Otley (1987) that the effectiveness of such feedback will, to a considerable extent, be dependent on employee characteristics and the nature of the feedback given. Such findings imply that management should think very carefully about the form in which the control feedback is given, and in particular they should consider such factors as how often the feedback is given and whether it is in numerical, narrative or diagrammatic form. With the ever-increasing availability of affordable, easy-to-use computer software, the opportunity for management to tailor their feedback reports to the specific needs and abilities of each user is a very real one.

Measures

Management should always ensure that the measures of performance used in the control system are appropriate and fair. Most hospitality organizations concentrate on objective and verifiable measures of financial and physical performance, including for instance departmental sales revenue, occupancy levels and average spend rates, gross and net profits and return on capital employed. However, it is being increasingly recognized that performance measures used must also support the evaluation of more qualitative – and hence, it is likely non-quantifiable – aspects of performance. Moreover, as has already been noted, Umbreit and Eder (1987) strongly suggest that to be fully effective, performance measures should also recognize, and indeed reflect, the link between desired outcomes and the behaviour which may lead to those outcomes.

Training

It has been suggested, by for instance Argyris (1953), that management – and especially those closely involved in the design and implementation of the management control system – should be trained to appreciate more fully the human implications of their control system. In particular it is suggested that the managers involved should regularly participate in training in such areas as handling conflict, status systems, counselling and effective leadership.

Groups

The possible negative impact of employee groups – established in an attempt to counteract the effects of perceived pressure that may prevail in some management control systems – has already been noted. However, it is important also to note that not all employee groups involve such negative implications. Indeed, Mullins (1993) has pointed out that a possible means for management to exercise more positive control is by their encouragement and support of the development of informal work groups and communication links. This recognizes the fact that informal group agreements and standards can be a powerful and positive control technique. Such informal groups give employees more freedom and discretion in how they go about their work, which has been found to be a source of considerable motivation and job satisfaction.

Conclusion

Management control is an inherent and essential feature of all organizations – not least in the increasingly 'complex' hospitality industry – involving every employee in the organization.

However, if control systems in hospitality organizations are to prove effective there are a number of important considerations that management must keep in mind when designing their control systems. First, it is essential that the control system and the balance of control tools it comprises are matched to the particular context in which the organization operates. In particular, management should ensure that their management control system is closely matched to such contextual contingent variables as environment and culture, organization size and structure.

Second, management control systems should also incorporate certain conditions – as indicated by Otley and Berry (1980) – and characteristics, such as flexibility and timeliness, which have been found to be associated with effective control systems.

A third important area for consideration by management in the design of management control systems, which is all too often neglected, is that of their impact on both management and employee behaviour. As Mullins (1993) states, 'By their very nature, control systems are concerned with the regulation of human behaviour'. Therefore, it is vital for the design of effective management control systems that an awareness of the potential behavioural implications associated with the operation of management control systems is demonstrated.

Finally, however, it can be argued that even such an awareness is unlikely to be adequate to support an effective management control system. Consequently those involved in the design of management control systems for use in the hospitality industry must ensure that they incorporate into the control system appropriate actions and techniques both to minimize the dysfunctional effects of management and employee behaviour and to maximize their positive behavioural implications.

References

Abernethy, M. A. and Stoelwinder, J. U. (1991). Budget use and task uncertainty, system goal orientation and subunit performance : a test of the fit hypothesis in not–for–profit hospitals. *Accounting, Organizations and Society* 16: 105–120.

Argyris, C. (1953) Human problems with budgets. *Harvard Business Review,* January/February, 97–110.

Audit Practices Committee (1980) *Operational Guideline 3.204 Internal Controls.*

Chartered Institute of Management Accountants (1991) *Management Accounting Official Terminology.* London, CIMA.

Ferguson, D. H. and Berger, F. (1986) The human side of budgeting. *Cornell HRA Quarterly,* August, 87–90.

Flamholtz, E.G. (1983) Accounting, budgeting and control systems in their organizational context: theoretical and empirical perspectives. *Accounting, Organizations and Society,* **8**: 153–169.

Hofstede, G.H. (1968) *The Game of Budget Control.* London, Tavistock.

Hopwood, A. G. (1972) An empirical study of the role of accounting data in performance evaluation. *Empirical Research in Accounting, Supplement to Journal of Accounting Research,* **10**, 156–182.

Merchant, K.A.(1981) The design of the corporate budgeting system: influences on managerial behaviour and performance. *The Accounting Review* LVI: 4, 813–829.

Merchant, K.A. (1984). Influences on departmental budgeting: an empirical examination of a contingency model. *Accounting, Organizations and Society* 9: 291–307.

Mullins, L.J. (1993). *Management and Organizational Behaviour.* Pitman Publishing.

O'Dea, W. (1985) Budgetary control – a behavioural viewpoint. *International Journal of Hospitality Management,* 14, 179–180.

Otley, D.T. (1978). Budget use and managerial performance. *Journal of Accounting Research* **16**: 122–149.

Otley, D. T. (1987) *Accounting Control and Organizational Behaviour.* Butterworth-Heinemann.

Otley, D.T. and Berry, A.J. (1980) Control, organization and accounting. *Accounting, Organizations and Society* 5: 231–246.

Rusth, D.B. (1990). Hotel budgeting in a multinational environment: results of a pilot study. *Hospitality Research Journal* 14: 217–222.

Schmidgall, R.S. (1990) *Hospitality Industry Managerial Accounting.* Educational Institute of the American Hotel and Motel Association, East Lansing, MI.

Schmidgall, R.S. and Ninemeier, J.D. (1987) Budgeting in hotel chains: co-ordination and control. *Cornell HRA Quarterly* 79–84.

Umbreit, W.T. and Eder, R.W. (1987) Linking hotel manager behaviour with outcome measures of effectiveness. *International Journal of Hospitality Management,* **6**: 139–147.

Wallace, M.E. (1966) Behavioural considerations in budgeting. *Management Accounting,* August, 3–8.

11 The use of accounting information in hotel marketing decisions

Nina J. Downie

Introduction

Key features of the hotel industry include fluctuating demand, high fixed costs, product perishability and profit instability. Therefore, in the 1990s there is a strong justification for companies to adopt a marketing-oriented approach to operating their hotels. Indeed, current thought concerning the management of hotels identifies the satisfaction of customer needs as a paramount key to success (Lewis and Chambers, 1989). If this marketing orientation is to be achieved, then decisions must be made, and information gathered throughout all levels of the organization.

Traditionally the appropriate information for marketing decisions is collected from market research data, customers' wants, needs and satisfaction, and what competitors are doing. This market research is then considered in terms of what the organization is capable of offering in the marketplace. With all of these individual elements constantly changing, it is a dynamic operating environment where little remains static.

The focus of this chapter is the provision of accounting information for marketing decisions made by managers in hotels. Fieldwork which has been undertaken to investigate the use of accounting information in hotel marketing decision-making suggests that, to ensure they receive the information they require, many managers devise their own supplementary systems within the company information system. The conclusion that can be drawn from this is that group accounting systems are designed to meet the corporate needs of head office, rather than the needs of the individual hotel managers.

In an international context, this approach to collecting information for marketing decision-making within hotels is the same throughout the world. Whilst the type of accounting systems and the external reporting requirements will vary, the process of making decisions, using the information available, remains the same. Managers in hotels receive innumerable reports, information and statistics, and therefore, the purpose of this chapter is to investigate how these can be designed to facilitate more effective marketing decision-making.

Marketing decisions

Marketing demands that decision-making is determined by the needs and wants of the customer (Kotler,1988); therefore hotel managers must constantly anticipate and respond to changes in demand for their products and services. Lewis and Chambers (1989) suggest that the customer is the soul and substance of marketing, and any decisions being made that affect the customer should be considered as marketing decisions. Taking this viewpoint, it is reasonable to suggest that marketing decisions are not just made by marketing managers, but by any managers in hotels making decisions which affect the customer.

Taking an even broader view, if marketing leadership is to be attained, then there must be a high level of commitment and understanding throughout every department and every level of the organization. Davidson (1987) suggests:

> The marketing approach challenges all members of a business, whatever their specialist function, to relate their work to the needs of the market-place and to balance it against the firm's own profit needs.

One of the main tasks of managers in hotels is to estimate and influence demand for their products and services, ensuring effective use of the available resources. The most common way to investigate the marketing mix of a business is through the concept of the four Ps proposed by McCarthy (1964). In this instance, it is the most appropriate method because it identifies the areas where it is possible for a manager to initiate change. For example:

- *Product decisions* – developing the products and services to be offered, e.g. the menu, in room facilities, or service standards.
- *Price decisions* – implementing a market-oriented pricing structure, or monitoring the prices charged by the competition.

- *Place decisions* – selection of distribution channels, or organizing logistics, e.g. setting stock levels.
- *Promotion decisions* – planning promotional activities, or planning staff training to support promotions.

If effective decisions are to be made that will generate custom and profit for the company, then two main sources of information are required. Marketing information on customer needs and competition will be needed to assess the acceptability of the action to the customer, and accounting information is required to assess the financial viability of the decisions for the company. The marketing activities of an organization are usually formalized, coordinated and evaluated through the use of a marketing plan, which then becomes the blueprint for the marketing of the business.

The role of the accounting function in marketing decisions is to support rather than control the actions taken. Ward (1989) suggests that what is needed is:

> a close level of communication and co-operation between the marketing function and accounting, so that both areas understand the full implications of specific decisions and ensure that the correct relevant financial information is supplied and used appropriately.

There are barriers to this actually taking place within companies, though the benefits would seem to outweigh the costs of developing such important communication and exchange of information.

The interface

Marketeers and accountants have traditionally been considered as two unlike poles in their approach to the management of an organization. This view is now changing, and rightly so. Development of the interface is fundamental to facilitate effective marketing and operational decision-making within today's dynamic business environment.

Initially, there are interesting comparisons between the two professions of accounting and marketing. Accountants are traditionally production-oriented, concerned with cost controls and adherence to budgets. Elbert Hubbard provides an amusing description of a typical accountant (Sizer, 1989):

> A man past middle age, spare, wrinkled, intelligent, cold, passive, non committal, with eyes like a codfish: polite in contact but at the same time unresponsive, calm and damnably composed as a concrete post or a plaster of Paris cast: a petrification with a heart of feldspar and without charm of the friendly germ, minus bowels, passion or a sense of humour. Happily they never reproduce and all of them finally go to hell.

Although extreme, the general perception of the accountant as being a detached, rather clinical member of the organization, concerned about control and targets, is perhaps still commonly held.

On the other hand, the marketeer has been caricatured by Williamson (1979), who describes the marketing manager in the eyes of the accountant to be:

> A bit of a rogue, not very bright, rather less reliable than others, and his accuracy is definitely suspect. He is a shade more professional than his personnel manager friend, but slumps to the bottom again where social responsibility is concerned.

Once again, rather an extreme description, but highlighting the marketeer as rather a colourful character who is concerned with spending rather than controlling money.

When considering the differences between the accounting and marketing professions, they do appear to be two unlike poles both in terms of their approach to the management of an organization, and also in the types of people that undertake the two functions. It is perhaps not difficult to see why the interface between these disciplines has been difficult to establish. This aspect is described by Trebuss (1977):

> Thus, marketing and finance may deal with each other every day, but can do so with clenched teeth and a grimace – an attitude not productive for either function or for the company as a whole.

Job (1992) suggests five related areas on which work has been published so far concerning the interface:

1. Cultural lag.
2. Knowlege gap.
3. Organizational structure and design.
4. Accountants on advertising and marketing.
5. Accounting information for marketing.

With the exception of 'accountants on advertising and marketing', which is concerned with the promotion of accounting services, all the above factors will have a considerable effect on development of the accounting – marketing interface, and must be given new consideration within organizations. Clearly there is much that has been written on the interface which demands further investigation.

To date, the interface between accounting and marketing has not attracted specific attention in the hotel industry. However, within the two professions of accounting and marketing, work has been undertaken to ascertain how this important aspect can be developed. The stimulation for this move seems to have followed the shifting strategic focus of organizations towards the marketing concept (Meldrum *et al.*, 1986).

To bring together the two professions of accounting and marketing, thought should initially be given to the training they receive. This would enable both professions to understand, and act on, the other's needs (Ratnatunga, *et al.*, 1990). In fact, this is a good example of how the concept of internal marketing can be implemented to the good of the employees, and the company as a whole.

The Cranfield School of Management has created a Marketing Accounting Research Centre in response to the developing strategic marketing focus of business (Meldrum, *et al.*, 1986). The term marketing accountancy is used to describe the subsequent change in the type of accounting information generated for internal decision-making and reporting. A change in job scope or title would also seem to be a good first step towards recognizing the need to integrate the two functions.

The role of accounting

Accounting within an organization encompasses many roles, mainly concerned with the functions of planning and control. These roles generally stem from the core function of being a provider of information, the accounting system usually being the major quantitative information system in a company. This role concept can be further divided into two types of information provision, the focus being whether the information is required for internal or external use; in terms of professional accounting roles, financial or management accounting. The interest in accounting information for this work is clearly centred on the information being used by managers in making marketing decisions, generally in the field of management accounting.

The orientation of a business should determine the focus of accounting information which is required by management in order to support decision-making effectively. Kotas (1973) states that there are essentially two kinds of business orientation – cost orientation and market orientation – the key determinants for the orientation being:

- Cost structure.
- Demand for the product or service.
- Capital intensity.
- Nature of the product.

He describes how this orientation then directs the emphasis of accounting:

> In terms of accounting procedures, the difference between the cost orientated and market orientated approach is this: in the cost oriented situation we are essentially concerned with the debit side of the profit and loss account, our approach is inward looking; cost manipulation and cost control are our main weapon. In the market oriented situation we recognise that most of our costs are fixed and uncontrollable; we therefore shift our attention to the credit side of the profit and loss account.

In traditional types of ownership, hotels are generally capital-intensive, operating with high fixed costs and variable demand for perishable products and services. These factors justify a market, rather than a cost orientation. The best course of action thus is to try and influence the demand, paying more attention to managing the revenue side of the profit and loss account. That is not to say that the expenses should simply be accepted – a market orientation does not preclude the control of costs. Indeed, currently cost-cutting campaigns are commonplace within many company strategies, particularly during periods of recession.

The two major sources of accounting information which managers use in their decision-making are the budget and performance reports. The budget is the formal quantification of management's plans, and performance reports show a measurement of the activities achieved.

In hotels, accounting information is usually received by managers through the profit and loss account, with an analysis of the figures presented (this format is also usually used for the layout of the budget). The revenue and expense figures and sales analysis outlined in Figures 11.1 and Table 11.1 are generally used by managers to support their decision-making.

Revenue
   (Total and by departments)

Less: Cost of sales

Gross profit
   (total and by departments)

Less: Expenses
   Labour cost (total and by departments)
   Other identified direct operating expenses by department
   Undistributed operating expenses

Profit /Loss
   Total

Figure 11.1 Accounting information in the profit and loss account

Table 11.1 Sales analysis

Accommodation related	Food and beverage (F&B)-related
Average room rate	Average spends
Accommodation / total sales	F&B sales / total sales
Accommodation sales mix	F or B sales / total F&B sales
Room occupancy percentage	Stock turnover
Bed occupancy percentage	Number of covers
Yield percentage	F&B sales mix
Number of sleepers	Sales per employee

The emphasis on revenue information appears to be consistent with that of a market-oriented approach. In addition to the above accounting information, revenue and expenses are also often analysed in percentage terms, and perhaps some cost behaviour or variance analysis will also be provided.

The major use of the profit and loss information shown in Figure 11.1, and the sales analysis information shown in Table 11.1, is to analyse the historical and current performance of the hotel and its departments; for example, to monitor the current activity against last week, last month, last year or against budget. It will probably also be used to set the budget for the next year's trading, perhaps being used and amended on a rolling forecast basis.

In a market-oriented company, it seems logical that the approach to the management of revenue generation should also be carried through to the measurement of management performance. Within an operation, the budget often becomes the main quantifiable performance indicator of management. Whilst the most effective method of setting a budget is beyond the scope of this work, it is appropriate at this stage to question the most effective method of using the budget to measure management performance.

Having established the type of information that managers use to support their decision-making, it is necessary to identify when and where the interface between the two departments actually takes place. Ward (1989) suggests that this happens within the function of the marketing activities, as shown in Figure 11.2.

So the interface takes place within the marketing activities of an organization, rather than within a specific department. Ward (1989) outlines the key financial involvement in marketing decisions in three phases:

1. Financial analysis.
2. Financial planning.
3. Financial control.

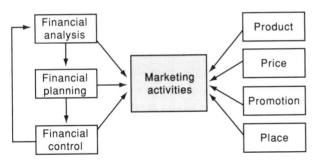

Figure 11.2   Financial involvement in marketing. From Ward (1989), with permission

Horngren (1982) emphasizes the role of accounting in terms of information provision for decision-making through reporting. It could therefore be argued that a fourth financial phase should be added to the above three, this being financial reporting as this is the usual method of disseminating the information to users.

Buttle (1986) classifies the main concerns of marketing management:

- Analysis of the business environment.
- Planning for future achievements.
- Implementation of plans.
- Control of plans and staff.

There are clear similarities between accounting and marketing roles within marketing decision-making. Both functions are involved with analysis, planning and control: the managers are then responsible for implementing the plans. McDonald (1989) describes marketing planning as being 'concerned with identifying what and to whom sales are going to be made in the longer term to give revenue budgets and sales forecasts any chance of achievement'. Surely this must be sound common ground on which to start building the interface between the two functions? Whilst the two professions may have different backgrounds and objectives, they do have the similar core activities of planning, analysis and control within marketing activities.

Developments in accounting information

In the last decade, there have been considerable developments in the techniques available to managers to assist their decision-making in hotels. The following methods have been selected on the basis that they improve the provision of accounting information for marketing decision-making in hotels:

- Cost-volume-profit (CVP) analysis.
- Yield management.
- Rooms value engineering.
- Market segmentation profit analysis.

Each technique is discussed and its contribution to the development of the accounting and marketing interface highlighted.

Cost-volume-profit (CVP) analysis

As the name cost-volume-profit analysis suggests, this technique is concerned with investigating the interrelationship between cost, volume and profit. It is an important tool which managers can use to assist them in both profit-planning and budgeting. By monitoring the interaction between these three factors, alternative courses of action can be evaluated in the light of the levels of profit which would be generated.

In order to undertake CVP analysis, it is necessary first to identify and classify costs according to the fixed and variable elements that are incurred through generating revenue. Following this classification, a CVP worksheet can be produced. To gain maximum benefit, this should be carried out using a spreadsheet model, so that 'what if' questions can be tested.

The main barrier to using CVP analysis is often a reluctance to attempt the task of classifying cost and revenue variability. However, Harris (1992) points out that:

> In dealing with CVP relationships, precision is almost an illusion, so that while the analysis should be as accurate as possible, it should also be simple to use, otherwise the costs will outweigh the benefits.

The information generated is invaluable in assisting managers in decision-making, its versatility being a key strength. CVP can be used to evaluate alternative courses of action in terms of the generation of profit for a period of time, a single department, a promotional package or for the operation as a whole.

CVP analysis also enables calculation of the break-even point. This is the point at which all costs (fixed and variable) have been covered, and any further sales will contribute directly to profit. Harris (1992) suggests that this has important motivational benefits for managers, through knowing that they have achieved break-even point, and that subsequent sales will be contributing to profit. Once again this calculation can be applied for any selected purpose, whether it is for a new promotion or a specific department.

This technique provides an analysis of figures which is suited to both historical and future-oriented decision-making. It offers new insights and support for managers planning and developing their business, whether it is showing areas where they have made good decisions, or areas where opportunities can be found to generate profit.

Yield management

Arguably, the major step forward in accounting information has been centred on the concept of yield management, initially through manual systems, and subsequently sophisticated computerized programs.

A major task of managers is to achieve the best possible return on the space available to them, whether this is bedroom, restaurant, leisure or conference space. Jeffrey and Hubbard (1994) suggest that for most hotel establishments 'a principal marketing objective is the achievement of high and stable room and bed occupancy rates.' Achieving this objective is obviously closely linked to the actual demand for the space. Lockwood and Jones (1990) draw attention to the complexity of the demand for hotels:

> In reality, hotel managers have to cope with wide variations in demand from many different sectors of their market who may be offered different product packages at many different prices all at the same time.

In yield management, the concept of selling the most space possible is combined with also considering the rate or price at which the space is sold. This type of strategy is linked to the maximization of revenue. Broadly, it is assumed that when demand is high, selling space at a discount should be avoided, maximization of the revenue is achieved through charging a higher average room rate. In situations when the demand is low, then the return on the space is maximized through increasing the occupancy by reducing the rate charged.

It is a way of managing the demand for space, products and services, and is operated through an understanding and interpretation of the particular demand patterns, trading the rate with occupancy, according to fluctuations in demand for the space. In hotels, these principles are most readily applied through systems for accommodation sales. These customers usually book in advance, so booking patterns can be established, and market segments with similar needs can be identified. However, if the benefits were considered to be cost-effective, the concept could easily be used for other types of space.

The yield is simply the product of occupancy and average room rate (Lockwood and Jones, 1990). This statistic can be further refined by converting it into a yield percentage: expressing the actual revenue as a percentage of the total revenue that would have been achieved had all the rooms been sold at full rack rate (Orkin, 1988). Thus, yield management is a market-demand pricing technique used to monitor and maximize revenue, though it is also an indicator of the level of revenue achieved by the management.

Due to the complexity of demand for hotels, often the most effective way of implementing yield management is through the use of a computerized system, such as Fidelio. Computerized systems are designed to assist in the calculations of forecasting demand and setting rate bands for market segments, usually on a daily basis. A yield management system manager will often be appointed to take responsibility for coordinating, interpreting and managing the system.

A supplementary benefit of the approach of yield management is that it encourages the exchange of information within a company between marketing and accounting. The system manager will require information from both the marketing plan and the budget in order to input the required information. This process could perhaps be used as a first step towards formally integrating the marketing plan with the budget.

The computerized systems usually incorporate a reporting function which can be used to analyse the sales achieved, for example, which promotions generated the most sales, or how successful weekend packages were. Indeed, the forecasting capabilities of the system have limited benefits if they are not checked against the actual results. The International Hotel Association (1993) stresses: 'Don't leave yield management reports on the shelf. They are one of the best business planning tools a hotelier can have'. Perhaps analysis of variances in yield management results is also another area where marketing and accounting could or should be working together.

A major problem of the yield management approach is that it may encourage heavy discounting, which could be detrimental if used for longer-term pricing decisions (Dunn and Brooks, 1990). The technique is useful to monitor and achieve the maximization of rooms revenue, and evaluate sales and pricing alternatives. However, because it ignores the levels of profit generated by the decisions, it is not effective for the longer-range profit goals of a company. The need for the development of the yield management approach is summed up well by Dunn and Brooks (1990):

> Yield management has been a successful short term technique for adjusting prices to market conditions. In the long term, however, pricing decisions must be based on a more thorough analysis that includes profit margins.

Rooms value engineering

Menu engineering (Kasavana and Smith, 1982) has demonstrated and established the benefit of understanding the profit implications of selling different individual items on restaurant menus. Lockwood and Jones (1990) have now developed a framework to apply the concept of value engineering to rooms management.

Hotels offering different types of rooms at different rates – often a prerequisite of market segmentation strategies – should find the technique particularly relevant. The aim is to identify the levels of profit generated by sales of different types of rooms. To apply rooms value engineering:

> The variable costs of accommodation operations are examined and a matrix is constructed to identify areas of operation which can be improved to increase profitability (Lockwood and Jones, 1990).

Much of the required data is readily available and can be analysed using a computer spreadsheet. There are two variable cost elements of selling rooms – the cost of servicing and the cost of materials. Lockwood and Jones (1990) provide a method for establishing these costs, which need to be identified for each room type.

Following this identification of costs, an analysis can be carried out by using a spreadsheet model to calculate the profit contributions according to room type. This information helps managers improve their pricing decisions, because they are aware of the profit rather than the revenue implications of their decisions. For example, when pricing a special package which includes a bottle of champagne or a trip to a local tourist attraction, these costs could be included in the calculations. The sample matrix shown in Figure 11.3 demonstrates how the matrix can be used to display the relative popularity and the contribution to profit for different types of

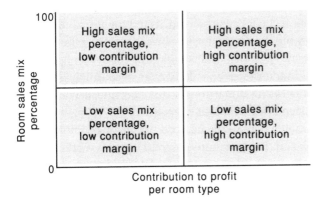

Figure 11.3 Sample rooms value engineering matrix.

rooms. Appropriate quadrants need to be identified for individual operations so that the various room types are allocated to quadrants which are meaningful to the managers making the decisions.

Rooms value engineering also helps managers decide which rooms to give priority to during busy periods, decisions being made according to which room types generate the most profit. Using the technique also helps managers identify room types which may not be generating sufficient profit, in which case decisions can be made to improve the profit contribution.

Discounting can have a considerable effect on profit contribution. The matrix can be further developed to provide an analysis of the effects of discounting on profit generation:

> An after the event analysis using the actual achieved average room rate for each room type would provide considerable insights into the performance of the rooms department and the sales expertise of the hotel (Lockwood and Jones,1990).

In addition to the need to identify the profit implications of decisions, this approach is also required as a consequence of the rising costs of preparing a room for sale. It helps managers identify areas where they can make improvements to the profitability of their operation, through creating a heightened awareness of costs and their effect on profit. It is an excellent example of how accounting information can be actively used to improve marketing decision-making. In the longer term, a yield management system which makes this type of calculation, rather than applying a yardstick approach, which is currently possible, will be a powerful tool for the hotel manager of tomorrow.

Market segmentation profit analysis (MSPA)

Marketing planning in hotels usually focuses on market segments, with specific marketing activities and packages being directed towards individual market segments (for example, business, leisure or conference guests). The marketing plan also generally shows the marketing activities planned according to the identified market segments. However, accounting provides information according to operating departments (for example, accommodation, restaurant or bar), instead of by market segments.

There is an obvious mismatch here in the use and provision of information for planning and control activities in hotels – marketeers working and planning with market segments, and accountants recording and reporting by operating department. In addition to this, two separate methods of recording and evaluating the planning and control functions are used – the marketing plan and the budget. There is thus a need to consider how accounting information can be designed to support marketing decisions more effectively. Kaplan and Atkinson (1989) suggest that the ultimate challenge of an accounting system should be:

> To develop management accounting practices that support the basic managerial tasks of organising, planning, and controlling operations to achieve excellence throughout the organization.

MSPA is a technique developed by Dunn and Brooks (1990) which will help to approach the development of the accounting–marketing interface in hotels, improving the current provision of information, and subsequent decision-making. The main difference of the MSPA system is the identification and reporting of direct and indirect costs (overhead) by market segment, rather than by operating department. Present accounting systems usually allocate costs to operating departments (profit centres), e.g. room, food and beverage, and service departments (cost centres) e.g. administration, marketing and energy. In order to create a MSPA model it is necessary to complete three stages of analysis:

1. Identify target market segments for profit reporting.
2. Report all revenues by market segment.
3. Distribute overhead costs to market segments.

To implement the MSPA system it is necessary to change the approach to cost allocation, by using an activity-based approach to reporting and allocating costs. For this system, the costs need to be allocated first from cost centres to activity centres, and then to market segments. So to calculate the allocations, cost drivers have to be identified, based on the use of resources for all the activity centres. Figure 11.4 illustrates the concept of distributing the expenses from cost centres to the market segments.

Implementation of this model would demand a fundamental change in the current financial reporting procedures of hotels. Prior to attempting full implementation of MSPA, it should be viable to test recording revenue information by market segment, as well as by operating department. This could easily be achieved with a spreadsheet model, and may show interesting results concerning revenue sources which would stimulate further investigation of the total system.

The main problem of developing this system lies in the difficulty of identifying, apportioning and allocating costs to market segments. Activity-based costing is difficult to develop accurately so that the figures generated are precise. Perhaps an interim measure is needed to test the application of

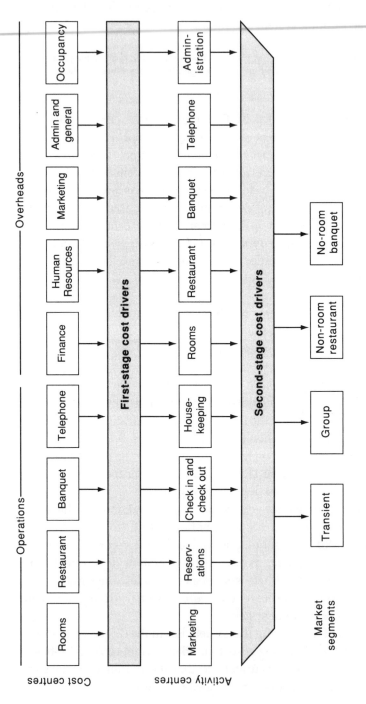

Figure 11.4 Flow chart of how expenses are distributed from cost centres to market segments. Costs incurred by the nine cost centres on the top row are reassigned to appropriate activity centres (middle row) using arithmetic formulas called first-stage cost drivers. The costs are distributed to market segments using another set of cost drivers. For example, some of the rooms-division costs are assigned to housekeeping, based on the number of employees. That expense is then divided between the transient and group segments according to the proportion of room-nights purchased by the two segments. From Dunn and Brooks (1990), copyright Cornell University. Used by permission. All rights reserved.

MSPA. This could be achieved by using standard costs within the activity costing, e.g. the costing of room check-in or room servicing. The results could then be evaluated and developed as more information on the cost structures was identified.

MSPA offers numerous opportunities for improving the accounting information for marketing decisions in hotels. The focus on longer-term profit maximization objectives and the integration of accounting and marketing activities are the key benefits. The system also provides the framework to develop further the information provision for management in the areas of:

- Profit rather than revenue maximization strategies.
- Pricing guidelines, and testing pricing assumptions.
- Investigating the interdependence of department sales.
- Evaluation of capital investments.
- Forecasting future profitability.
- Analysis of revenue and expenses by market segment.
- Break-even by market segment.
- The effectiveness and focus of cost management.
- Profit projections based on the perceived impact of marketing and financial plans.

In the longer term there would seem to be considerable benefits to developing a system which coordinates the accounting and marketing activities of the company. Mossman, *et al.*, (1978) suggest that:

> The objective of a marketing/accounting information system is to facilitate decision making by market segments. The analytical methods used must assure not only that decisions made for a segment are optimal for the segment but also that they maximise the total profit of the firm.

MSPA would seem to be the best route towards helping companies achieve a competitive edge in this increasingly competitive environment, through improving decision-making within the firm by adopting a more integrated and cohesive approach.

The way forward

The techniques of CVP, yield management, rooms value engineering and MSPA are just examples of the tools available to managers today to improve their decision-making. A powerful aspect of these approaches is that they provide managers with information which is suitable for historical analysis of performance, and will also improve the current provision of relevant information for planning activities. They all involve the interface between accounting and marketing, which is considered to be the main thrust behind developing the management of profit in hotels.

Marn and Rosiello (1992) present an interesting emphasis on the importance of managing pricing. They suggest that managers are 'leaving significant amounts of money – potential profit – on the table at the transaction level'. The transaction level is the point at which the product meets the customer. In hotels, numerous transactions take place, customer by customer, minute by minute, and every transaction is a profit opportunity.

Managers must therefore have information on the profit implications of their decisions to use in conjunction with their marketing knowledge. This is a concept which has not been developed so far, but would seem to have considerable benefits for hotels because of the numerous transactions which take place on a daily basis. Marn and Rosiello (1992) suggest that getting 'the pricing right' is 'the fastest and most effective way for a company to realise its maximum profit'. Considering the number of transactions which take place in hotels, the concept of managing price offers numerous opportunities for companies to develop their approach to 'pricing for profit'. It would also seem to be a sound fundamental concept to adopt when attempting to improve the present provision and use of information for management decision-making in hotels.

Sizer (1989) suggests that the increasing power and capabilities of technology offer the opportunity to provide the type of financial analysis which managers need in business today. To identify these needs and provide more effective accounting systems, Johnson and Kaplan (1987) suggest that what is lacking is the knowledge, but that is now being developed.

Lewis and Chambers (1989) consider that hotel information systems are currently poor in providing critical marketing information which is required for marketing decisions, for example, in the areas of marketing planning and product development. Geller (1984) conducted research into executive information needs in hotel companies. He found that, whilst executives were generally satisfied with the historical operating and financial statistics they received, they did feel that they lacked the specific information they needed to support their planning activities, particularly in the area of marketing. The conclusion that can be drawn from these views suggests that what is needed is more specific information about market segments. For example, which segment is expected to spend the most in the restaurant, or which segment is the most costly to attract to the hotel, so that products and marketing efforts can be designed in line with customer needs, and more accurate forecasting of revenue achieved.

Perhaps the main reason for the lack of this type of information is that accounting systems are designed to meet the needs of corporate office reporting functions, rather than those of individual hotel managers. Johnson and Kaplan (1987) suggest that this results in a narrow focus on producing monthly earnings reports, rather than information to support decision-making. If internal reports are to help control the business, then their nature and frequency should be dictated by relevant decision-making time scales and needs of the users, rather than head office requirements (Ward, 1989).

The first step towards developing accounting systems is the acknowledgement of the actual, rather than the perceived, information needs within all departments of the hotel. This is best achieved through the awareness that functional areas within a hotel are internal customers to each other, so internal services need to focus their actions on the requirements of those that require them. From the accounting service point of view, a good example of this type of consideration is the method in which the information is presented to managers. Perhaps graphical presentation would be more appropriate than tables of figures, or relevant summaries of information provided instead of full reports.

There is clearly a need for change in the type of information provided by the accounting function to support marketing decisions in hotels. This should be focused on:

- The identification of marketing decisions being made, which could be supported by accounting information
- The specific type of information required by marketing decision-makers.
- The timing, frequency and appropriate presentation of the required accounting information.
- An emphasis on information and reporting which provides managers with the profit implications of their decision making.
- Reporting which is oriented to future rather than historical information.
- An investigation into the implications of information for pricing decisions, and the profit which is being lost.

Development of the accounting and marketing interface demands an integration of all departments within a hotel, and a new approach to decision-making within the business:

> Integrated means combining parts into a whole and may sound like just another meaningless buzz word, but it is not. When marketing is integrated the whole company participates, not just the marketing department. Every part of the business combines to satisfy customer needs at maximum profit. (Davidson, 1987).

If there is to be a buzz word for the 1990s in hotels, then it has to be *profit-planning*. Managers now have the technology, the marketing concept, including the dimension of service quality, and are beginning to develop the knowledge to start making more informed decisions in every area of the business. This will enable managers to actively plan for customer satisfaction and profit. The approach has far-reaching implications for how managers will receive and use information, make decisions, and be assessed on their performance – but it will be worth the effort!

References

Buttle, F (1986) *Hotel and Foodservice Marketing – A Managerial Approach.* Cassell Educational, London.

Davidson, H. (1987) *Offensive Marketing*. Penguin Books, London, p. 96.

Dunn, K. and Brooks, D. (1990) Profit analysis: beyond yield management. *The Cornell HRA Quarterly*, **31**(3): 80–90.

Geller, A. (1984) *Executive Information Needs in Hotel Companies*. Peat, Marwick, Mitchell, USA.

Harris, P. (1992) Hospitality profit planning in the practical environment. *International Journal of Contemporary Hospitality Management*, **4**(4): p.24–32.

Horngren, C. (1982) *Cost Accounting: A Managerial Emphasis*, 5th edn, Prentice-Hall.

International Hotel Association (1993) The ABCs of yield management. *Hotels*, p. 55–56.

Jeffrey, D. and Hubbard, N. (1994) A model of hotel occupancy for monitoring and marketing in the hotel industry. *International Journal of Hospitality Management*, **13**(1): 57–71.

Job, J. (1992) *Marketing/Accounting Literature Review, Research and Discussion Paper Series*, South Australia Discipline of Accounting and Finance, Flinders University of South Australia.

Johnson, H. and Kaplan, R. (1987) *Relevance Lost – The Rise and Fall of Management Accounting*. Harvard Business School Press, Boston, MA.

Kaplan, R. and Atkinson, A. (1989) *Advanced Management Accounting*, 2nd edn, Prentice-Hall, Englewood Cliffs, NJ., p. 14.

Kasavana, M. and Smith D. (1982) *Menu Engineering: A Practical Guide to Menu Analysis*. Hospitality Publishing, East Lansing.

Kotas, R. (1973) Market orientation. *HCIMA Journal*, **19**: 5–7.

Kotler, P. (1988) *Marketing Management – Analysis, Planning, Implementation and Control*, 6th edn, Prentice-Hall, Englewood Cliffs, NJ.

Lewis, R. and Chambers, R. (1989) *Marketing Leadership in Hospitality – Foundations and Practices*. Van Nostrand Reinhold.

Lockwood, A. and Jones, P. (1990) Applying value engineering to rooms management. *International Journal of Contemporary Hospitality Management* **2**(1): 27–32.

McCarthy, E. (1975) *Basic Marketing: A Managerial Approach*, Homewood III: Irwin, 75–80.

McDonald, H. (1989) *Marketing Plans – How to Prepare Them: How to Use Them*, 2nd edn. Butterworth-Heinemann, p. 41.

Marn, M., and Rosiello, R., (1992) Managing price, gaining profit. *Harvard Business Review*. **70**(5): 84–94.

Meldrum, M, Ward, K and Srikanthan, S (1986), Can you really account for Marketing? *Marketing Intelligence and Planning UK*, **4**: 39–45.

Mossman, F, Crissy, W and Fischer, P (1978) Budgeting for operational planning and control. In: Shapiro, S and Kirpalani, V (1984), *Marketing Effectiveness – Insights from Accounting and Finance*, Allyn and Bacon, Boston, MA, p. 415.

Orkin, E.B. (1988) Boosting your bottom line with yield management. *The Cornell HRA Quarterly* **29**(4): 52–56.

Ratnatunga, J., Hooley, G. and Pike, R. (1990) The marketing–finance interface. *European Journal of Marketing* **24**: 29–43.

Sizer, J. (1989) *An Insight into Management Accounting*, 3rd edn., Penguin Books, London, p. ix.

Trebuss, S. (1977) Organising for the marketing/finance interface. In: *Business Proceedings*. LaPlaca, P.J. (ed.), Chicago, American Marketing Association, p. 228.

Ward, K. (1989) *Financial Aspects of Marketing*, Butterworth-Heinemann, Oxford, p. 16.

Williamson, R. (1979) *Marketing for Accountants and Managers*. Butterworth-Heinemann, in association with ICMA, Oxford, p. xii.

Part IV Financial Management

12 The hotel financial controller: a member of the management team

Catherine L. Burgess

Introduction

The hotel controller's role has changed dramatically during the last 10 years, from being regarded as a pure accountant who sat in an office all day to becoming a full participatory member of the management team. This chapter presents some of the results of a research project which initially investigated the role of the controller over a 10 year period to 1990. Subsequently the effect on the financial function which had resulted from the technological and other developments, and the economic recession of the early 1990s, was reviewed.

Methodology

The research project was structured in three stages. The first stage required the review of the literature available on the topic. The second and third stages entailed the acquisition of primary data, first by means of a mailed questionnaire to hotel industry financial personnel, and second by a series of semistructured interviews with a subsample of the questionnaire respondents. Results of the survey and interviews were then compared to published data, and conclusions drawn. A small proportion only of the findings of the final thesis are discussed here, in terms of the controller's experience and responsibilities, and relationship with other members of the management team.

The previous role of the hotel financial controller

Literature survey

The review of literature has examined the information available relating to hotel (or hospitality) accounting, including previous published research. Little information has been forthcoming, there having been few primary research projects conducted in this field (particularly in the UK). A few quotations regarding the role of the controller have been found in hospitality textbooks and journals, but the majority of recent material represents individuals' opinions rather than proven facts.

Cote (1988), in defining *hospitality accounting,* says that:

> Internal control comprises a plan of the organization and co-ordinated plans and measures adopted within a business to safeguard its assets, check accuracy and reliability of its accounting data, promote operational efficiencies and encourage adherence to prescribed management practice.

Reading and consultation indicate that an *accountant* is seen as a person who is formally qualified (and hence a member of one of the professional accounting bodies), whereas a *financial manager* has a wider role. A *financial controller* is a type of financial manager who may be a qualified accountant, but often has different qualifications, specific to a particular industry (e.g. hotels) or to general business. This title is used here as it reflects the operational nature of the responsibilities of many hotel accountants.

There has been little research published which investigates the role of the hotel controller. The primary investigation for industry in general has been performed by Sathe, whose survey (1982) concentrated principally on controllers at corporate level. He suggests that:

> controllers are staff managers and not measured on the profit and loss [bottom line]... they must be actively involved in the business decision-making process to ensure that specialist knowledge and expertise get proper consideration when business decisions and actions are taken.

He stresses that strong controllers are essential to corporate strength, being responsible for the integrity of the information supplied. He concludes that, in the areas he was able to observe, companies where controllers are involved in the decision-making processes were generally more successful in their various fields.

Many of the textbooks which are written about various aspects of the hospitality industry devote sections to the accounting function, although many of these are now somewhat outdated. Few expand on the role of the controller, concentrating on the function rather than the manager. Gray and

Ligouri (1980), in discussing the role of controller in hotels, highlight the changes in priorities since the 1970s, particularly the influence of computerization, and stress that the 'new' managerial responsibilities now being undertaken by controllers have not superseded the traditional responsibilities, but are additional to them. The primary responsibility of the controller is still to maintain controls within the accounting function.

A major piece of research on the role of the hotel controller was performed by Geller and Schmidgall (1984), with results being further updated in 1990. Although the study relates to controllers in the USA, it has relevance to the industry in the UK, as there are many hotel companies which operate on an international basis with similar responsibilities worldwide. This study concentrated on the controller's work, looking at education, skills, salaries and benefits and responsibilities.

The journal of the International Association of Hotel Accountants, *Bottomline* devoted an entire edition (1988) to the role of the financial controller. This consisted of a series of articles by various industry writers, who discussed the past, present and future status of the controller. Opinions tend to be expressed, rather than the results of primary research. For instance, Ferree (1988) regards the role of the controller as being originally seen as that of a 'beancounter' or glorified bookkeeper, interfering with management rather than acting as a member of the management team. However, the role has now developed into a multifaceted activity as a result of changes in the structure of the industry. Computerization has had a marked influence on the tasks performed. Responsibility for solving operational problems, managing systems and evaluating trends rather than performing typical accounting activities is now commonplace. As a consequence there has been an influx of more non-accounting managers into this area, such as those qualified in hotel and catering.

Little research has been performed in the UK. The research of Jones (1991) examines the financial information needs of various managers within an international hotel company. Financial controllers were one section of management questioned, principally at unit level. She identifies common goals concerned with the various aspects of management information, where the controller is seen as a service provider to other members of the management team, to the head office and for statutory bodies.

Other sources of information also relate opinions rather than facts, several articles having been published which discuss hospitality financial control as a career. As an example, Afiya (1993) discusses the differences between the hotel controller and an accountant in professional practice, highlighting the people-oriented nature of the industry, and the fact that the accounting office is 'at the heart of the establishment'. This article includes comments from industry practitioners, which emphasize the communication skills required in working 'closely and constructively' within the operational areas, and with other members of the management team.

Results of the questionnaire survey

This study required the comparison of responsibilities for a wide range of hotel financial controllers primarily within the UK. A questionnaire was mailed to all 463 members (which included financial personnel at all managerial levels) of the British Association of Hotel Accountants (BAHA), which compared the responsibilities of individuals for 1980, 1985 and 1990. Ninety respondents were currently employed as hotel financial controllers, of whom one-third were female and two-thirds male, and these form the basis of the results discussed below.

The survey encompassed a wide range of questions relating to the type of establishment in which controllers work (and had worked), their experience, work and managerial responsibilities, training and education. Limited results relating solely to managerial experience and responsibilities are presented here.

Experience in the industry

Respondents were requested to state their job titles in 1980, 1985 and 1990, giving an indication as to the breadth of experience of controllers. In 1985, for instance, 10 respondents held a non-accounting management position of some sort, in 1980 13 held such posts. The most popular specific area quoted was hotel front office. This will be discussed later in the chapter when reviewing the current and future status of the controller with other managers. Within the industry, 53.3 per cent had worked for more than 10 years in the hotel sector, and another third for between six and 10 years. Over 40 per cent had worked for the same company for six years or more, only eight respondents having changed company within the last year (1990). Initial research had also suggested that the majority of staff joined the industry at an early stage in their careers, with little exposure to other industries. However, responses suggest a different view – over half (56.2 per cent) had worked outside the industry at some time, the vast majority for longer than a nominal few months (which could have suggested holiday jobs whilst studying, for instance). Of the respondents with other industry experience, the highest number had been in some area of accounting, with others having worked in manufacturing and retailing.

The hotels where controllers work

The majority of respondents worked in London or another major city or airport location. Under a quarter worked in an area defined as the 'rest of the

UK' (Table 12.1). The definitions of what constitutes a hotel are varied, but research suggests that this mix reflects the general overall balance of location within UK hotels. When analysed by size, a third worked in hotels with over 300 bedrooms, and another 53 per cent had more than 100 bedrooms. These statistics perhaps reflect the responsibilities of the role, and the necessity of the larger hotels to employ a person for this office, although it should be noted that four out of the 90 controllers worked in hotels with fewer than 40 bedrooms. Over half regarded their hotels as being of four star status, and two-thirds classed their main function as being 'commercial' (rather than conference or leisure). In ownership terms, two-thirds belonged to a chain, the rest being owner-occupied, operated under management contract or run independently.

Table 12.1   The hotels where controllers work (1990)

Location	%	Size (bedrooms)	%
London	41.1	Over 600 bedrooms	13.5
Other major city	17.8	300 – 599	18.9
Airport	5.6	100 – 299	52.7
Resort	6.7	40 – 99	9.5
Rest of UK	21.1	Under 40	5.4

Percentages do not include those results which were not applicable.

Computerization and self-accounting

One of the areas shown in the literature survey to be influential in the changing role of the controller was the extent to which hotels were computerized, and had converted to self-accounting systems. The great majority of hotels surveyed used computerized systems to facilitate their operations, with the 8.9 per cent which were not computerized being generally smaller in size. In 1980, only 42.1 per cent were computerized.

Of the hotels where controllers work, 70.5 per cent claim to be self-accounting – they complete the hotel accounts up to final profit and loss/balance sheet status (although they may well employ a firm of professional accountants to finalize the published accounts for audit – a statutory requirement). Only 13.0 per cent have centralized accounts (where the management and statutory accounts are prepared by head office), with 16.5 per cent operating a combination of the two. There has been a progression towards the use of self-accounting during the last ten years – in 1980 59.0 per cent were self-accounting, 17.9 per cent were centralized and 23.1 per cent had a partial system.

Controller responsibilities

There have been many changes in responsibilities of controllers during the last 10 years. Generally, there has been a trend away from this person being responsible directly for departmental activities (revenue control, night audit) towards more financial responsibilities (budgets, cash management). There is also an increasing trend for controllers to become involved in areas such as hotel development (Figures 12.1–12.3).

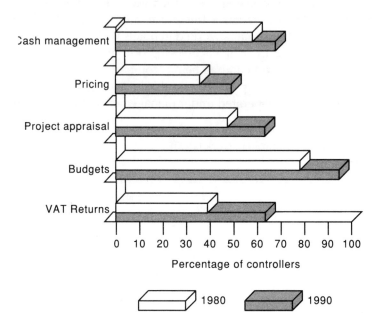

Figure 12.1   Financial responsibilities of controllers

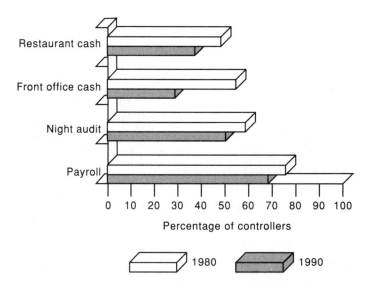

Figure 12.2   Departmental responsibilities of controllers

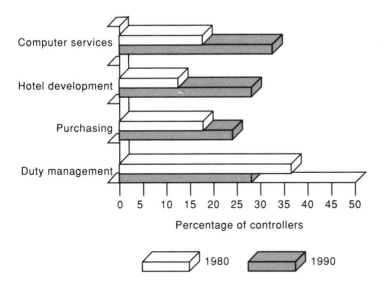

Figure 12.3 Other areas of controllers' responsibilities

There do not appear to be many variations in responsibilities dependent on the type of hotel ownership. However, in self-accounting units controllers are responsible for more areas than centralized hotels. Larger hotels generally have more departments than smaller ones, although the functions still usually need to be performed and are often combined with other duties. These changing duties are reflected in the amount of hours controllers spend at work – over 80 per cent claim to work more than 45 hours a week on a consistent basis. In 1980 this figure was only 64.1 per cent.

The future of the hotel industry and the controller

The second section of the research process investigated the effect of the recession on the hotel industry, and the consequent future of both hotels and of the financial controller. This required a survey of the published data, followed by a series of in-depth interviews with a selected subsample of hotel financial controllers and head office financial personnel.

Literature survey

This literature survey required an assessment of how hotels have changed in recent years, particularly as an effect of the recession of the early 1990s, and to ascertain what outcome this might have on the future management of hotel businesses. There has been little research published to date which has looked at the effect of the recent recession on the hotel industry. Industry statistics are the principal source of data, and these indicate a shortfall of occupancy, average room rate and hence profitability over recent years (Table 12.2).

Table 12.2   Comparison of results for average hotels in the UK

	1988	1990	1992
Average annual room occupancy	67.3 %	65.1 %	48.0 %
Total turnover (millions)	£ 5,700	£ 7,000	£ 6,100
Business trade (millions)	£ 2,793	£ 2,940	£ 1,952

From Mintel Leisure Intelligence (1994), with permission

Parkinson of Horwath Consulting (who also publish annual statistics relating to hotels), speaking at the 1993 Hotel Accounting Conference, quotes:

> the worst three years' trading since the great depression of the 1930s... profitability has been impacted by a downturn in revenues but cost savings have reduced the proportionate impact...cash flows have suffered...[this has]proved too much for many businesses.

The International Hotels Association undertook a worldwide survey *Hotels of the Future* on the future of the hotel industry. The results were published in 1988 and, although economic factors have changed, many of the recommendations are still highly relevant. These recommendations covered all aspects of the hotel industry, but those relevant here highlight the increased importance of technology and the need for change in the organization of human resources. Management structures are likely to need to be reorganized, deleting layers of hierarchy, and the labour force will be required to be multiskilled wherever possible.

Results from the interviews

A subsample of 27 controllers, head office personnel and recruitment specialists was selected for further detailed questioning. These represented a wide range of hotel characteristics, including a variety of size, type, ownership, location and management structure. The general consensus of opinion, given by over two-thirds of the interviewees, was that hotels had become vastly overpriced during the 1980s, and that the major effect of the recession would be to deflate room rates back to more sensible levels. Never again would hotels be able to be so 'greedy' and would now have to offer far more value for money in a much more competitive marketplace. London hotels, in particular, had 'priced themselves out of the market', and that it would be several years before average room rates returned to the levels of previous years.

Additionally, as a result of the recession, business customers had implemented measures of economy within their own organizations and had found other ways of conducting business from a distance. These influences have resulted in a reduction of the length of stay for business travellers, with the consequent lack of occupancy causing hotels to offer increasingly competitive room rates. Tourism has also suffered, there being less disposable income available for leisure travel. This market was expected to regenerate, but customers will continue to seek cheaper accommodation. The effect of price competition, plus decreased occupancy, would (say the interviewees) have a major impact on the upper three- and four-star markets in particular. Five-star hotels will survive, there still being a demand for the highest quality of accommodation and service, but hotels of a lesser standard will face increasing competition for a static (or diminishing) market. Only in the budget sector (low three-star and below) will hotels see growth, customers opting for the cheapest accommodation of a particular standard.

The effect of decreasing revenue (from lower average room rates, occupancies and consequent food and beverage spends) will necessitate maximization of cost controls, in order to maintain acceptable profit levels and service debts incurred during the high-spending 1980s. The implementation of systems to manage all aspects of the business will increasingly take over from previous human control, reducing costs in all areas, with hopefully little effect on the service provided to the customer. One major cost area in any hotel is seen to be that of food, and there has been an increasing awareness of the need for effective control of these largely perishable products, which has also been impacted by new food hygiene regulations. Careful planning and utilization of food stocks can minimize losses, and hence improve costs in this sensitive area. Another large cost for consideration is that of payroll and associated benefits: if the cost of employing staff can be minimized (again, without affecting service) then a major reduction of expenditure can be effected. Nearly all the interviewees reported reductions of headcount during the recession, with the adoption of variable working practices to ensure that all functions were adequately performed. Managers are seen to be far more active in the hotel, increasing their communication with all levels of staff and promoting a less class-oriented hierarchy. This is often seen to be beneficial to staff relationships, and results in an improved attitude towards all staff. Even with an upturn in business, these flexible working patterns are unlikely to be abolished in the future – managers have found them to be far more effective than the previous more rigid methods. This has affected controllers, particularly in the area of duty management. From the mailed survey it was seen that they were becoming less likely to perform duty management shifts in 1990 in addition to their normal duties: this trend has now reversed and is now seen as one way in which controllers can do their bit in assisting other managers and hence restricting payroll costs. However, they still in general work shorter, and less unsocial, hours than most of their colleagues in the operational management fields.

Management control will, as a result, be increasingly important for the future of hotels. A shortfall of available business will result in an increasingly competitive market, with value for money the most important criterion to the customer. This will necessitate a strong maintenance of standards which can only be implemented by the increasing use of effective computerized systems, with controls of paramount importance to the business.

The controller as a member of the management team

The need for control of costs to maximize profitability affects all areas of management. Departmental managers have been made aware of the requirement for effective supervision in this area, and the resultant need for practical control mechanisms. They have realized the necessity of liaison with the experts in this area, namely the control staff. Controllers also have been proactive in encouraging an exchange of information and resultant improved communication between the control and operating departments.

The controller's role has traditionally been split into the areas of management and financial accounting, with cost control being regarded as a financial function (production of numerical data) rather than a managerial function (analysis and interpretation of the data produced). The increase of technology has resulted in more and better systems being available for use, for many different functions within the hotel environment. For instance, computerized systems are now commonplace in the areas of hotel reservations, point of sale, purchasing and nominal ledger. These new systems have had a great effect on the operation of the hotel, but on the responsibilities of the controller in particular. They produce a great deal of data, previously unavailable to managers (or only with a high degree of labour and effort), which now require utilization. Traditional manual accounting tasks have generally disappeared, enabling controllers to concentrate on the investigative and consultative approaches of the data produced.

The operational managers within the hotel unit have also taken advantage of the new facts available. With more sophisticated systems the amount and type of information produced can be daunting, and many managers require assistance in the interpretation of the statistics produced. Additionally, the need for managerial control has also increased, new ways of circumventing systems having emerged which result in new methods of fraud and potential abuse. The performance of many managers is now partly measured on the financial results achieved by their department, and hence optimum performance and knowledge are desired. The availability of advice and perhaps more formal training from the accounting area is essential, so that they may make the best use of the material available.

An ability to forecast future business is also of paramount importance to the various departments of the hotel, and to the organization as a whole. Accurate predictions of occupancy can ensure correct staffing and purchasing of supplies in all areas, and hence minimize excesses of expenditure. The consequent maximization of usage of these items ensures that costs are kept to the optimum for the level of service provided. The controller can assist in forecasting levels of future business, based on the wide range of past and future data now available, and knowledge of industry demand. The informal meetings required in order to produce the necessary forecasts also improve the level of contact between the control and other functions of the hotel.

All the interviewees felt that operational experience was, and would continue to be, of paramount importance to the controller. Only with knowledge of all the departments of the hotel could they perform their job successfully, both in control terms and as members of the management team. They would be able to converse far more easily with other managers if they had a degree of operational knowledge about the various departments, preferably gained via a working environment rather than purely by observation. This knowledge, combined with financial expertise, facilitates the analysis and interpretation of the accounting data produced. As a consequence, managers may be made aware of the problems occurring in their areas, and of potential solutions. Experience of other industries is also helpful in finding alternative solutions to management problems, hotels often being seen as 'blinkered' in their approach.

Additionally, the organization (and the hotel) also requires accurate data in order effectively to manage flow of cash in and out of the company's accounts. The shortfalls of revenue of recent years, combined with high interest rates and other factors, have ensured that the cash inflows to the organization have shown a downturn for many companies. Effective management of credit at the hotel level minimizes the negative effects of this. Also, control of cash being paid out (for payroll, supplies and to statutory bodies) must be competently managed if the company is to remain solvent. The majority of controllers now take a prime role in the management of cash, and require the commitment and cooperation of other managers if this task is to be effective. Accurate and timely billing of invoices, for instance, can minimize the problems of customers paying their accounts, and hence improve the flow of funds into the organization.

The level of communication required of the controller has, as a result, increased considerably, both in the field of financial information and as a working manager, with the ability to interpret data being as important as the information provided. This improvement in communication has increased the status of the controller with other managers within the operating unit. It is important, however, that this relationship is correctly handled by all parties. A demonstration of knowledge and an understanding of the operational pressures resulting from a service environment by the controller will facilitate a tactful relationship with other managers.

For the individual this increased status has had a consequent growth of personal confidence and perceived importance within the operation, which in turn has increased his or her importance to the organization as a whole. As a result, the controller is now perceived as being a major service provider to other managers, within both the hotel and the organization as a whole. This person is no longer perceived as being an adversary, but much more of an adviser and colleague. Increased communication and commitment between the accounting and operational functions have ensured an improved level of management, reduction of problems and consequently may well have minimized the negative effects of the recession on profitability.

The future controller

The interviewees were also asked to give their predictions as to the type of knowledge and experience required of the controller of the future. Only with an awareness of development in management can companies train and develop their staff to service current and prospective hotels.

Successful controllers of the future will be knowledgeable about industry developments, be aware of modern hotel management trends and be able to identify how these might well be used to maximum advantage within their own establishment. Communication with other controllers would assist with this increased knowledge, as well as awareness of alternative solutions from other areas of the industry, and of other industries. The controller will need to be proactive in identifying the need for change in all areas of management, aware of the consequences and able to act as a mediator between the various departments. There is a necessity for the organization as well as the hotel to recognize the importance of this function.

Accounting skills will also continue to be of paramount importance within the hotel business. Shortfalls of profitability, often combined with cash flow difficulties, have necessitated an increased awareness of the importance of forecasting as an accounting skill. The ability to forecast revenue and expenditure on a short- or medium-term basis gives advanced notice of further action required in order to minimize any shortfalls. With this information, departmental managers will then be able to revise their activities where possible, decreasing the likelihood of severe financial difficulties. Additionally, as profitability is not a guarantee of liquidity, cash flow may be forecasted and hence managed more effectively.

Future controllers, therefore, will need to have an extensive knowledge of all aspects of the hotel operation, as well as the financial techniques necessary to maximize profitability and liquidity. They will be expected to liaise between the head office and hotel, and between different departments within their own establishment. An ongoing awareness of current trends, together with the ability to identify and implement changes where required, will be essential for any controller wishing to pursue a successful career. Experience and stability within the industry will lead to increased knowledge and consequent perceived value to the employer.

Conclusion

The higher concentration on cost control (in all areas of the business) has increased the emphasis made on the cost accounting area of the hotel controller's role, which has only served to enhance the status of the controller in the organization. The research revealed a change in attitude towards controllers' position in their organization, managers from the various disciplines viewing them as a resource rather than as an adversary. However, it is important that controllers themselves acknowledge the need for tact and diplomacy when communicating with all levels of management, recognizing the essential 'customer-first' service element of the hotel operation.

Managers increasingly require accurate and timely information as to the state of the business. Information relating to all areas of revenue and expenditure, plus non-financial statistical information, is required for the constant monitoring of the organization and for future predictions. The ability to forecast future business trends is crucial if shortfalls are to be avoided, and profitability maintained. Most controllers have responded positively to the challenge of increased financial information needs as well as the control of costs, and see this as improved participation as part of the management team. Their status is now seen as much more than the 'beancounters in ivory towers' of a few years ago.

The increasing importance of the controller as a member of the management team, combined with an ongoing awareness of current trends, will make their occupation increasingly popular. It is essential that the image of the industry as an employer is improved, with potential recruits being made aware of the importance of the service areas of the establishment. The level of ability required, increased status and stability of the position, combined with shorter and more sociable working hours, will make the control department increasingly attractive, particularly for women. Overall, the future of the financial controller is seen to be that of an increasingly important member of the management team within the hotel and company hierarchy.

References

Afiya, A. (1993) A wealth of opportunities. *Caterer and Hotelkeeper Careers Guide*, p. 20.

Bottomline (1988) Journal of International Association of Hotel Accountants. October/November.

Cote, R. (1988) *Understanding Hospitality Accounting II*. Educational Institute of the American Hotel Association, East Lansing MI, p. 282.

Ferree, T. (1988) Trend analysis: expanding the role of the controller. *Bottomline*, pp. 16,17,22.

Geller, N. and Schmidgall, R. (1984) The hotel controller, more than just a bookkeeper. *Cornell Hotel and Restaurant Administration Quarterly*, August, pp. 91–97.

Geller, N., Ilvento, C. and Schmidgall, R. (1990) The hotel controller revisited. *Cornell Hotel and Restaurant Administration Quarterly*, November, pp. 16-22.

Gray, W.S. and Ligouri, S. (1980) *Hotel and Catering Management and Operations*. Prentice Hall, Englewood Cliffs, N J. p. 49.

International Hotels Association/Horwath and Horwath (1988). *Hotels of the Future*, London.

Jones, T. (1991) *Financial and Operating Needs of Managers in Hotel Companies*. Oxford Polytechnic: MPhil Thesis.

Mintel Leisure Intelligence, *(1994), Hotels*, Vol. 1. Mintel International Group, pp. 4,5,7.

Parkinson, G. (1993) Presentation at Hotel Accounting Conference. London: November, unpublished.

Sathe, V. (1982) *The Controller's Involvement in Management*. Prentice Hall, Englewood Cliffs, NJ.

13 Financial management in an international environment: Hotel 2000 NV – a case study

Ian C. Graham

Introduction and summary

Based in Brussels, Hotel 2000 NV is a hotel-owning, managing and brand-franchising company. The finance function is concerned with the management of hotel and franchisor accounting and reporting for more than 160 hotels in countries as far afield as Iceland and South Africa, Portugal and Muscat. The company produces:

1. A weekly flash revenue report showing key performance indicators such as Revpar, occupancy and average rate,
2. Monthly operating statistics, profit and loss account, balance sheet and cash flow reports and forecasts and quarterly published accounts,
3. Monthly and annual statutory financial filings in almost twenty different countries.

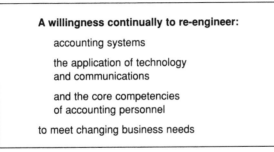

Figure 13.1 Financial management in an international environment

The company's financial management system is underpinned by a continual re-evaluation of business processes better to address the changing environment, including accounting systems, information technology and communications and the human resources engaged in financial management (Figure 13.1).

This chapter will outline the infrastructure (Figure 13.2) and cycles of control and analysis employed.

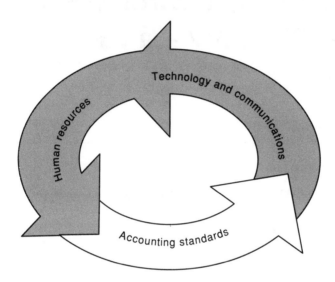

Figure 13.2   Infrastructure

Infrastructure accounting

The company has standardized certain aspects of accounting systems to facilitate the production of timely and accurate management information. Central to the success of these efforts are the disciplines which have been imposed from the corporate office, including a common chart of accounts, management report layouts, internal controls manual, language and terminology, and a reporting timetable (Figure 13.3).

The company has adopted the eighth edition of the Uniform System of Accounts for Hotels (1986) as the foundation for its common chart of accounts in all company managed hotels. The chart has been enhanced to improve analysis of revenues but is otherwise comparable to the charts used by most other international hotel chains. In addition to facilitating the financial analysis of operations within the company, this allows for benchmarking performance on a comparative basis by both city and country. The company uses published information such as is provided through Pannell Kerr Forster and Associates and Horwath Consulting for this purpose. The company's internal control manual contains definitions of rooms available, rooms occupied and room revenue, as well as other data. The standard franchise agreement contains references to these definitions, thus ensuring that, at least as relates to the basis of the franchise fee, common definitions are also adopted by its franchisees.

- Standard chart of accounts
- Standard report formats
- Common internal control manual
- Centrally defined reporting timetable
- Single language
- Strictly limited number of software applications

Figure 13.3   Critical success factors

The standard chart of accounts has been used to allow the preparation of management reports in the style dictated by the Uniform System, but also extended in the style and layout determined by local legislation for both tax and statutory requirements.

Ownership of the company's chart of accounts is held centrally, with occasional working parties established to obtain input from all users for suggested modifications and additions. Control of a core number of reports (at a hotel, area and divisional level) is also maintained centrally. This approach ensures that skills are focused appropriately and avoids hotel-based controllers spending time modifying the system. However, this does require occasional working parties to be established to agree amendments and improvements at all levels.

The internal control manual was developed cooperatively by a team composed of corporate executives, internal audit and hotel controllers. It is against the procedures established here that internal audit appraises company-managed hotels. Waivers are permitted, with appropriate authorization, in those countries where procedures cannot be implemented, or in small hotels where staffing constraint limits segregation of duties, etc.

The manual is slowly becoming out of date as cost-cutting measures change staffing structures in the hotels and require compromises in areas such as segregation of duties. In addition, as technology increasingly influences the way hotels are managed, the policies established in earlier, more manual times become obsolete. For example, the added value of a night audit function is brought increasingly into question. In the near future, Hotel 2000 NV plans to re-engineer the manual.

Additionally, the parent company, a UK-quoted company, has published a finance manual establishing umbrella accounting policies and focusing in particular on compliance with UK generally accepted accounting principles (UK-GAAP) and disclosure requirements. Because it primarily concerns UK published accounts, the manual has a limited circulation in Brussels. However, the conflict between UK and non-UK reporting requirements is an area that gives rise to permanent reconciling differences between the books of account maintained for UK consolidation purposes, and those used for local country reporting. The issues of revaluation of property and the lack of depreciation of hotel buildings (which are uniquely accepted in UK-GAAP) constitute areas of continual confusion. Senior finance managers must therefore ensure that appropriate compliance to both UK and local GAAP is achieved in each country.

Whilst the company's internal control manual is currently in loose-leaf binder format, thus permitting new policies to be distributed and added by the holder, the group finance manual has recently been rewritten in CD-ROM, allowing easy interrogation, easier updating and lower distribution costs.

In order to ensure effective reporting, the company has adopted English as the language of internal communication. Thus, manuals are in English; the master version of the chart of accounts, and internal audit reports are all in English. It is therefore imperative that only staff with adequate comprehension of technical English are employed in the finance function in non-English-speaking countries. Clearly, in each country, most external correspondence and compliance reporting is in the local language and thus there is also a general requirement for bilingual staff. As progress has been made in standardizing software, attempts have been made to provide local-language screen formats for junior-level accounting staff members. This, together with other obligations, constrains the choice of common computer software, as does the requirement in many of the Middle East countries for reporting and invoicing in Arabic.

The divisional office establishes reporting timetables up to five years in advance, reporting calendars are issued identifying the accounting month end. Like many other international companies Hotel 2000 NV uses a 4–4–5 week calendar ending on a Friday night. Periodically, the accounting year has to be one of 53 weeks rather than 52 weeks. All reporting entities are advised of the due dates for individual reports according to a standard number of days after the month end.

The preparation of the company's five-year strategic plan is a corporate office activity which is not delegated to hotels. However, once a year the revenue and capital budgets are prepared to tight timetables by each hotel and consolidated centrally. The process starts in month 5 of the fiscal year and is completed at a hotel level by month 9; during months 11 and 12 group approval of the budget is obtained.

During the fiscal year itself, each hotel reports a monthly standard set of numbers in local currency that quantify the monthly differences in values in each balance sheet and profit and loss account balance; hence it is referred to as the net change. Additionally, each quarter the hotel updates its forecast of full-year trading with a summarized projection of key trading variables.

From this monthly net change process, the divisional office prepares a standard suite of management reports, including a profit and loss account, full-year profit and loss projection, and cash flow projection. This is compiled and transmitted within 14 days of the hotels' closings for consolidation into the group's results.

Finally, statutory reporting is typically an annual event, although quarterly summarized information is made available to the group for eventual publication. Several hotels and cost centres may constitute a single legal entity, for which local statutory reporting obligations must be met. Such statutory accounts are developed from the same database as the management accounts. These accounts will also typically form the basis of the numbers required for tax filing, and for submission to workers' councils, supervisory boards, etc.

Infrastructure – technology

The company has computer software needs for bookkeeping, consolidation, budgeting, capital expenditure control, and cash management (Figure 13.4). There is common accounting software used across the majority of hotels, with progress being made to limit the software used elsewhere to a list of not more than two recommended packages.

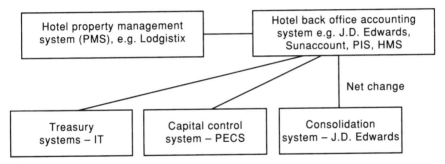

Figure 13.4   Software linkages

The accounting software J.D. Edwards Version 5.2 is installed as the workhorse for both multicurrency consolidations but also for accounting (accounts payable, general ledger) in Belgium, France, Germany, Holland, Italy and UK. The software resides on two IBM computers (AS400s), one in Brussels and one in Wiesbaden (retained to respect German requirements for books of account to be in country and in German). Elsewhere, historically, the company has extensive installed bases of the proprietary HMS accounting software (now completely unsupported), PIS and several other locally supported packages, primarily residing on stand-alone personal computers. Throughout, accounts receivable accounting is maintained on a variety of property management system software packages, principally HMS and increasingly Lodgistix. Payroll solutions are country-specific. Recently installed is a piece of software addressing capital expenditure control (PECS) which is now out in most hotels on stand-alone personal computers. In the Brussels divisional office, Excel is used exclusively for the development of projections, plans, etc., although the raw data are also maintained in J.D. Edwards.

Like the accounting infrastructure, technology is a resource that is constantly being improved upon. Several initiatives are in place. The most important is probably the development (with Systems Union) of a Hotel 2000 NV version of Sunaccount; the pilot installation of this client server-based back-office package was completed in late 1994. Client server technology is generally forecast to be the hardware platform which will become an industry standard. Thus a client-server-based software is essential for the company going forward and likely to be the company's key accounting software in the near future. Over the next five years, Hotel 2000 NV anticipates swapping the AS-400 based accounting system for a client server-based system using either Sunaccount or J.D. Edwards Version 7 (promised for 1995) throughout the division.

Second, Hotel 2000 NV is actively looking for a more suitable (relational) database software to replace J.D. Edwards as the tool of consolidation. This too is likely to be client-server based.

Thus, overall, Hotel 2000 NV would like to take advantage of the installation of the client server environment supporting Lodgistix (now established as Hotel 2000 NV's preferred property management system (PMS)) by putting in integrated business solutions that not only address PMS needs, but also accounting and office system needs in hotels.

Budgeting and planning software comes in a variety of shapes and sizes; no attempt has yet been made to standardize in-hotel office systems, with the result that projection and budget software are prepared on Symphony, the lowest common denominator, and sent out to all hotels from here. The hotel manager and controller are required to budget for each revenue and cost centre (department) in the chart of accounts and to summarize the key financial and non-financial results on the budget software. On receipt by divisional office, by modem link, leased line or simply by returning the disk, the hotel budget is uploaded. When these are combined with similarly prepared budgets for cost centres and franchise income, the divisional consolidated budget can be produced. The company regards Symphony as an outdated mechanism for budgeting and is likely to nominate Excel as the standard for all aspects of spreadsheet analysis, including budgeting, in the near future.

Extensive use is made of telecommunications; all company-managed hotels in Belgium, France, Germany, Holland, Italy and the UK access the AS400 using IBM-leased lines and elsewhere good progress is being made in installing modems to allow reporting hotels to download standardized files directly into the divisional databases.

Already, this technology infrastructure minimizes rekeying and ensures that consolidated results have in-built integrity, and may eventually almost eliminate rekeying of data. However, communications costs associated with the AS400/J.D. Edwards solution are now a significant cost to the business and Hotel 2000 NV is questioning the approach currently adopted. A possible variant would be to have intelligent terminals at each hotel for batch-processing of accounts payable and nominal ledger with dial-up facilities for uploading. Such dial-up facilities would be cheaper than the leased line (although perhaps not so secure), but the solution requires an investment in hardware at each hotel and awaits the production by J.D. Edwards of such software.

Infrastructure – human resources

The finance department in Brussels (Figure 13.5) that administers this structure is composed of the following individuals, all reporting to the Vice-president finance, legal and information technology:

- Vice-president – legal counsel.
- Director – financial control.
- Director – management information.
- Director – corporate finance.
- Director – information technology.
- Director – tax.

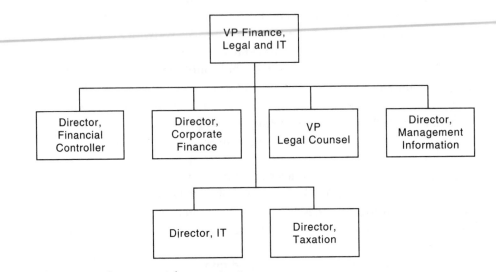

Figure 13.5   Structure of the organization

Additionally, an internal audit department is based in Brussels but, to preserve independence, the Manager does not report to the Vice-president Finance, Legal and Information Technology. This case study will not focus on the legal and information technology departments, but a short analysis of the roles in each of the other areas now follows.

The financial control function is responsible for all aspects of accounting for cost centres (except those under the directorship of the Vice-president company-managed hotels and his subordinates) ensuring full compliance with UK and other statutory requirements. Additionally, they report financial results (except those under the directorship of the Director–Management Information and his subordinates), ensuring timely and accurate reporting of historic results. Compliance with Hotel 2000 NV and group accounting policies is an important aspect of their responsibilities, as is the development of new or changed policies. As with all other staff members, they monitor cost levels and institute changes to minimize cost wherever possible, consistent with their responsibilities.

The management information group compiles, verifies, analyses and distributes regular reports on a timely basis to Hotel 2000 NV management, to include the company's management profit and projection analysis, company-managed hotel performance, overhead cost centres review, franchise hotels trading summaries and sales, marketing and frequency programmes reporting. Additionally, they compile, verify, analyse and distribute on a timely basis to company-managed hotel management, profit and loss, balance sheet and statistical summaries and including the annual budget. Furthermore, they work on regular reports for group management, to include the strategic plan and annual budget. Finally, and perhaps most importantly, they work on *ad hoc* reports, to include analysis of aspects of the business, providing management with thoughtful analysis of distribution, brand value, efficiency issues, with a view to adding to both short-term profits and long-term shareholder value (Figure 13.6).

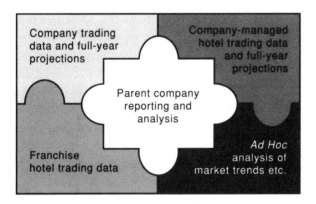

Figure 13.6   Putting it all together: management information department

The corporate finance group is concerned with several aspects of asset management. They have the skills to assess the economic viability of various proposed acquisitions and development deals. They implement and maintain appropriate controls and reporting to ensure that Hotel 2000 NV's owned and leased assets are maintained in the appropriate condition and control capital expenditure reporting. Asset management also includes responsibility for managing ongoing and new joint venture investments, with a view to maximizing shareholder value. Pan-European treasury activities aimed principally at ensuring surplus funds are invested for maximum profit commensurate with risk, are also managed by the group from Brussels. Systems are in place to ensure, for example, that surplus pesetas in Spain can be swept and swapped to provide needed lire in Italy.

Closely associated with the treasury and accounting activities is the corporate requirement for minimizing the effective tax rate, including general tax management and the optimization of the utilization of withholding taxes. In addition to these areas, the tax department is also concerned with compliance filing and with planning for all corporate taxation, including corporation tax, value-added taxes and capital taxes.

Hotel controllers are part of the management team of each hotel and thus report to the general manager of the respective establishment. Each is responsible for maintaining adequate systems of internal control over assets, liabilities, revenues and expenditures, and of reporting regularly (daily, weekly, monthly and annually) certain standard reports as established by the Hotel 2000 NV. Because not all hotel general managers are technically strong in accountancy and finance, a strong dotted-line relationship exists directly between the hotel controller and the corporate office finance staff. Hotel controllers, rather than hotel managers, will frequently call corporate office for guidance on reporting and accounting matters, as well as support for treasury or capital control matters. Additionally, to support young or less experienced hotel controllers, a network of peer groups has evolved by which informal support can be offered on a country or area basis. Finally, support to the hotel managers and controllers is offered through a regular series of balance sheet reviews, at which senior corporate finance executives conduct a half-day review of current balance sheet accounts and ensure that appropriate guidance is given. For example, the appropriate level of accrual for a cost, or the interpretation of a company policy on depreciation of a newly acquired asset, can be reviewed and agreed.

The hotel controller thus has to have the core competencies associated with compiling a comprehensive series of financial records, but the willingness to accept a considerable degree of guidance (e.g. standard chart of accounts, standard reports, standard software, standard reporting timetable) that comes from being a part of an international organization. Hotel controllers are generally unqualified accountants, although Hotel 2000 NV has supported the attainment of local qualifications in such countries as Germany and the UK. Technical training and corporate programme guidance are provided through annual controller conferences at which corporate finance staff make presentations and hotel controllers have the opportunity to question and exchange ideas.

Control cycles

Hotel 2000 NV seeks to affect financial management through a continual process of control and reporting. For the purpose of this chapter, the focus will be on the level of detail, i.e. transactions, which are monitored on the basis of elapsed time, from daily and weekly control and analysis, through monthly and annual reports (Figure 13.7).

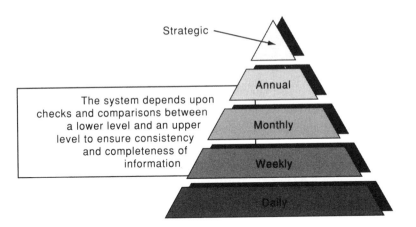

Figure 13.7 Control and reporting

Daily control and analysis

Daily control is exercised over revenue and expenditure capture and surplus cash balances (Figure 13.8).

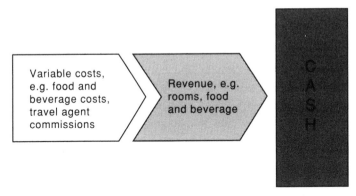

Figure 13.8 Daily aspects of financial management

Within each hotel, all revenue-generating departments record revenues earned through the Lodgistix or other PMS or one of the subsidiary point-of-sale systems that are interfaced to the PMS. Thus the restaurants, bars, leisure and telephone departments report revenue as it is earned and these values are built up in the PMS to provide a comprehensive picture of the total revenue of the business throughout the day. Room revenue is generally input to the PMS during the night so that by early morning total revenue has been captured within the systems. Wherever possible, e.g. in banquets, bars and rooms, the potential revenue can be calculated independently so that management has comfort that the revenue reported in the system is complete. The PMS incorporates an end-of-day function that closes the revenue, cash and credit entries for the day automatically but this is generally subject to additional human over-review by night audit and/or income audit functions.

Additionally, the end-of-day function includes the automated transmission of a guest daily check out record (DCO), by modem or satellite, to a data warehouse. The DCO summarizes revenues, key performance indicators, guest history summaries, guest buying patterns, source of business data, travel agent commission data, credit card commission data and corporate account data. As explained later, the corporate office in Brussels accesses this database to generate franchise fee invoices, credit card receivables and travel agent payments, and derives key marketing information for tactical promotions and effectiveness of sales and advertising programmes.

The balance sheet is adjusted by the movements on cash and accounts receivables. Revenue is recorded in the relevant revenue centre.

Hotel management has the ability either to interrogate the system directly to determine revenue, cash and credit summaries, or rely upon hard-copy reports generated in the end-of-day routines. These summaries may either already include budget variance analysis or such analysis can be added manually. The reports focus on the day just elapsed and also summarize the results for the month to date and effect a comparison to prior year results.

Thus, on a daily basis, after a review of space availability in the rooms, restaurants and banquet facilities, the daily reports produced by the PMS can identify profit opportunities in the forthcoming trading period and management will adjust the sale mechanisms (price, package, etc.) to optimize overall gross profits. For example, in periods of high demand, low-priced room categories (e.g. travel agent discount) will be closed; in periods of low demand, the banqueting room rental charge will be waived.

Expenditure capture is also exercised daily through the activities associated with goods received. As items of food, beverage or other supplies (variable costs) are received at the hotel, they are logged on a receiving report. This will normally detail the supplier and the quantities received, together with details of the underlying purchase order. With this record, together with the purchase order unit price, the hotel controller calculates the potential liability, and this will be recorded on the hotel's balance sheet. Once the invoice is delivered, the accrual and inventory values are adjusted as necessary. Completeness of expenditure capture is achieved through regular reconciliation of supplier statements to unpaid invoices, and by ensuring that the function of recording of the invoice is separated from the recording of the delivery.

Management is provided with a flash food cost report on a daily basis that discloses the percentage gross margin for the day and month to day compared to budget and prior year. This is indicative only because it does not take account of inventory movements.

The other variable cost that is controlled daily is travel agent commission. Until the evolution of the global distribution systems (GDS) bypasses them, the success of the travel agent, a key element in the promotion of the hotel, will be closely linked with the success of the business. As guests check out, the PMS records travel agent commission liability and part of the end-of-day routine is to control and validate this report.

The final aspect of financial management that is effected daily is the management of surplus cash. All cash takings are banked daily by each hotel, generally using the services of a security company. Arrangements are made with debit and credit card companies, which may account for more than 20 per cent of revenue, for electronic batch transfer of charge summaries as part of the end-of-day routine, and for daily bank transfer of receipts, net of commission due. As far as possible, electronic payment methods are in place to ensure that supplier obligations and salaries are made on the date negotiated, and not earlier.

Thus, banking arrangements are largely automated, and have been further refined to ensure that on a pan-European basis, the balances are notionally swept together for overnight investment. This activity is managed directly by the treasury manager in Brussels. Each morning, the treasury workstation, using the IT (International Treasurer) software acquired from Bank of America, electronically polls the banks around Europe and reports balances held. Decisions are made during the morning in respect of notional or actual swaps and currencies are lent or borrowed accordingly at money-market rates. For example, the need to settle contractors' works in Italy may be in excess of cash flow generated by the Italian hotels, requiring surplus Deutschmarks to be swapped into lire and lent from the German company to the Italian company.

In light of the magnitude of the values concerned, and the skill-set required, hotel management thus plays no role in cash management.

Weekly control and analysis

Hotel 2000 NV prepares weekly analyses of revenue and estimated profitability, together with updated forecasts of trading results for the current month that is in progress for all company-managed hotels. Additionally, most hotels monitor labour cost weekly.

The hotel controllers compile month-to-date reports of revenue from the PMS end of day reports, and once a week send a summarized report to

Brussels setting out key trading data for the period to date. A second part of the report revises the full-month projection of trading results under the same captions. The release of such revisions of projected trading results is approved by the management committee at each hotel in advance.

Cumulative week No. No. of weeks in month – 4 or 5 Data in US$ and local		Hotel 2000 NV Total	Analysis by			
			Country	Type of ownership	Brand	Hotel
Room revenue						
Actual						
Variance from	Budget					
	Projection					
	Last year					
Total revenue						
Actual						
Variance from	Budget					
	Projection					
	Last year					
Gross operating profit						
Actual						
Variance from	Budget					
	Projection					
	Last year					
Net operating profit						
Actual						
Variance from	Budget					
	Projection					
	Last year					
Occupancy						
Actual						
Variance from	Budget					
	Projection					
	Last year					
Average room rate						
Actual						
Variance from	Budget					
	Projection					
	Last year					
Revenue per available room (RevPAR or rooms yield)						
Actual						
Variance from	Budget					
	Projection					
	Last year					
GOP per available room						
Actual						
Variance from	Budget					
	Projection					
	Last year					

Figure 13.9   Weekly performance report

The reports are prepared in a standard file format and then either transmitted through the J.D. Edwards/IBM leased line or using a fax facility installed in the personal computer. Upon receipt of the file, Brussels management information department consolidates the files into a report, the weekly performance report (Figure 13.9).

Because this process focuses on consolidating preformatted files (i.e. files that cannot be altered by the compiler except to the extent of entering the required data), the process is largely macro-driven with little human interface. Nevertheless, there is a requirement to review the output to ensure both completeness of reporting and to identify keying errors. The report, which summarizes the situation as of the month to Friday midnight, is distributed on Monday afternoon to the managing director and team electronically, using the office local-area network that includes Excel as a spreadsheet application available to everyone. Those not connected to the system are provided with hard copies of the reports.

The report identifies potential softness (worse than budget or last year) or hardness (better than budget or last year) to the full-month projection of profitability. An analysis of the key performance indicators at each hotel enables the key trading issues to be identified. The corporate management team is thus enabled to respond immediately with support, counselling and direction to underperforming hotels, whilst encouraging further successful results from hotels trading above expectations.

The major costs at a hotel that are controllable weekly by the hotel manager are the variable costs associated with food and beverage sales, and labour cost. Labour costs are typically controlled daily by departmental management with a weekly overview provided to senior management. The reports are compiled on the basis of hours worked and total hours are then converted into full-time employees (fte) through application of the standard working week in the country concerned. This technique addresses the various categories of part-time and casual labour as well as sick leave and vacation, and provides management with the key performance indicators of department revenue per fte and estimated gross profit per fte. It is these statistics that, when taken in the context of guest comments, enable hotel management rationally to address areas of over- or under-staffing.

Monthly control and analysis

All profit and cost centres close their books on a Friday evening according to the 4–4–5 week calendar previously distributed. Whether it is using J.D. Edwards or some other software, the hotel or cost centre will make use of recurring (the same accounts are used each month) and reversing (entries made one month are reversed the following month) journals to simplify data entry, and subledgers (e.g. purchase) are, wherever possible, interfaced into the general ledger. Thus the monthly close is generally a smooth operation that can be concluded by the Tuesday evening. The draft results are presented to the hotel general manager or cost centre manager, and subject to revisions identified, the results are net changed to Brussels by the Thursday.

As explained earlier, the hotels and cost centres are accessing software residing on the same AS400 and the same software is also used for the corporate consolidation, so the net change is not from one computer to another, but from one environment on the computer to another. Those hotels and cost centres that are not using J.D. Edwards send Brussels a standard file by modem in a layout that allows for consolidation without rekeying.

In addition to the net change generated by each of the profit and cost centres (about 200 in total), a net change is generated to record franchise fee income from hotels that have entered into a franchise agreement with Hotel 2000 NV. The DCO record database is interrogated to derive readings of room revenue at each such hotel, and a fee calculation is applied based on the applicable contract. A standard journal is then generated to record the franchise fee earned and offsetting receivable, and these results are net changed for each hotel. This accountancy work is performed in Brussels, where the company's receivable function is located.

Thus, about five working days after the cost and profit centres have closed their books, the company has all the new data residing in the environment used for consolidation. This is then amalgamated into the legal entity reporting and responsibility accounting reporting. Whilst the former will be prepared in local currency, a significant challenge to the process of preparing management information is the translation by J. D. Edwards software of opening balances, year-to-date results and month results into the functional currency, which is the dollar.

The funding of all the legal entities is largely via intercompany loans. Additionally, many marketing costs, and certain other costs, e.g. insurance, are managed centrally and charged to hotels and cost centres through intercompany accounts. Finally, intercompany accounts are used to process the allocation of head office costs to the various legal entities as required by the allocation agreements (this is to ensure that tax deduction for the overhead is obtained). Thus, a critical element of the month-end process is the discipline of agreeing intercompany accounts by all parties before the books are closed in the centre. Upon consolidation, the director, financial controller will require that the net intercompany zeros out.

The system generates a trial balance that provides senior finance management with a view of the draft results for the month. Where the draft results

	Period			Actual	Cumulative		Projection	Full year protection	
Actual	Budget Variance	Prior Year Variance			Budget Variance	Prior Year Variance		Budget Variance	Prior Year Variance
Hotel 2000 NV									
Monthly management accounts summary									
Revenue									
Owned and leased hotels									
Managed hotels									
Franchise hotels									
Other									
Current operations									
Development									
Exchange variance									
Hotel 2000 NV consolidated revenue									
Operating profits									
Owned and leased hotels									
Managed hotels									
Franchise hotels									
Other									
Sub total									
Overheads									
Current operations									
Development									
Non-recurring items									
Exchange variance									
Hotel 2000 profit before interest and tax									

Figure 13.10 Monthly management accounts summary

appear to throw off unexplained variances to budget or prior year, the hotel controller or cost centre accountant will be challenged. Any resultant adjustments will be net changed and the final results now run. Importantly, therefore, those responsible for the consolidation process do not normally make entries in any environment other than their own; this ensures that adjustments are owned by the custodians of the books, not corporate office.

The monthly results for Hotel 2000 NV are then transmitted in a standard file format to the parent company for consolidation.

The suite of monthly reports is then generated and distributed. The management information department compiles and distributes:

1. Profit before interest and tax and projection analysis (Figure 13.10).
2. Company-managed hotel performance.
3. Overhead cost centres review.
4. Franchise hotels trading summaries.
5. Sales, marketing & frequency programme reports.
6. Key performance indicators.
7. Benchmark analysis.

Each suite of reports is accompanied by a short written overview of key issues and analysis of variances.

Additionally, the financial control department, supported by corporate finance, completes the suite of monthly reports, including:

1. Working capital movements.
2. Debt/interest schedules.
3. Capital expenditure.
4. Cash flow forecast.
5. Balance sheet.

For the preparation of these analyses, corporate office receives additional reporting from hotel and cost centre controllers as appropriate.

Once the month-end reporting is complete, all controllers prepare balance sheet account reconciliations which form the basis of journal entry corrections in the following month.

Financial briefings are given to the company's board of management by the vice-president finance, legal & information technology each month; additionally a presentation is made by the vice-president of key financial data to the monthly meeting attended by all corporate office employees. Similar presentations are made to each hotel executive committee and staff by hotel controllers. Thus the company achieves full dissemination of key performance data on a regular basis.

Annual control and analysis

Processes are in place to ensure that Hotel 2000 NV addresses certain issues at least annually. These include audit of internal control systems, the preparation of statutory filings of accounts and tax returns, preparation of operating and capital budgets and reviews of tax and treasury structures. It would be misleading, however, to suggest that these processes are only conducted once during any 12-month period. Rather, the reader should understand that the focus of these processes is longer-term and more occasional.

The focuses of the internal audit function are twofold – to give assurance to the group audit committee that the company's internal control systems can be relied upon and to provide services that add value to Hotel 2000 NV management. The latter might include the review of repair and maintenance expenditure to ensure that value for money is being obtained. On the basis of an annual assessment of risk, a programme of audits is developed. Each audit is preceded by the agreement of a scope of audit. As the audit work is completed, an exit meeting is conducted at which management respond to the points that have arisen and commit themselves to address the weaknesses identified within a given time frame. A monthly status report of outstanding audit points is circulated to Hotel 2000 NV management and the group audit committee (Figure 13.11).

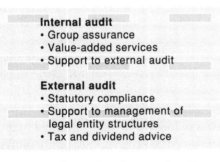

Internal audit
- Group assurance
- Value-added services
- Support to external audit

External audit
- Statutory compliance
- Support to management of legal entity structures
- Tax and dividend advice

Figure 13.11 Internal and external audit

External audit is engaged to meet statutory requirements and, increasingly, to support Hotel 2000 NV in meeting its tax reporting obligations. Hotel 2000 NV meets with the coordinating partner of the audit firm in mid year to plan the audit work required in each country at year-end external

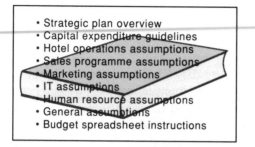

- Strategic plan overview
- Capital expenditure guidelines
- Hotel operations assumptions
- Sales programme assumptions
- Marketing assumptions
- IT assumptions
- Human resource assumptions
- General assumptions
- Budget spreadsheet instructions

Figure 13.12   Budget instructions

audit. This meeting will determine the extent to which internal audit can support external audit. As far as possible, the external auditors work with documents and summaries prepared by the client. Increasingly, they audit directly against files generated by the J.D. Edwards software. Once the audit is completed, an exit meeting with the vice-president finance, legal and information technology establishes the internal control weaknesses identified.

Tax and treasury skills are applied to dividend policy proposals for each legal entity. Work then commences on preparing the statutory filings throughout the company. Since the parent company Hotel 2000 NV has more than 50 subsidiaries, this work has been largely contracted out to the audit firm, although there is still a need for the various company annual general meetings, directors' resolutions, etc. to be arranged and documented by the company's officers.

The annual budget exercise commences in month 6 of the fiscal year with the production of a revenue budget booklet (Figure 13.12), in which are detailed instructions, guidelines and a timetable. The budget is prepared in the context of HOTEL 2000 NV's strategic plan; budget-holders are provided with an overview of principal strategic initiatives that will influence trading, together with a review of prospects for key economies.

The capital expenditure plans are conceived centrally with a view to supporting the general strategic direction. Individual hotels compete for the allocation of maintenance capital (funds required to maintain profitability, as opposed to expansion capital being funds designed to increase profitability). Maintenance capital needs are compared to levels of depreciation. Maintenance capital is allocated to elements of the business that can demonstrate the highest shareholder value or earnings potential, or which can be demonstrated to be defensive of shareholder value or earnings. Thus, a hotel that can demonstrate that improved shareholder value can be gained by acquiring the televisions rather than leasing them will be allocated funds in priority to a hotel that wishes to redecorate a two-year-old restaurant but cannot demonstrate any profit improvement.

The hotel operations budgets are focused on improving earnings by looking at ways of improving trading results against benchmark key performance indicators and also improving guest satisfaction. The sales and marketing initiatives aimed at improving revpar and business mix are detailed, with assumptions as to how these will impact hotels.

With information technology becoming a dominant mechanism for improving operating performance, guidelines are provided as to how improvements and initiatives can be expected to impact hotel performance. Consistency in salary budget assumptions is assured through the provision of central instructions. Levels of investment in training are also established in the budget instructions.

The hotels and cost centres are provided with a diskette containing the budget software and instructions on its use. The completed diskette is due back in the Brussels office by early month 8. It is then loaded into a J.D. Edwards ledger in which the budget is constructed. Several levels of review are completed before the managing director reviews a first consolidation of the budget in early month 9. After any further refinements, the budget is forwarded to group headquarters in mid-month 9. A meeting with group executives is scheduled for early month 10 to review the budget proposal for Hotel 2000 NV and, after any further changes, the budget is incorporated into the parent group budget during month 11. This final budget will include a cash flow and balance sheet budget as well as the profit and loss account budget.

Hotel general managers and their teams work against a bonus plan that is targeted at budgeted GOP (gross operating profit, also known as income (profit) before fixed charges). Hotel 2000 NV group executives work against a bonus plan that is targeted at budgeted cash flow and budgeted profit after tax and interest.

Each major element of capital expenditure is subject to an annual postcompletion review which determines whether the project has been completed on budget and whether the incremental profit impact has been achieved. The lessons learnt from the project are documented.

Conclusion

This chapter has examined the bases of financial management in a complex international organization. Critical areas of success, such as proper capitalization of local legal entities, management of investment balances in joint ventures, financial appraisal of expansion projects, restructuring to minimize effective tax rates, have not been addressed. Not only are the topics technically complex – each solution is typically unique.

In addition, this chapter has excluded areas already covered in this book, e.g. the application of key performance indicators, the support to marketing that finance offers, the development of the people involved in financial management.

Instead, focus has been made on the essential foundations for successful financial management – a combination of accounting standards, technological infrastructure and human resources that will be different in its elements in any single case study. What is, however, unchanging is the necessity of the senior managers continually to question the structure and to implement appropriate changes.

Useful addresses

Bank of America NT & SA, 26 Elmfield Road, Bromley, Kent BR1 1WA, UK.

BDO Hospitality Consulting, Hotel Industry Benchmark Reports (monthly and annual), 8 Baker St, London W1M 1DA, UK.

J.D. Edwards, 8055 E Tufts Avenue, Denver, Col 80237, USA.

HMS, Holiday Inn Worldwide, 101 rue Neerveld, 1200 Brussels, Belgium.

Lotus Development Corporation (dba Lotus Symphony), 55 Cambridge Parkway, Cambridge, MA 02142, USA.

Microsoft Corporation (dba Excel), One Microsoft Way, Redmond, WA 98052, USA.

Norton Waugh Computing Ltd. (dba PECS), The Old School, Weston under Lizard, Shifnal, Shropshire TF11 8SZ, UK.

Pannell Kerr Forster Associates, Hotel Industry Benchmark Reports (monthly and annual), New Garden House, 78 Hatton Garden, London EC1N 8JA, UK.

PIS, PO Box 53015, Riyadh, Kingdom of Saudi Arabia.

Sulcus (dba Logistix), 3875 N 44th Street, Suite 200, Phoenix AZ 85018, USA.

Systems Union (doing business as Sunaccount), Northampton Lodge, Canonbury Square, London, N1 2AN, UK.

HMS, Holiday Inn Worldwide, 101 rue Neerveld, 1200 Brussels, Belgium.

Uniform System of Accounts for Hotels, 8th edn (1986) Hotel Association of New York City, 40 West 38th Street, New York, NY 10018, USA.

14 Financial management implications of hotel management contracts: a UK perspective

Howard M. Field

Introduction

This chapter focuses on the impact on management structures and objectives, and the relationships between owners and operators, arising from the growth in hotel management contracts in the UK and internationally.

For an area which has provided the basis of such a great part of the development of the hotel industry over the past 30 years, and is performing an even more important role in the 1990s, there has been remarkably little published research into the impact of management contracting within the hotel sector.

This chapter approaches the subject from an essentially practical viewpoint, complemented by references from available published material, and with the aim of summarizing key considerations of parties to such arrangements, and to provide an informative guide.

It is based on experience which includes:

- Direct involvement in operations being managed under such agreements.
- Evaluation of proposals for management of a variety of hotels by established groups and independent operators.
- Assistance to parties, including those such as banks, who became enforced owners during recent economic crises.

- Designing management agreements suitable for short-term recovery requirements.
- Formulating terms for management contracts for non-hotel-industry experienced owners, lenders and investors.
- Comparing competitive proposals for existing and new projects.
- Assessing values of hotels operated under management contracts.
- Monitoring the performance of hotels operated under management contracts.
- Administering the owning entities of hotels owned by non-industry investors, operated on their behalf by hotel management companies.
- Arbitration in respect of disputes arising between parties to such agreements.
- Lecturing on the subject to undergraduates and postgraduate students studying for UK and international hospitality management degrees, and to professional accountants within the hotel industry.

Ownership and operation of hotels

To place into context the emergence of the hotel management contract, the starting point is a review of who owns hotels and an examination of the nature of the hotel as a physical asset.

There are several types of owners. They can generally be categorized as one of the following:

1. *Corporate and commercial hotel operators* – including hotel companies such as Hilton/Conrad International, Hyatt, Marriott, Forte, Accor, New World/Ramada; or conglomerates with hotel divisions, such as Bass/Holiday Inn, Seibu Saison/InterContinental, ITT/Sheraton, Ladbroke/Hilton International.
2. *Individuals/state* – the typical owner/operator; family trusts; wealthy entrepreneurs; heads of state, public, government or parastatal organizations; local authorities.
3. *Property developers* – who, for example, may have included a hotel in a multiuse scheme for strategic or planning purposes, and who may be short- or long-term portfolio owners.
4. *Financial institutions* – banks; development and venture capital funds; insurance companies; pension funds.

To consider the asset itself, a hotel comprises a site, a building, plant and equipment, furniture and operating inventories.

The site can comprise land either dedicated to the hotel, or encompassing other properties which incorporate or complement the hotel. In the latter cases, examples would be office/retail complexes in which the hotel is located, or golf/leisure/resort complexes with a hotel element.

The form of the owner's interest in the assets can vary significantly, and may include:

1. *Freehold* – that is outright, with all the related benefits and obligations.
2. *Leasehold* – as the landlord of a property leased to a tenant, giving limited residual obligations, with the tenant liable to maintain and restore the ownership at the end of the lease; the owner relies on receipt of the rental income.
3. *Security/trustee* – such as a financial lessor, a lender whose loan is in default, or as a trustee on behalf of other parties.

A combination of these elements can exist for any one hotel, such that the land may have a landlord who receives a ground rent. The building may be owned by a property fund which pays the ground rent, and which then leases the hotel building to the operator. The furniture and equipment may be separately owned by a financing institution, which rents them to the operator.

Occasionally, a hotel may have more than one operator. This can arise if certain facilities are under separate management from the main accommodation business. Examples might be where there is a casino, a leisure club, a golf course, a marina, an exhibition centre. Some hotels have restaurants or night clubs which are operated independently from the core hotel.

It can therefore be seen that hotel ownership does not necessarily mean the same as operating the business. And there can be several owners or operators involved in the elements of one hotel. Highlighting the distinction between owning and operating and the operator's role in managing the business of the hotel leads to further consideration of the nature of the relationship between the owner and the operator, and to identifying the factors which influenced the emergence of the hotel management contract.

The emergence of the hotel management contract

Rapid growth of national hotel chains took place in the USA during the 1950s and 1960s. At the same time, international expansion was taking place. The original US household-name groups such as Hilton, Sheraton, InterContinental, Holiday Inn, Hyatt and similar groups emerged as market leaders, and as strong brands which attracted guest loyalty and high-profile recognition in their chosen locations. This not only generated momentum from within the companies, to grow their chains and to compete with the others, but also created interest from new parties to participate in the opportunities to profit from this sector. Communities, cities and countries wanted their prestige hotels. Investors and developers wanted to get in on the act and to benefit from the inclusion of chain-operated hotels in their portfolios, and the ability to invest directly in this growth business.

Hotels involve real estate. In this period, and in subsequent economic cycles, hotels have been seen as providing secure property assets, together with income streams that generally at least keep pace with inflation. For many, they create an image of glamorous properties in glamorous locations, and therefore not surprisingly, owning hotels is often seen as an attractive proposition. Hotels are costly to build; they are complex businesses, requiring knowledge of technology and craft skills, and of marketing and professional management in specialist areas.

In order to address the varying interests of owners, operators, investors, lenders, communities and many other parties in the development of the hotel sector, an arrangement was needed which incorporated the elements required to create an effective commercial relationship. The factors which emerged provided the basis for a new way to achieve the objectives of the interested parties – the hotel management contract. These can be summarized as:

- Formation of professional hotel management groups, offering marketing strength, brand names, buying power, systems and procedures, project design and management, technical services, training and management development.
- Owners' need for experienced and established operators, for their own peace of mind, and to satisfy investors or lenders.
- Operating companies' desire to expand; reduction of the exposure to the investment and political risks of national and international expansion.
- Enhancement of the infrastructure for tourism and international commerce; political prestige for the developing regions and countries.
- Recognition of the separate interests of property and operations of hotels; the emergence of more sophisticated investors.

What is a hotel management contract?

There is no standard definition, but the following incorporates Eyster (1988). 'A hotel management contract is a formal arrangement under which the owner of a hotel employs the services of an operator to act as his agent to provide professional management of the hotel, in return for a fee. The operator assumes full responsibility for the management of the business, in the name of the owner. Under such an arrangement the ultimate legal and financial responsibilities and rights of ownership of the property, its furniture and equipment, its working capital and the benefit of its profits (or burden of its losses) remain those of the owner.'

Before examining how the management agreement is formulated, it is useful to highlight alternative forms of operation of hotels.

One choice open to an owner is self operation, either where the owner is also the manager of the business, or where the owner employs his or her own manager and staff, but maintains a master-and-servant relationship. Managers and staff can be hired or fired, and how they work is directly controlled by the owner. An alternative choice is leasing to an operator, where the owner depends on the operator to pay the agreed rent, but has no involvement in the business itself. A third choice is contracting with a management company; this option is explored in more detail in this chapter.

The operator's choices mirror those of the owner, with the general observation that the greatest risk/rewards arise from direct ownership. The least risk, but not necessarily the lowest rewards, is derived from the management contract.

In either case, consideration has to be given as to whether the hotel business is to be operated wholly independently, or with affiliation to consortia or referral systems for reservations, marketing, purchasing or other purposes. Also important is whether the hotel will be 'hard-branded' with a recognized name on the door, or 'soft-branded' with a chain affiliation attached to its own name. An example of the former would be a Holiday Inn (such as the Holiday Inn, Kings Cross, London), and of the latter the Hyatt Carlton Tower, London. The considerations surrounding the question of branding could occupy a chapter of their own. Franchising is a related subject, which will not be explored here.

In the context of management contracts, it is relevant to state that most such arrangements are driven by the need for a hotel to enjoy both the benefits of professional management and the strength of a referral system or brand. It is particularly these marketing advantages which can add value to the business compared to an independent, self-operated property.

A management contract agreement requires there to be a formalized structure incorporating the rights and obligations of the parties. Five key aspects covered in a hotel management contract are explained below.

Operators' services and obligations

These will generally cover the complete range of management, marketing, personnel, accounting, purchasing, maintenance and whatever is required to operate on a day-to-day basis, keep the asset in good condition and comply with agreed standards, and required legal or statutory obligations of a hotel business manager. Reporting, forecasting and other responsibilities will be spelled out, together with operating and maintenance standards. Any restrictions to be placed on the manager and those areas where the owner's consent must be obtained will be identified. Examples of the latter might include changing the general manager, changing the name of the hotel and entering into long-term contracts.

Owners' obligations and rights

The most common obligation sought by the operator from an owner is to leave all aspects of the operation to the discretion of the operator. The principal right of the owner will be to receive the net cash flow generated by the hotel. Generally, provision is made for all known liabilities and for management fees payable before any cash is payable to the owner. The owner is normally responsible to ensure that there is adequate working capital and that funds are provided for agreed capital expenditure. There may be privileges available to the owner for accommodation and services, but this is surprisingly uncommon. The terms applying to the calculation of profits and cash available will be set out.

Term of the agreement and renewal options

The most common form of agreement preferred by the operating companies has in the past provided for anything from 15 to 25 years, with renewal options, often in favour only of the operator, which can be infinite.

Recent experience, and the circumstances which have arisen principally through recession and financial defaults, has shown that entering into management contracts for as little as a few months can be possible. There are very few long-term agreements currently being signed. Owners, especially those whose concern is focused on investment return and capital value issues, have become better educated about the nature of such agreements. In order to preserve flexibility to optimize the return from the asset, they prefer the opportunity to test the market for their property rather than be locked into a longer-term agreement with one operator. The owner may wish to sell outright, free of the operating arrangement – or to invite competitive bids for the management agreement in order to improve his or her share of the profits.

Defaults and termination provisions

Provisions leading to penalties or termination usually fall into categories of failure to perform in accordance with the agreement; financial failure of one of the parties; or changes in the ownership of a party to the original agreement. Depending on whether the defaults are self-induced or have arisen indirectly, there are often 'cure' periods, failing which the agreement terminates. Should such an event occur, and especially if a brand-name operator or hotel is involved, there may be provisions for the removal of signs, badged items and brand-related equipment. It may also become necessary for the general manager and other key staff to be removed or replaced.

Costs and penalties can be significant, and agreements in general reflect the reluctance of the parties to give up their rights without adequate compensation. There are many examples where high awards have been made to settle the loss of future fee potential to the operator; conversely, there have been some cases where an operator has been forced to write off fees or suffer damages.

Operator fee basis

Over the years when operators wrote their own terms for fees, the norm was for a percentage of gross revenues, up to 5% being common, together with an incentive based on a percentage of a defined profit level. This latter was usually described as the gross operating profit (GOP), more recently termed income before fixed charges (IBFC), and the incentive averaged around 10 per cent. The informed operator required the revenue and incentive fee elements to be calculated separately, with both to be charged after IBFC profit. A variation is for the revenue-based fee to be deducted before calculating the incentive fee.

Owners and competitive operators gradually reduced the level of fees, or introduced greater performance-related incentives and gearing to the operators' earnings. It is now possible to find examples where no fee is payable until certain profit levels are achieved; or no fee is payable until a defined cash flow is produced; or the operator guarantees a minimum return to the owner; or the operator receives only a base fixed fee.

In general, operators like to secure their base fee by reference to revenues, enabling them to enjoy the benefits of increases achieved both by inflation and growth of business volumes. The owner's interests are first, to ensure there is enough cash to pay interest and meet any other financial obligations, and then to achieve a combination of income and capital growth from the profits.

If a hotel is particularly attractive, perhaps because of its location or prestige (for example, the Lanesborough at Hyde Park Corner, London) the owner is in a strong position to secure an operator on very keen terms. In other situations, such as in a remote location, or where a hotel has been developed as part of the infrastructure in a location where there is no established market, the owner may have to allow for a generous fee formula to attract the right operator.

The variety of agreement terms now encountered reflects the evolution and adaptation of the principles to fit the aims and objectives of the parties in a range of circumstances. It is difficult today to define the norm for fee terms, without careful analysis of the parties and their particular circumstances.

Other management agreement provisions required will cover:

- Preopening phase for a new hotel.
- Technical services.
- Marketing/sales/advertising arrangements.
- Reservations networks.
- Brand names/franchises.
- Purchasing.
- Training and recruitment.
- Employee benefits.
- Accounting, systems and audit.
- Operating and capital budgets.
- Maintenance and repair standards.
- Working capital, profits and losses.
- Disputes and arbitration procedures.

Accounting and financial issues

The provisions of hotel management contracts concentrate heavily on operational management and marketing issues. However, the principal parties are at the end of the day concerned about the economic results of the business, and their respective rewards. A balance of objectives between the owner and the operator has to be reflected in financial terms.

As stated earlier, the operator generally seeks a basic remuneration for providing professional management services, normally related to revenue, and an element of incentive related to a share of the profits. The owner's financial concerns are usually to achieve an adequate cash flow from the operation to fund working capital and financing obligations and to produce an acceptable return on the investment. It is in the owner's interests to seek to achieve the best combination of operator and fee structure to optimize the return from his or her investment. The choice of the right operator is as important as the fee structure, as in the end the added value of the operator's effectiveness has to be greater than the cost of the fees if the owner is to derive benefit from the arrangement.

To address the financial objectives, management agreements incorporate provisions to cover the remuneration of the operator, the provision of funds by the owner, accounting and reporting standards, and the treatment of cash flow.

Accounting is generally the responsibility of the operator, at least for all aspects of the day to day operation of the hotel and compliance with requirements for sales, value-added tax (VAT), payroll and related taxes and administration. Owners may retain the balance of the accounting details for the property, and the owning entity and its financing, or they may build this responsibility into the agreement with the operator. The latter basis may well apply where the operator is a partner or shareholder with the owner. The minimum will be for the operator to compile a full set of management accounts and a balance sheet with cash, bought and sales ledger control account, stock and an owners' current account. Books of account suitable for compliance with the local business legislation have to be maintained, and computerized hotel systems will sometimes have to be supplemented to enable both management and financial accounting needs to be met.

Information and communications systems are normally computerized. Management agreements need to identify the level of authority and obligations of the operator in respect of major systems, so that it is clear who has the rights over hardware, software and the database. Technology implications were not an issue when early contracts were written. Now, the complexity of technology and its relationship with communications, reservations and other aspects such as fire, security, health, safety and in-house entertainment applications require consideration when establishing appropriate management agreement terms.

Reporting standards and frequency have to be agreed. Most hotel operators will have a procedure to produce periodic management accounts at least on a monthly basis. Good practice will ensure that these are available before the end of the next accounting period, and the more sophisticated systems will ensure that the data are available within as little as one to five days from the end of the relevant period. Owners are generally entitled to copies of these accounts within, say, 20 days of the period end, to give time for management review and comment.

The format of the hotel's accounts is traditionally driven by the standards of the operator. For most, this means use of the Uniform System of Accounts for Hotels. Many owners are unfamiliar with the detail formats, but the management agreement will tend to refer directly to profit, cost and related terminology derived directly from the Uniform System. One major advantage to the owner of acceptance of this format is the ability to compare the hotel's results with industry trends compiled and published by international hotel industry consultants.

Budgeting and forecasting provide the basis for establishing the operator's targets and the expected profitability and cash flows. From these, together with standards for inventory holding, credit policy, supplier payment frequency and other related balance sheet aspects, the hotel's working capital needs can be established. Generally, it is the obligation of the owner to ensure that there is adequate working capital available to the operator.

Provisions have to be made for the frequency of audits, the arrangements for internal and external audits and reasonable access to the books and records by the owner's representatives. In addition, practical matters such as the bank accounts to be maintained, whose signatures are permitted on cheques, and whether bank accounts are to be maintained in credit or with overdraft facilities, need to be addressed in the agreement. On the basis that profits are made, and the cash flow is positive, provisions then have to be agreed as to how often, and on what basis, the operator passes available surplus cash to the owner.

Careful definition of the treatment of certain expenditure on items such as major repairs, asset additions and replacements is required to ensure both parties understand their obligations as to the provisions of finance to cover these, and what will be the resulting accounting implications. Operators will want to exclude as much as possible from the expenditure, which will impact the profit level on which incentives are based. The owner will have both this and considerations such as tax and external reporting standards to address.

The above points illustrate the necessity for a comprehensive approach to the agreement when covering key areas of concern between the owner and operator as to how the hotel operation will be controlled and accounted for.

On the principle that the operator is running the business as the agent of the owner, the contract provisions must ensure the operator maintains adequate controls and records for the business. The owner must be able to rely on the accuracy and timeliness of reports and accounts, to be able to monitor the performance of the business and fluctuations in working capital and cash flow, particularly so that financing obligations can be met.

The operator will have to address accounting implications for the fees earned and other payments receivable. Key issues for the operator include the frequency and basis of calculation of the fees (basic fees tend to be earned based on monthly or periodic results; incentive fees may be based on cumulative results, or on year-end results). What happens in periods where there are operating losses needs to be considered, as well as how failure to achieve agreed performance standards is to be treated, if this has a bearing on the amount of fees earned; also, how and when fees are payable. Calculating fees earned is one stage in the process. Dealing with payment of the fees earned can be complex. Operators prefer to have the right to deduct their fees from the hotel's operating accounts and to make payments to themselves, in the same way as for any routine supplier.

Problems can arise if there is insufficient cash available. Maintaining relationships with suppliers, and the need to keep payroll and related taxes up to date and to ensure the continuity of the operation, often result in management fee payments having to be delayed where cash flow is tight. At what point such late payments give rise to interest or are recognized as defaults between the owner and operator should be addressed in the management agreement, and disagreements can arise as to whether the circumstances have been contributed to by the actions of the operator or external influences outside the operator's control. Where the owner is unable to honour financial commitments, the operator is faced with both the problems of collecting amounts due, and the potential loss of goodwill if the hotel is unable to meet its normal trading obligations and is known publicly to be in trouble. For overseas operations, additional issues such as those relating to currency fluctuations, exchange control, withholding taxes and the impact of VAT all add to the complexity of accounting for and control of management fees.

There are also situations where expenses are recoverable by the operator in addition to fees earned. These might include the travel expenses of specialist executives visiting the hotel to carry out inspections or project work. Sometimes the operator has a purchasing role, which can result in the generation of balances due for items purchased and supplied by the operator's company. Provisions as to how these charges are to be authorized and supported, and for the resulting debts to be paid, must be covered. Disputes can arise over charging rates and margins applied by the operator, and it is common for balances of amounts due to the operator to build up if an approval system for the charges and their payment has not been considered or operated routinely.

Certain operational costs to be recharged to the hotel, or to which the hotel contributes, which are in addition to the management fees but which form part of the operating arrangement, such as group sales and marketing contributions, central reservations and franchise royalties, are generally made the subject of separate contractual arrangements. If the operator is involved in preopening activities for a new hotel, a whole structure of how these costs are budgeted, how expenditure is to be controlled and accounted for, and how the costs are to be reimbursed to the operator, needs to be established.

There may be the need for the operator to provide owners with detailed accounts for expenses to which the hotel has contributed for a chainwide shared service. Often the owner has the right to representation, as a chain member, to a committee of owner representatives which influences the decision as to the level of expenditure to be borne by chain-operated properties. In addition, the operator might make local contributions to such costs to support its competitive market position.

In the larger hotel groups, especially those with worldwide operations, senior financial managers can be fully employed in controlling and accounting for chainwide programmes. The control of the collection of fees and other payments due to the operator can be a significant task within the operator's head office organization.

It can be seen that there are many complexities to be considered by the operator to ensure that these elements are all handled effectively. Recent UK hotel company corporate collapses (notably Queens Moat Houses and Resort Hotels) have exposed the importance of establishing appropriate accounting policies. This is especially the case where fees earned and other balances due to the operator have not been received, and where there is doubt about the hotel owner's financial stability.

The uniform system and management fees

As referred to earlier, the most widely used source of terminology relating to accounting issues in hotel management contracts is the Uniform System of Accounts for Hotels. This format of departmental hotel management accounts was established by the Hotel Association of New York City in 1926. The latest edition, the eighth, was published in 1986. Whilst reflecting practices and standards largely derived from US companies, the system has been adopted worldwide within the hotel industry. It is probably more widely accepted than any other industry-based standard accounting format. Not surprisingly, given its origins and continued existence and development, and the preponderance of US hotel management companies, many of the definitions and terms used in management agreements can be traced directly to the Uniform System. Indeed, it is common to see reference to the Uniform System as the standard for the production of management accounts by the operator for the owner of a hotel.

It should be recognized that, although for USA purposes much of the profit and loss and balance sheet will comply with US–GAAP (generally accepted accounting principles), this will not generally be the case elsewhere. Even if the Uniform System is acceptable for management accounting purposes, there will usually have to be a complementary system for the production of financial accounts for local compliance.

	£000
Operating departments – revenue	
Rooms	2,000
Food and beverage	1,500
Telephone	250
Garage and parking	50
Guest laundry	50
Other operated departments	100
Rentals and other income	20
Total revenue	3,970
Operating departments – income	
Rooms	1,500
Food and beverage	450
Telephone	100
Other	170
Total operating departments income	2,220
Undistributed operating expenses	
Administrative and general	240
Data processing	50
Human resources	50
Transportation	50
Marketing	120
Guest entertainment	60
Energy costs	170
Property operation and maintenance	160
Total undistributed operating expenses	900
Income before management fees and fixed charges	1,320
Management fees (see Figures 14.2 and 14.3)	
Rent, taxes and insurance	300
Interest expense	50
Depreciation and amortization	150
	500
Income before income taxes	820
Income tax	300
Net income	520

Figure 14.1 Hotel operating statement

The key factors common to most management agreements will be the definitions of revenue and profit for base and incentive fee calculations. Standards for the treatment of major repairs, replacement and renewals and capital expenditure will usually be addressed separately, as the Uniform System does not prescribe these. Essentially, the Uniform System concentrates on a responsibility accounting approach for the operating departments of the hotel, allocating sales, direct costs of sales and departmental payroll and expenses to the main profit centres; allocating payroll and direct expenses to each of the main service/overhead departments; and detailing as fixed expenses such items as rent, depreciation, financing and taxes, the latter being considered as outside the operating management's control, and as non-operational costs (Figure 14.1).

As indicated earlier, traditionally the operating profit level was called gross operating profit (GOP), a term still seen in many management agreements. In the eighth edition of the Uniform System, this level of profit has become income before management fees and fixed charges (IBFC), (Figure 14.2). A line item for management fees is now shown as a cost below what was the GOP level.

		£000	
Base fee	5% Total revenue	198	(5% of £3,970)
Incentive fee	10% Income before management fees and fixed charges	132	(10% of £1,320)
Total management fees		330	

Figure 14.2   Management fee calculation: alternative 1

Commonly the base fee is calculated at levels of between 3 and 5 per cent of revenue, and the incentive element at between 5 and 10 per cent of IBFC. Variations of the incentive element include application of the agreed percentage to profit after the achievement of a minimum level or IBFC, or to profit after deduction of part or all of the interest costs and/or depreciation. Sometimes actual capital expenditure or an allowance for such expenditure becomes a deduction from IBFC before the incentive fee applies (Figure 14.3).

		£000	
Base fee	5% Total revenue	198	(5% of £3,970)
Incentive fee	10% Income after base management fee, before fixed charges	112	(10% of £1,320 less 198)
Total management fees		310	

Figure 14.3   Management fee calculation: alternative 2

Management implications

The growth of management contracts has resulted in a whole range of implications for both hotel managers and financial managers. A number of relationships are affected by the existence of such contracts.

For instance, guests and customers, who need not be aware of the arrangement, may encounter the consequences when, for example, establishing credit, making insurance claims, negotiating terms. There may be participation in chainwide promotional schemes which have to be honoured by a managed hotel.

Staff of the hotel will normally be employees of the owner. Operating companies do not wish to accept the statutory and legal obligations which arise from being the employer, and the owner may need the flexibility to switch operators without the complications of having to re-employ the staff. The employees will have to be made aware of the legal position, and their employment contracts will specify who is their employer as well as to whom they report for management purposes. It is however common for the general manager, and sometimes the financial controller, to be specified as being employees of the operator. In these cases, the employment costs are recharged by the management company to the operation. Operating companies have to establish how chainwide career and benefit programmes apply at hotels which are separately owned. Owners will need to be involved in any cumulative or longer-term employee programmes such as pension arrangements and the relevant cost and funding implications.

It may be specified by the owner that some right of refusal is retained in respect of the senior management appointments. Enlightened owners also prefer management agreements to have some limitation on the operator employing management or staff at pay rates, or granting pay increases, which can be shown to be in excess of local norms. Internationally, operators are sometimes restricted as to those positions which can be filled by non-local employees.

Suppliers may need to be aware that the operator for a particular hotel is agent for the owner and not liable in his or her own name. Problems often arise because suppliers assume an operator whose name is familiar is the party with whom they are contracting.

Professional advisers for a hotel operated under a management agreement will generally be well aware of the relationships of the parties. However, the managers may have to deal with additional professionals as there will often be those acting for the owner as well as those acting for the operator.

Banks and other financial parties should also be well aware of the arrangement, but there are many levels of day-to-day contact which may blur the distinction between the owner's affairs and the operating of the hotel.

Personal contacts with the hotel can be numerous and confusing to management. Apart from executives from the operating company, there may be representatives from their key advisers, suppliers, customers or the like, who have to be accorded due recognition. Then there will be contacts derived from the owner's organization and relationships, which can often introduce a whole range of people needing to be accommodated, sometimes literally, by the hotel management. Apart from necessary business contacts, it can be surprising how many friends or relatives, shareholders or others, claiming connections with the owner deem themselves entitled to attention and favours.

An important role has been created for industry-experienced professionals with the relevant expertise to act as the owner's representative or as an independent adviser, to oversee the operation of the management contract and to balance the interests of the parties to the arrangement. In the case of disputes, arbitration by knowledgable and experienced professionals is often preferred to complex and expensive litigation.

Having encountered and dealt with many of these relationships, it is possible to make some observations about the impact and ongoing evolution of hotel management contracts for operators and managers.

For instance, management contracts for a long time largely reflected the drive of hotel operators to expand, taking advantage of the marginal costs of adding a managed hotel, and the reduced investment risk involved. The operators said: 'We will manage; build the hotel this way; these are our terms; we will decide how long we will stay'.

However, there is now more competition for locations between operators, and there are also more sophisticated owners of hotels. In future, the owner is likely to be the party who drives the terms of the management contract, ensuring there is greater obligation on the operator to perform, and that there is more flexibility to change operator if necessary. He or she will say: 'You manage; this is my project, and any changes must be justified; these are the terms I will accept; if you want to stay, you must meet the agreed performance criteria.'

The rate of growth in number of independent management companies has increased, although not yet internationally. These include groups which are not themselves part of established chains, and which operate for a variety of owners. They may eventually emerge as recognized companies with stock market attractions in their own rights.

Hotel general managers will have to respond to the additional challenges of representing the flag for the operator, and successfully and profitably managing the unit for the owner. Managers will bear a greater share of the risk involved than would be the case for only one master. Unit managers will also have to understand both the owner's and the operator's objectives for the hotel. Short-term recovery; rebadging; changes of owner – all are examples of factors which will have an impact on the manager's responsibilities.

In essence, as a result of all of these challenges, the successful manager of a hotel operated under a management contract is likely to possess a far more well-rounded business background than many of his or her industry colleagues.

References

Eyster, J.J. (1988) *The Negotiation and Administration of Hotel and Restaurant Management Contracts*, 3rd edn., School of Hotel Administration, Cornell University, Ithaca.

Hotel Association of New York City (1986) *Uniform System of Accounts for Hotels*, 8th edn. New York: Hotel Association of New York City.

15 The hotel management contract: lessons from the North American experience

Paul Beals

Hotel investors, those deep-pocketed, 'patient money' entrepreneurs who fund the lodging industry, are often seen gnashing their teeth because of the treatment they receive at the hands of hotel companies. Consider, for example, two recent demonstrations of hoteliers' arrogance and incomprehension.

Corksniffing

The scene is a worldwide conference of hospitality educators. We academics are pleased to have the chief executives of several multinational lodging and catering firms address us on the topic of how we can better prepare our students for the industry's changing environment. The president of an international hotel company rails against instruction in 'corksniffing' as part of our curriculum, advocating instead greater attention to business disciplines such as financial management and strategic planning. He summarizes his argument against the emphasis on technical skills that characterized his own professional training by observing that 'we're in the real-estate business, not the hotel business'.

Sage remarks, representing a profound understanding of strategic issues? Some present thought so, and applauded the executive's perceptiveness. But this writer could not help but reflect on the irony and annoyance hotel owners would express had they been present to share in the executive's wisdom. Irony because the company president proudly acknowledged a 30-year career in the hotel business. Why did it take him three decades to come to the fundamental proposition that hotel operation is a real-estate undertaking? What did he think owners engaged his firm to do?

Owners' irony would have progressed readily to annoyance, especially for those who employed the executive's firm to manage their properties. Among investors, the executive's firm is perhaps the most frequently cited as being arrogant and unresponsive to ownership's concerns when hotels it manages perform badly. Owners (and lenders) complain that the executive's company is too willing to invoke its contractual 'right to quiet enjoyment' and the term remaining in its well-crafted 20-year contracts, while giving short shrift to investors' cash flow needs.

Putting on the Ritz

The business press, perhaps reflecting the preoccupations of its writers and editors, is more likely to sing the praises of de luxe hotels than to reveal their financial realities. Not so a recent article on the Ritz-Carlton chain, where it was reported that only 20 per cent of the company's properties are profitable for their owners (Hirsch 1994).

The investors' complaints against Ritz-Carlton are well-known to any participant at an owner-operator meeting: lucrative management fees too heavily weighted to reward sales, not profitability; building the brand image at the expense of owners; selling rooms and services below cost; and entering markets inappropriate to luxury hotels. Horst Schulze, Ritz-Carlton's president, describes all the properties managed by his company as successful because they achieve excellent operating profits and, without apparent irony, observes: 'Whoever owns a Ritz-Carlton must consider themselves very lucky that we're running it'.

After some 25 years' experience with management contracts, investor–owner relations should have advanced to a more harmonious, more productive level. The intent of the present chapter is to explain why they have not and to indicate, based on the North American experience, tactics to mitigate similar conflicts in the future development of the hotel management contract concept.

As the preceding scenarios suggest, hotel investors do reserve a certain rancour for hotel operating companies as we emerge from the débâcle of the early 1990s. However, responsibility for the friction between investors and hoteliers rests with both parties to the transaction, although neither participant demonstrably acted in bad faith. Rather, what characterizes the evolution of management contracts is the playing out of a new strategy. As investors and operators, each for their own reasons, implemented the strategy of separating ownership from management, unforeseen implications and permutations surfaced. Arguably, no amount of planning or analysis could have anticipated or forestalled the tumultuous evolution of management contracts.

A deal with the devil?

First principle

As will be demonstrated below, there are a number of reasons why the strategy of separating hotel ownership from operations is a dangerous proposition. Perhaps the most fundamental reason is that the strategy runs the risk of obscuring the first principle of asset valuation: the sole means to realize value from hotel real estate is through its operation as a hotel.

Various real-estate practitioners and commentators try, unsuccessfully, to give the lie to this premiss. The appraisal profession, for example, is sometimes commissioned to value the going concern component of a hotel separately from its improvements. Although this is an interesting intellectual exercise, it has little to do with the economic reality of the hotel business. We may as well attempt to value a bottle of fine wine by decomposing its market price into a drinking-pleasure component and a cost component (grapes, packaging, vintner's labour, etc.).

Real-estate owners attempt vainly to obscure the principle by two self-deluding stratagems: the 'cost/elegance' argument and the 'bigger-fool theory' of investment. Under the former, owners ignore the relative magnitude of the income (profit) stream a property promises to produce, preferring to concentrate on the costs incurred and the beauty of a hotel's wall sconces to justify their estimates of value. It is interesting to observe that such owners, confronting the inverse situation, where the present value of expected future cash flows exceeds their costs, happily embrace market-determined prices but scorn reasonable offers inferior to their costs as contrary to economic logic (and justice).

Practitioners of the bigger-fool theory expect of course always to find a future buyer prepared to pay an appreciated price for the assets they purchase at already unseemly prices. In the real-estate business, these delusions are abetted by the practice of using market-derived capitalization rates. Since 'cap' rates are determined by comparing current cash flows to selling prices, they obscure the fact that today's prices are in fact determined by future cash flows, which can quickly become unrealistically inflated when markets overheat.

Evidence of the bigger-fool theory at work in real estate is not limited to confirmed speculators (called flippers in a parlance ominously suggestive of the turf). When Donald J. Trump's difficulties meeting debt service on his Atlantic City hotels were first reported, one of his executives explained blithely that Mr Trump's forte was not managing properties for their cash flow but rather trading them to benefit from their appreciation. Since Mr Trump was unable to sell his hotels, presumably he and his associates comprehend better the relationship between cash flows and appreciation potential, at least until the next market upturn.

Finally, students in this writer's classes attempt to violate the principle that the only source of value for a lodging property is its operation as a hotel, by proposing alternative uses. Notwithstanding their creativity and their willingness to confound their instructor, it is difficult to identify alternative uses for a structure consisting primarily of 300–600 contiguous cubicles, each with a bath. Although students cannot cite too many existing conversions, they inevitably identify some marginally feasible physical uses, such as office space (class B at best), dormitories, minimum-care facilities for the elderly, etc. Of course, what students are temporarily permitted to ignore, but which the market does not, is that such uses represent steep discounts from the market value had the property operated as a hotel.

Whether it is the egotism of owners, an overheated market, or the obstinacy of students, there are numerous ways to obscure the first principle of hotel asset valuation, but none to refute it. When the operation of a hotel is the only means for ownership to realize value, it is necessarily risky to put operations in the hands of another party unless ownership can be sure that both parties' interests coincide completely. On reflection, and in retrospect, it would have been naive to expect a conflict-free relationship when the role of the hotel management company is so centrally important to the success of investors, yet the two entities are separate. Moreover, the distinctly different outlooks of the two entities all but ensure a clash between investors and hoteliers.

Mentalities

The divergent mentalities of investors and hoteliers are tellingly illustrated by observing that they even count using two different methods. Except as it affects taxes, profit is an abstraction for the hotel investor. They count in cash flow and measure outcomes on an absolute basis – cash inflows versus capital outlays. Hoteliers count in terms of accounting profit, and measure it on a relative basis at intermediate steps (departmental profit percentage, gross profit percentage, income before fixed charges as a percentage of revenue), emphasizing cost control over revenue generation. Most investor–operator conferences, when they are confrontational, reflect this divergence: the owner and/or lender plead for cash while the hotelier, echoing Mr Schulze (above), cites ratios – a 28 per cent food cost, 32 per cent income before fixed charges, etc. – as evidence that they have done their job.

Like beings from foreign cultures, operators and investors also have different perspectives on time. The investor values immediacy (forever asking, according to one set-upon hotelier: 'What have you done for me lately?'), and discounts future cash flows. Hoteliers are trained to concentrate on outcomes achieved over a longer, more fluid horizon. They value customer service (the more personalized the better), their franchise with consumers and repeat business. Thus, where investors see frequent-stay programmes as discounting, the hotelier sees a made-to-order marketing tactic enabling him or her to achieve numerous important objectives.

The fundamental conflict between investor and hotelier perspectives is succinctly summarized by the debate that so often ensues when capital projects are reviewed. Hoteliers insist that an upscale restaurant or a lobby renovation will enhance the hotel's image and yield new business. Investors, to the frustration of operators, seek precision that goes beyond assembling cost estimates to forecasting concrete benefits in terms of increases in net operating income measured over a specific time line. Not surprisingly, operators frequently complain that investors fail to provide adequate capital to realize the full potential of the hotels they manage, and investors accuse hoteliers of misspending capital.

Hoteliers need investors to exercise their profession, while investors need operators to realize value from their assets. Yet their outlooks are sufficiently incongruent to make each entity's participation resemble the proverbial deal with the devil: a bargain that promises the fulfilment of every objective but entails onerous, unforeseen costs. What compelling reasons existed for the parties to enter into a relationship bound to be discordant?

Strategic needs

The bromide that 'all good ideas are obvious' describes the appeal both investors and hoteliers found in the concept of separating ownership and operations. The strategy, as shown below, not only provided the solution for the immediate challenges both entities faced but also promised long-term expansion as investors and hotel companies exploited the growth potential of the North American lodging industry in the late 1960s and early 1970s.[1]

Expensive capital

Before the advent of management contracts, hotel companies found themselves in a capital-markets squeeze that severely limited their expansion possibilities. Older, successful properties in hotel companies' portfolios showed accounting profits, but combined federal and state income tax rates in excess of 50 per cent reduced cash flows and reported earnings. Newer hotels provided greater tax-shelter benefits and conserved cash flow, but at the expense of reported earnings. Thus, regardless of the mix of assets a hotel company held, stock-market evaluations were anaemic, and capital therefore expensive.

A way out

By remaking themselves as management companies, hotel companies achieved numerous desirable objectives, including especially:

- The potential for rapid expansion without the requirement to raise capital.
- Rapid market penetration and hence greater brand recognition among consumers.
- Fee-based earnings without the drag on earnings of depreciation charges.
- Streamlined balance sheets as mortgage indebtedness was removed.
- The ability to attract scarce management talent to the advancement opportunities offered by chains.

Insulating investors

While meeting their strategic needs, the transformation of hotel companies to fee-based operators also created opportunities for various entities either foreclosed by regulation from managing hotels (e.g. insurance companies) or unwilling to shoulder the complexity of hotels as operating businesses. Consider, for example, that hoteliers promised effectively to insulate owners from the day-to-day management of a highly labour-intensive business employing a low-tech delivery system that is difficult (at best) to rationalize and control. Consider, too, that hoteliers promised to simplify for investors an industry that provides not only shelter but diverse, intangible services, most of which yield only small contribution margins, to shifting, fickle markets.

In addition to freeing them from the quotidian demands of a complex retail activity, the advent of management contracts allowed ownership interests to optimize their financial returns. Investors structured private entities that concentrated on cash flow and property appreciation, not earnings per share. They maximized leverage and minimized taxes through the use of various pass-through entities (e.g. real estate investment trusts, limited partnerships). Hotels' special characteristics, comprising a relatively large proportion of the capital cost invested in personal property eligible for accelerated depreciation and operating losses in the early years of operation, also contributed to their tax-shelter appeal. The combined effect of these factors was the realization of the classic real-estate strategy: maximize cash flows while deferring income recognition.

Too good by half

Because the new structure of the lodging industry was so convenient strategically to both participants, few paused to reflect on its implications: wealth (real-estate ownership) was being separated from operations, the source of the wealth. Not only did participants overlook this fundamental risk – they ignored the potential for conflict if either party gained ascendancy over the other.

The upper hand

Success

As one investor remarked, 'hoteliers are entrepreneurs, especially with other people's money'. As this characterization suggests, hotel management companies did gain the upper hand over investors early in the development of management contracts, although the capital sources funding the lodging industry share some responsibility for the ascendancy operators achieved.

As the lodging market expanded, management companies' success bred success. Operators expanded the number of rooms they managed, leveraging their market penetration and customer franchise to reassure investors. Moreover, true to their entrepreneurial nature, management companies were not adverse to practising a certain self-promotion and mystification intended to enhance their perceived value and their bargaining position with investors.

Similarly, in a financing market rife with inexperienced hotel lenders, the chains' reputation and experience were important sources of reassurance to underwriters. The so-called comfort letter, announcing the management company's willingness to operate the developer's project, became a requisite preliminary to the opening of serious negotiations between the developer and prospective money partners.

In comparison to today's perhaps overcrowded hospitality education market, there were few sources of trained operators or executives for the lodging industry, and even fewer means for managers to gain formal educational qualifications while on the job. Management companies provided a structure and a way out of this talent shortage, and investors welcomed this solution to a long-standing problem.

As a result of the above factors, operating companies handily carried the day in the formative stages of the development of the management contract concept. Operators commanded significant fee income, relatively unfettered control over day-to-day operations, and long contract durations.

Complicity

If the early operator–investor relationships too frequently favoured the management companies, it was at least in part because investors, through their inattention, contributed to the imbalance. As it so often is today, lodging development was capital-, not strategy-driven. Many investors poured money into hotels but failed to provide the management companies with specific operational and financial goals to meet. As one veteran lodging-industry investor at a major American insurance company observed of this period: 'The management contract was just another [loan] closing document'.

Growth in the demand for lodging, inflation and the availability of long-term fixed-rate financing permitted equity investors the luxury of ignoring the cost of management services and their impact on operational cash flows. In addition, many owners were also developers, driven by up-front fees and the prospect of leveraging minimal (or negative) equity to achieve property appreciation. Like practitioners of the bigger-fool theory of investment, such developers were not overly concerned with the operational cash flows a property produced, and thus did not monitor attentively the performance of the management companies they engaged.

The balance shifts

Although management companies enjoyed an advantage as the number of contracts in place expanded during the first decade of their use, the balance began to shift perceptibly to improve the position of investors during the 1980s. At least four factors contributed to this shift.

The recession induced by the monetary tightening necessary to bring inflation under control made investors more attentive to the operating cash flows their hotels produced. As investors scrutinized the performance of operators, the low barriers to entry in the management contract business provided an increasing number of competitors, enlarging investors' choices and diminishing the bargaining power of management companies.

The proliferation of lower-cost, independent management companies also provided greater flexibility to investors because they were able to purchase brand identities and management expertise separately. As franchisees of major hotel companies that enjoyed strong consumer acceptance, owners reduced their risk and reassured lenders, but also reduced the overall cost of their management services by employing smaller companies offering more competitive fees than chain operators.

Finally, a natural evolution in the understanding of the management contract instrument occurred. Investors and their advisers grew more experienced in the use of management contracts, identified inadequacies in the contractual arrangement, and demanded more of operating companies to redress perceived inequities.

Performance clauses

The combined effect of the forces favouring investors was that new management contracts, while still giving significant base fees to operators, required higher standards of performance before incentive fees were paid. By moving further down the income statement in establishing benchmarks for operator compensation, investors attempted a better alignment of the management company's interests with their own. The contractual devices, in increasing order of onerousness for the operating company, included the following.

Subordination to debt service

Under these clauses (sometimes called stand-asides or 'subject to's'), operators' incentive fees were calculated based on a percentage of income before fixed charges (IBFC) but payable only out of cash flow remaining (if any) after the payment of debt service. The key point of such contractual arrangements was to establish the operator's claim on incentive fees earned according to the percentage-of-IBFC calculation, but unpaid because of cash shortfalls. Fees could be deferred and accrue as a liability, be deferred and accrue with interest, or simply be forgone. Obviously, the latter option favoured investors and exerted continuing pressure on operators to improve performance if they wished to receive the incentive portion of their compensation. Conversely, a deferral of fees, especially if interest also accrued, sometimes placed investors at a distinct disadvantage if the liability mounted to a significant sum and they attempted to change operators, refinance or dispose of their property.

Subordination to debt service and return on equity

Some seasoned investors, especially insurance companies experienced in hotel financing, required operators to subordinate their incentive fees to debt service *and* a fixed cash-on-cash return to equity. Typically, such clauses required management companies to forgo definitively any year's incentive fees if there was insufficient cash to pay them after satisfying debt service and return-on-equity requirements.

Cure provisions

These clauses, when successfully negotiated by investors, required operators not only to subordinate their claims on cash flow to investors' claims, but to fund shortfalls. If the operation of the hotel did not provide adequate cash flow to pay debt service, the operator received a cash call, requiring him or her to advance cash to cover debt service. Depending on the individual negotiations, such cash payments could accrue as a liability of the investors, accrue with interest or simply provide the operator with no claim in exchange for their contribution.

Equity, and the management companies' negotiating skills, provided for a counterpoise to the contractual devices intended to align operators' interests with investors'. In exchange for incurring greater risk, operators began to propose various compensatory rewards. They sought higher overall fees by maintaining their base fees while seeking greater percentages of residual cash flows; they demanded longer contract durations and more substantial termination penalties; and they attempted to share in ownership returns by seeking equity positions or sharing in property appreciation on the sale or refinancing of the hotels they managed.

A speculative bubble

Although the evolution of investor–operator relations in the 1980s put more pressure on hotel management companies to enhance operating results, in general they prospered as they participated in the expanding lodging market. The expansion was to prove a speculative bubble in the 1990s, further adding to the pressures on operators, but few paused to contemplate the prospect of overbuilding in the overheated lodging market of the 1980s.

The 1980s development scene

The environment creating the bubble of the 1980s had its origins in legislation enacted early in the decade to stimulate the economy through deregulation and accommodative tax policy. The push to deregulate various institutions helped some sectors, but proved disastrous to the banking industry. Savings and loans, formerly small, local institutions specializing in home mortgage lending, suddenly found themselves competing for deposits in an industry that posed few barriers to entry. Venturing into real estate allowed savings and loans to offer the competitive returns necessary to attract new depositors. At the same time, more traditional hotel lenders, encouraged by rising market values and attempting to compete with savings and loans, moved out on the risk curve, structuring more aggressive deals.

The result of this overheated market, as the crash of the early 1990s revealed, was that many financing structures assembled represented, in real terms, negative equity for owners and loan-to-value ratios greater than one for lenders.

Tax policy designed to stimulate the economy featured rapid depreciation schedules and the possibility for individuals to offset their ordinary income with accounting losses from real-estate holdings. The lodging industry had special appeal for those seeking to take advantage of this liberal tax treatment because, as noted earlier, a relatively large percentage of the lodging investment is in furniture, fixtures and equipment, subject to rapid depreciation allowances and because new hotel developments typically yield operating losses in their start-up periods. This fiscal stimulus incited owner-developers, many of them inexperienced in hotels, to ignore the management-intensiveness of the lodging industry. Only when the market became overbuilt did they realize that creating value (and survival) depended on operating expertise.

Hotel management companies, ever the entrepreneurs and ever ready to expand the number of rooms managed, responded to the opportunities by creating new products. Flying the banner of market segmentation, many firms 'backed and filled', moving up and down the gamut of property types in response to capital availability rather than to their clientele.

The débâcle

The mixture, leavened by generous appraisals, of eager capital sources, tax-driven developers and operators bent on expansion, yielded artificially inflated property values and more hotel development than the lodging market could sustain. The overbuilt situation was further exacerbated by a shrinkage in demand for lodging that accompanied the recession of the early 1990s. For the lodging industry, the early 1990s proved the most difficult period since the Great Depression of the 1930s.

The frenzied activity of lodging development had managed to divert attention from the excess of supply during the 1980s, but by the 1990s the industry's problems were clear. Hotel occupancy rates reached their lowest point during 1991, posting 60.2 per cent nationwide, after declining from 70.6 per cent in 1980. Local occupancies in some markets were reported as low as 35 per cent – far below break-even for even the most conservatively financed hotel. Liquidity all but evaporated as hotel property values declined precipitously; when sales of hotels were consummated, prices ranged as low as 15–40 per cent of replacement cost (Rushmore, 1994).

Mortgage delinquencies for hotels surpassed those of any other property type, reaching 18.5 per cent of all hotel loans in 1991, (Isenberg and Zucker, 1993).

The squeeze on operators

The industry shakeout led to many foreclosures and many changes of ownership, frequently accompanied by the removal of the management company. Losing the prospect of property appreciation to create value, investors turned increasingly to their management companies, demanding that they improve operating performance. In some cases, management companies were unfairly blamed for poor operating results when no amount of creativity or diligence could turn around an overleveraged, ill-conceived product in an overcrowded market. As Beals and Engel's (1995) research has demonstrated, thoughtful investors do recognize that they shared responsibility for the industry's inadequate performance because they frequently did not have an explicit strategy for their lodging assets and therefore did not charge operators with achieving specific, measurable results.

At the same time, however, investors cite specific inadequacies that they maintain are too widespread among management companies. Chief among the complaints voiced is the operator's lack of a strategic focus on two fronts: an understanding of the investor's need to create value and the ability to adjust the product to the realities of a changing market. Thus, investors fault operators for emphasizing operations and operational performance criteria (e.g. food cost, departmental profit, percentage income before fixed charges, etc.) while failing to appreciate the importance of cash flow as the most pertinent test of a hotel's ability to fulfil investors' strategic objectives. Similarly, investors charge that when operators find their products losing favour with the market, they are unable to view the problem strategically and make meaningful changes in the product to respond to their clientele (Beals and Engel, 1995). 'Management companies manage', observed one investor, 'but when they get into trouble, they can only do more of the same thing.'

These perceived deficiencies in operating companies, plus the need of inexperienced owners-in-foreclosure to engage advisers to help engineer turnarounds of distressed properties, have increased the use of hotel asset managers. In the employ of investors, asset managers help their clients understand the particular challenges of hotels as an asset class and develop strategies to maximize value. As the investors' representative, they counsel and monitor the operators responsible for day-to-day management of lodging properties, ensuring that the necessary tactics are implemented to create value.

The wider use of asset managers is arguably the result of operators' inability or unwillingness to comprehend the investor's perspective. Food-service contracting firms have long understood the distinction between customers (the patrons who consume the meals they produce) and clients (the entities that engage them to manage their food-service operations). Too often, hotel management companies have failed to understand this fundamental distinction and wilfully ignored the interests of their clients, concentrating instead on providing more and better service to their customers, even as customers signalled their reluctance to pay for the incremental features foisted on them.

Similar arrogance is displayed by management companies when they respond to investors' entreaties for improved performance by invoking their 'right of quiet enjoyment', the standard management-contract legal phrase intended to describe the degree of control over day-to-day operations ceded to the management company. Investors report that some operators demonstrate little inclination to attempt new strategies to create value for investors, preferring instead to protect their interests and prevent their removal from contracts by citing the length of the remaining contract term and the penalties due on unilateral termination of the contract by owners.

A limited number of investors, exasperated by the obduracy of management companies, have attempted to terminate their contracts by suing operators for breach of contract. The adjudication of the disputes to date (one was settled out of court; the second continues) suggests a pyrrhic victory for hotel investors. Although a fundamental precept of agency law holds that a principal retains the power to revoke an agency relationship such as is created by a management agreement, an owner who terminates an operator may be liable for damages if the operator can prove that the termination is wrongful. The termination of an operator may be complicated further if the operator has an investment in the hotel because an 'agency coupled with an interest' is irrevocable. The question of whether or not an operator's equity contribution constitutes an interest has not been definitively decided.[2]

At this writing, the practical import of the legal skirmishes is limited. Investors are, however, watching developments carefully, and some may have been influenced to eschew equity contributions from operators (see below).

Investor precautions

The hard-earned experience of investors in the early years of the decade has led to a new caution on their part when hotels are purchased and new management companies installed, or in the limited number of instances when they succeed in renegotiating a contract. The contract terms sought by investors are intended to achieve two broad objectives: to incite better the management company to produce the operational cash flows investors seek, and to maintain the investors' flexibility when a management change or disposition of the asset is in the investors' best interest.

Savvy investors are now using the fee structure as their most powerful device to force the alignment of the operator's interest with their own. Investors acknowledge that it is not in their long-term best interest to deprive hotel management companies of a reasonable fee for their services. According to Beals and Engel (1995), fees deemed adequate to ensure operators' viability and an appropriate profit are in the range of 4–6 per cent of total revenues. However, investors insist that fees be calculated to weight net cash flow from operations more than revenue generation. As one veteran hotel investor argued to justify the fee structure he perceived as equitable to owners and operators: 'They [management companies] are better off with one and twenty-five than three and ten'.

As the preceding commentary suggests, the fee structure investors consider desirable, and which they are imposing on operators, provides for only a small percentage-of-revenue base fee and calculates incentive fees as a significant percentage of available cash flow *after* payment, however, of debt service and a return to equity participants.[3] Thus, except for situations where the management company is a caretaker-operator charged with improving performance enough to facilitate the sale of the property, investors are prepared to pay a base fee in the range of 1–2.5 per cent of revenues. The percentage of available cash flow paid to the operator varies depending on a property's financial structure, but is calibrated to bring the operator's total compensation into the 4–6 per cent of revenue range, but only if investor cash-flow objectives are met.

The use of performance clauses such as stand-asides and the subordination of fees to debt service is obviated by a fee structure that awards incentive fees as a percentage of residual cash flows. The use of cure provisions is also currently less attractive to investors, who reason that the object should not be to extract cash from management companies in lieu of performance, but to select competent operators who are able to produce adequate cash flows from operations.

In the place, however, of performance clauses designed to address cash shortfalls, some investors are formally setting objectives above income before fixed charges. Performance criteria, for example, that evaluate departmental profit are becoming more common, as are non-financial criteria such as measuring operator performance in terms of market share and market penetration. To the extent that such performance measures reinforce the fundamental principle that successful operations are the sole source of value, they promise to moderate investors' return expectations and contribute to stability in an industry subject to boom-and-bust cycles.

Maintaining flexibility

The illiquidity of lodging assets earlier in the decade was often exacerbated by the existence of a long-term contract with an operator who could only be removed at a substantial cost, thus driving market values down even further. Hotel investors have been marked by this experience and seem determined to avoid its recurrence by maintaining the highest degree of flexibility possible, while ensuring adequate commitment from the management companies engaged to operate their properties. Investors generally insist on contract durations far shorter than the 20-year periods that were once standard, and some investors assert that they will not enter contracts that exceed five years. Similarly, contract termination clauses, while still providing for some compensatory fees to management companies if they are unilaterally removed, are far less onerous to investors, effectively increasing the marketability of lodging properties.

Investors' desire to keep at hand an exit strategy for their lodging assets is illustrated by their changing attitude towards operator equity contributions. Once considered a desirable way to increase operator commitment by 'holding his feet to the fire' if the asset underperformed, an equity investment from the management company is now considered of questionable value by some veteran hotel investors. Noting that, on a relative basis, the investments were more symbolic than monetarily significant, these investors reason that the commitment they signal is overshadowed by the risk of giving the operator a potentially dangerous security interest in the property. 'All the operator does [when he makes an equity contribution],' observed one investor, 'is buy an annuity stream. Do you expect him to give it up willingly when I want to sell or change managers?'

Conclusion

The evolution of hotel management contracts was the result of a fundamental imbalance, as well as a sign of the times. So long as operators were adequately compensated through basic fees, or through a formula of basic fees and incentive fees calculated without regard for the cash flow generated for investors, they were not sufficiently incited to maximize the value of the assets they managed. In fact, as one investor observed, 'if an operating company performed too well, its success could prove its own undoing'. If the hotel were sold to realize the value created, the management company might find itself out of a contract or, at best, reporting to a new owner demanding continued superior performance to protect and enhance the value of the acquisition.

The development of hotel management contracts also parallels trends observed in the wider spectrum of business in North America, where the concept of agency has been severely tested. After the rash of management-led buyouts of the 1980s, it is no longer believed that agents will act in the long-term best interests of their firms merely because they have contracted to do so. Instead, it has been found necessary to create a system of rewards that aligns managers' interests with owners' by compensating them on the basis of increases in shareholder value. Thus, a complementary stick is used if the carrot is not effective: let shareholder value slip and managers quickly find their firm 'in play' and their jobs at risk.

When viewed as a part of this larger context, it seems unlikely that hotel investors' current outlook will change and that they will relent in their efforts to control the performance of management companies more tightly. Some investors in fact have definitively ensured their control over management companies by purchasing them. Others have entered into strategic alliances that give management companies an inside track in the operator selection process, but also tie them more closely to the perspective and objectives of their affiliated investors. Despite this trend towards greater control over operator performance, some investors express concern that, as current contracts expire over the next decade, North America will have entered another period of aggressive hotel development. If the consolidation of hotel management companies continues, they reason, the remaining operators will be in high demand and will once again be able to negotiate favourable contracts, to the detriment of investor returns. Since the last period of such ascendancy by management companies contributed to a lodging-industry upheaval injurious to all participants, a recurrence is to be resisted vigorously.

Endnotes

1 Portions of the discussion that follows draw on material presented by James J. Eyster (1988) *The Negotiation and Administration of Hotel and Restaurant Management Contracts* (Ithaca, NY: Cornell University School of Hotel Administration), pp. 191–206.

2 For a full discussion of the wrongful termination and agency-coupled-with-interest issues, see: Butler, J.R. Jr. and Benudiz, P.P. (1994) The

Marriott decision: increasing a hotel's value with a management agreement audit. *The Real Estate Finance Journal*, **9**, 57-69. A counterbalance to the Butler and Benudiz view, which demonstrates a perceptible bias, can be found in a reply from Howard A. Allen (1994) in *The Real Estate Finance Journal*, **10**(1), pp. 5-6.

3 It should be noted that intelligently negotiated management contracts provide for renegotiation of the subordination of operator incentive fees if the hotel's financing structure changes. Like so many issues in the evolution of management contracts, this is the result of hard-won experience. In some instances, operators, after accepting subordination to the payment of debt service, found themselves 'leveraged out' of any possible incentive fees when refinancing increased debt service significantly.

References

Beals, P. and Engel, T. (1995) Investors' perspective: the future of the lodging industry. *The Real Estate Finance Journal* **11**(1), 13–19.

Beals, P. and Engel, T. (1995) Investors' demand hotel management contracts. *Real Estate Review* **25**(1), 32–36.

Hirsch, J.S. (1994) Of luxury and losses: many Ritz hotels are in the red. *Wall Street Journal* 22 April, B3.

Isenberg, W.L. and Zucker D.L., (1993) Strategies for unintentional owners of hotel assets. *The Real Estate Finance Journal*, **8**(3), 41.

Rushmore, S., (1994) An overview of the hotel industry: past, present, and future. *The Real Estate Finance Journal* **9**(4), 6-7.

16 Hotel profitability – critical success factors

Frank J. Croston

Introduction

It is difficult to discern why certain hotels are consistently more profitable than their direct competitors. Reasonable arguments can be advanced concerning the impact of location, or brand affiliation, or the superior quality of the physical product, and the consequent profit improvements which may result. In reality, however, these factors do not seem to provide the whole answer.

In order to provide an objective framework within which to examine the factors which contribute to superior profit performance, an analysis has been prepared which draws upon operating results from hotels contributing data to *EuroTrends*, a survey published annually by Pannell Kerr Forster Associates (PKFA). The hypothesis advanced is that similarly sized hotels, offering a comparable range of facilities and amenities, located in close proximity to each other and operated by an internationally recognized brand, ought to produce comparable levels of profit. To test this hypothesis, 10 pairs of hotels have been selected from 10 European cities, which meet the criteria set out. All of the more profitable hotels from each pairing, as measured by profit per available room, have then been grouped together as *winners*. All of the less profitable hotels have been grouped together as *losers*.

The results of this analysis, as presented in Figure 16.1, demonstrate that the winners produced 46 per cent more profit than the losers. This staggering level of profit variance, given the criteria employed, suggests that further analysis and understanding of the underlying causes are merited.

It should be emphasized that the screening criteria did not seek to identify hotels with dramatically different profitability profiles, in fact, quite the

	Winners		Losers		
	Per available room	Ratio	Per available room	Ratio	Variance
Revenue					
Rooms	55,480	57.6%	50,825	55.5%	4,655
Food	25,027	26.0%	23,484	25.6%	1,543
Beverage	6,045	6.3%	8,712	9.5%	(2,667)
Telephone	5,109	5.3%	4,972	5.4%	137
Other operated departments	4,029	4.2%	2,918	3.2%	1,111
Rentals and other income	560	0.6%	708	0.8%	(148)
Total revenue	96,250	100.0%	91,619	100.0%	4,631
Departmental costs and expenses*					
Rooms	14,519	26.2%	16,098	31.7%	(1,579)
Food and beverage	26,431	85.1%	28,211	87.6%	(1,780)
Telephone	2,320	45.4%	2,063	41.5%	257
Other operated	2,036	50.5%	1,600	54.8%	436
Total costs and expenses	45,306	47.1%	47,972	52.4%	(2,666)
Total operated departmental income	50,944	52.9%	43,647	47.6%	7,297
Undistributed operating expenses					
Administrative and general	7,715	8.0%	9,709	10.6%	(1,994)
Marketing	5,055	5.3%	4,727	5.2%	328
P.O.M.	4,190	4.4%	5,045	5.5%	(855)
Energy	3,085	3.2%	3,056	3.3%	29
Total undistributed expenses	20,045	20.8%	22,537	24.6%	(2,492)
Income before fixed charges	30,899	32.1%	21,110	23.0%	9,789
Operating statistics					
Occupancy	64.5%		61.7%		
Average rate	235.64		225.76		
Yield	152.01		139.20		
Number of rooms	308		303		

* Percentage costs to departmental revenue

Figure 16.1   Comparative performance analysis of 10 pairs of hotels operating in major western European cities in 1993. All amounts are in Deutschmarks.
Source: PKFA EuroTrends Database

reverse was the case. Whilst the individual hotel identities cannot be revealed for reasons of confidentiality, Figure 16.2 lists the cities analysed and indicates the level of profit differential recorded. This demonstrates that the pairings selected in certain cities, such as Berlin and Madrid, came close to supporting the hypothesis. In other cities, however, the winners outperformed the losers by nearly three times, as shown for Lisbon and Vienna.

City	Profit variance *	Revenue variance †	Size variance ‡
Amsterdam	38.1%	32.8%	9.9%
Berlin	7.2%	(32.7%)	25.7%
Brussels	35.4%	34.7%	4.4%
Frankfurt	52.9%	(11.8%)	8.9%
Hamburg	77.6%	11.2%	3.2%
Lisbon	188.3%	(17.9%)	8.6%
London	14.8%	13.9%	1.3%
Madrid	2.8%	(2.5%)	18.2%
Munich	36.2%	(39.4%)	5.3%
Vienna	183.2%	135.1%	2.6%
Average	46.4%	5.1%	1.7%

* Extent of superior profit performance of 'winners' as a percentage of 'losers' profit.
† Extent of superior or (inferior) revenue performance of 'winners' as a percentage of 'losers' revenue.
‡ Variance in the number of rooms available between each pair of hotels, expressed as a percentage of the smaller hotel's number of available rooms.

Figure 16.2   Analysis of profit, revenue and size variances within the sample.
Source: PKFA EuroTrends Database

Figure 16.2 also reveals a number of surprising failures to convert a significantly superior revenue performance into a superior profit performance. In five of the 10 cities, the eventual profit winners had inferior revenues to the losers. Many hoteliers live by the adage 'take care of the top line and the bottom line will take care of itself'. The variance analysis presented in Figure 16.2 does not support this contention, and begins to illustrate that the answer to superior profitability cannot lie in revenue-based issues alone.

Critical success factors

The simple answer to enhancing profit is to increase revenues and reduce costs. Rather more difficult is the task of identifying what precise methods and techniques can be employed, and the extent to which these can be utilized in different markets and styles of hotel.

By reference to Figure 16.1, the winners produced 5.0 per cent more revenue, spent 7.3 per cent less on costs, which in combination resulted in 46.4 per cent more profit being realized. The profit differential is particularly pronounced due to the much higher rooms revenue earned, which is by far the most profitable type of revenue. The overall profit performance is also underpinned, however, by better control of departmental costs and expenses and a lower base of undistributed operating expenses.

By reference to the results presented in Figure 16.1, and analysis of the underlying results, it is reasonable to conclude that the superior performance of the winners rests upon above average performance in one or more of the following areas:

1. Operating efficiency.
2. Marketing.
3. Product specification.
4. Service delivery.

The balance of this chapter will examine each of these four areas, and seek to identify what the superior-performance hotels are doing to produce higher profits. The analyses will refer to the performance of the sample hotels, where appropriate, to illustrate various issues. The analyses will also draw upon the experience gained by PKFA through undertaking numerous efficiency and profit improvement reviews.

Operating efficiency

Figure 16.3 sets out a diagrammatic representation of the factors which, in combination, are required to produce operating efficiency. Through observation, a hotel which operates efficiently always appears to be managed within

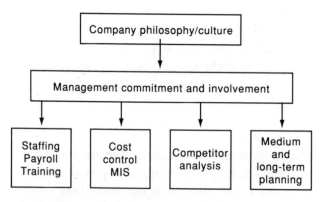

Figure 16.3 Operating efficiency. *Source:* PKFA

a culture which promotes efficiency through *top-down* involvement and management commitment. The specific areas and techniques set out along the bottom of Figure 16.3 are not particularly helpful if management fails to treat them seriously, or to act upon information on performance as it becomes available. As a minimum, better-performing hotels will encourage full management participation of all department heads in the preparation of budgets, the analysis of variances as they arise, all key decision-making and all guest service issues.

Payroll

Payroll has long been recognized as the largest single controllable cost in any hotel operation. Figure 16.4 shows the payroll performance of two of the pairs of hotels contributing to the sample, from Frankfurt and Lisbon.

	Frankfurt		Lisbon	
	Hotel A	*Hotel B*	*Hotel A*	*Hotel B*
Average rate	DM 255	DM 270	DM 180	DM 235
Room occupancy	58.0%	60.0%	53.0%	45.0%
Total revenue	DM 36.6m	DM 38.1m	DM 19.2m	DM 21.6m
Total payroll	DM 11.1m	DM 15.7m	DM 6.1m	DM 11.2m
Payroll percentage	30.3%	41.2%	31.8%	51.9%
Total profit	DM 12.2m	DM 7.3m	DM 7.0m	DM 2.2m
Profit percentage	33.3%	19.2%	36.5%	10.2%

Figure 16.4 Impact of payroll on profitability. *Source:* PKFA EuroTrends Database

By examining the Frankfurt data it can be observed that Hotel B operates with a payroll burden some 41.4 per cent higher than Hotel A, despite the fact that Hotel B is servicing only 4.1 per cent more revenue! In fact, Hotel B appears to be relatively efficient in other areas of cost control, as payroll accounts for nearly 94 per cent of the ultimate profit differential. This is a somewhat extreme example of the impact which payroll can have upon profitability.

Turning to the Lisbon data, the case for regarding payroll control as a critical success factor is further strengthened. The adverse payroll cost variance achieved by Hotel B is actually greater than the ultimate adverse profit variance.

```
Competitor analysis and benchmarking
The right balance of full-time/part-time staff
Flexible full-time employees
Reductions in staff turnover
Structured incentive schemes
Investment in and commitment to training
Creation of quality circles
```

Figure 16.5 Steps to a better performance in staffing, payroll and training

Figure 16.5 details the more important aspects of superior performance in the area of staffing, payroll and training. Considerable efforts have been made by all hotel groups to improve their performance in this area, particularly as a consequence of recessionary pressure on profits during the early 1990s. For some hotels this has resulted in a greater empowerment of staff and enhanced service to the guest, despite falling numbers of employees. For others, however, where the integration of training and incentivization have been less well-managed, the service delivery to the guest has fallen. This topic begins to reveal the linkage between effective cost control and enhanced revenues – properly managed payroll reductions can lead to improved revenues, while poorly managed payroll reductions will almost always harm revenues.

Cost control and management information systems

Table 16.1 presents comparative data from the pair of hotels selected from Hamburg. Hotel A is significantly more profitable, although it is interesting to note the similarity between the two payroll amounts. The conclusion must be that Hotel A is gaining a significant advantage through more effective cost control, particularly departmental costs.

This is certainly a dramatic example of cost control in action. How can this difference in performance be explained? Are the management of Hotel B incompetent? Perhaps this is so, but it is more likely that they, and their head office, are unaware of the performance of Hotel A, and they may not even be asked to explain their poor performance. Indeed, they may be receiving praise, as this performance was an improvement on the previous year.

It is doubtful that the management of Hotel B would claim not to have known any of the cost control and management techniques being employed by Hotel A. Indeed, if they sat through a presentation of Hotel A's business plan they would probably describe it as *motherhood and apple pie*. The point is that there is *no mystery* – Hotel A is simply applying well-known techniques consistently and thoroughly in every aspect of its operation.

Table 16.1 The impact of cost control on profitability

	Hamburg	
	Hotel A	*Hotel B*
Total revenue	DM 28.6m	DM 26.5m
Departmental costs	DM 12.7m	DM 14.4m
Ratio	44.4%	54.4%
Undistributed costs	DM 6.4m	DM 6.6m
Ratio	22.4%	24.8%
Profit	DM 9.5m	DM 5.5m
Ratio	33.2%	21.0%
Payroll	DM 10.3m	DM 10.1m
Ratio	36.0%	38.1%

Source: PKFA EuroTrends Database

Figure 16.6 sets out a range of techniques and activities which well-managed hotels apply in the execution of their business. These techniques are well-known, and widely applied – although obviously not by all. Speed of response by management is of particular importance, as it emphasizes to staff that performance is being monitored and that they will have to account for sub-standard performance.

```
Zero-based budgeting

Exception-based variance reporting

Efficient purchasing and controls

Well-trained and well-supervised staff

Involvement and commitment of management

Speed of response
```

Figure 16.6 Cost-effective cost control

Competitor analysis and benchmarking

Competitor analysis is an increasingly important element of operating efficiency. It needs to form a central part of a concerted effort to identify and attack areas of the business which are not performing as well as direct competitors. Figure 16.7 identifies the key elements of the benchmarking process, with the cyclical nature of the process being emphasized by the diagram. A frequent stumbling block in this process is the empowerment of the organization to implement the changes required. If management control is strongly centralized in a hotel chain, the empowerment must naturally come from the centre. This often requires a level of supervision and analysis beyond the resources of scaled-down head office operations. The result can be inertia. This can be resolved by the creation of project teams drawn from the units, or by the involvement of external agencies if the rewards for success appear sufficiently promising.

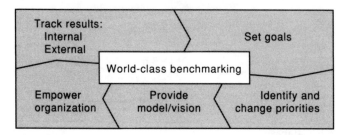

Figure 16.7   Competitor analysis benchmarking. *Source:* PKFA

Medium- and long-term planning

Although this is presented as the final element of the review of operating efficiency, it is by far the most important. If this vital area is properly addressed and managed it will, unavoidably, identify a strategy for all of the areas previously discussed, as well as those discussed in the balance of this chapter. Far too often, however, many hotels approach this area on a 'last year plus a bit basis', or regard it as a form of negotiation with head office, during which they will submit an initial low budget or plan, in the expectation of being asked to improve the numbers before the budget is accepted.

Figure 16.8 sets out the key inputs and outputs to the planning process. Most hotels simply fail to devote the time and resource necessary to this

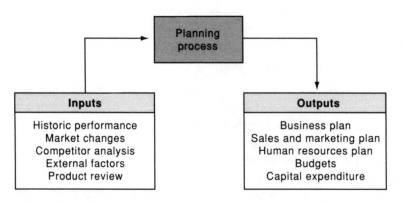

Figure 16.8   Medium- and long-term planning. *Source:* PKFA

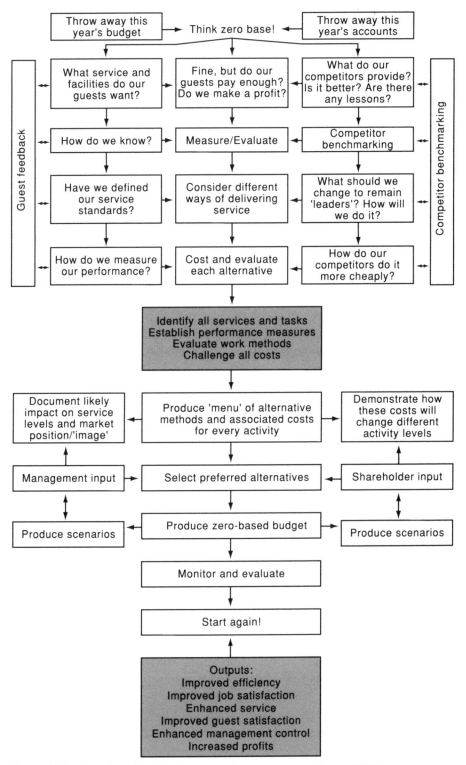

Figure 16.9 Zero-based budgeting: a continuous process. *Source:* PKFA

process, and consequently fail to reap the rewards available to the *excellent* hotels. A good example of this is the zero-based budget. This is a widely used phrase, but a rarely used technique. It is, however, an excellent example of the manner in which careful and diligent planning can lead directly to enhanced profitability. A practical overview of the use of, and processes involved in, zero-based budgeting is presented in Figure 16.9. The key elements of the process are the reliance upon external benchmarking and guest feedback, emphasizing that superior performance needs to be delivered in the context of a competitive and dynamic marketplace.

Ultimately the planning process is the starting point of attaining superior performance, and the mechanism by which it can be maintained once achieved.

Marketing

Figure 16.10 sets out the simple objectives of any hotel marketing activity, and the results which it is hoped will be attained. It is important to recognize that this process is continuous and cyclical, as markets are constantly changing and the marketing effort needs to change in response, as illustrated in Figure 16.11.

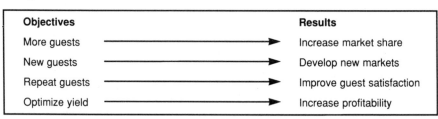

Figure 16.10   The aims of marketing

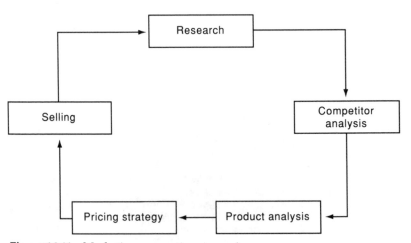

Figure 16.11   Marketing – a continuous cycle

Competitor analysis again emerges as an important element of this process. Customers generally are becoming more discerning, more price-aware, better educated about alternative purchasing methods and generally more difficult for hotels to hoodwink! No marketing strategy will succeed in a vacuum, but it is often surprising how little general managers know about their direct competitors in the same city, or the marketing strategies which they are using.

Table 16.2 sets out the issues which the marketing plan should address – a well-known analysis of the 5 Ps: product, place, price, promotion and perception. Information, and consequently informed decision-making, is the lifeblood of this process, and can give well-managed hotels a distinct competitive edge.

Table 16.2 Elements of the marketing plan

Product	Image, branding, segmentation
Place	Location, source markets
Price	Competition, VFM, time-pricing
Promotion	Advertising, CRS, sales force
Perception	Image, cachet

VFM = Value for money; CRS = computer reservations systems

Computer reservations systems

There are two issues, in particular, which currently and in the future will even more so distinguish excellent hotels from average hotels. These are yield management and computer reservations systems (CRS).

First, the major advantages and disadvantages of CRS are presented in Table 16.3.

The evolution of CRS

Since airline reservations systems came into existence in the 1950s, the opportunity has existed for other travel service providers to share the benefits of the airlines' investment in this technology. In the early 1970s airline CRS terminals started to appear in travel agent offices, and by the end of that decade, hotel and other travel services could be booked via the CRS. Throughout the 1980s the volume of hotel reservations made via airline CRS increased dramatically and, as hotels became automated themselves, agents were able to sell hotel room inventory directly in real time.

During this period, hotels themselves became automated in their front office, reservations, and other operational areas, and property management systems (PMS) were developed. Simultaneously, chain hotels sought to increase their sales distribution by opening central reservation offices (CROs), serving their clientele via tollfree telephone connections.

Table 16.3 Global distribution systems (GDS): advantages and disadvantages

---

Advantages

Representation to worldwide markets via travel agents and travel management companies using GDS

Ease and efficiency of booking for travel agents and travel management companies, who can book air travel, hotel accommodation and other travel services at one time

Availability of other marketing services via consortia or reservation service providers

Availability of marketing information from hotel CRS/PMS, group CRS or via GDS. Hotels gain a competitive advantage through access to information such as:

1. Source of booking
2. Geographic origin of clients
3. Market segmentation analysis
4. Client and client company history
5. Analysis of the effectiveness of promotions
6. Booking patterns via GDS

Cost savings through the integration of reservations and hotel front office/PMS

Disadvantages

Cost of bookings can be high, and can involve one or more of:

1. Travel agent commission
2. Booking fees to GDS
3. Consortia/reservations service provider fees

This can be particularly prohibitive for low-tariff hotels

Complexity of maintaining rate and available inventory records in multiple systems

Hotels must be equipped with compatible CRS/PMS of their own

Ongoing communication is necessary to keep hotels in the forefront of agents' minds

---

CRS = Computer reservations services
PMS = Property management system
GDS = Global distribution system.

In the 1990s, airline CRS have continued to evolve into what are now known as global distribution systems (GDS). These GDS have become increasingly more sophisticated and linkages continue to be developed between systems. They now allow hotels to be represented in more detail, with great flexibility of rates and availability in response to seasonality and demand being able to be accommodated. 'Seamless connectivity' between agents booking via a GDS and hotels' real-time rooms inventory and rates is now an everyday occurrence.

Today 96 per cent of travel agencies in the USA have direct access via a terminal to one or more GDS, although in European countries this figure varies between 20 and 85 per cent. In the future this usage will be even more widespread, and information available to agents and customers will be more sophisticated, involving complex images and sound. Several GDS already offer visual imaging via CD-ROM technology.

The question for hotel companies, particularly smaller cost-sensitive companies, is no longer whether to be represented via GDS, but how to do so, or which consortium or representative company to use in order to do so.

Yield management

This is still very much a buzzword in the hotel industry, and in many cases little more than lip service is paid to it. It is vitally important, however, and attention to maximizing rooms revenue through yield management is part of any profitable hotel's success.

The principle, borrowed from the airline industry, involves maximizing the revenue earned in the sale of a perishable product. A hotel bed (or an airline seat) which remains unsold at the end of the day generates no revenue. Thus there is a benefit to be gained from selling that bed or airline seat at any price (although there is a minimum cost in cleaning a hotel room) rather than not selling it at all. The challenge of yield management is to sell the maximum number of beds or seats at the maximum price which the market will bear for each particular bed or seat.

In reality, yield management for hoteliers is the short-term manipulation of the selling price in order to maximize revenue through the combination of the number of rooms sold (occupancy) and the price at which they are sold (average rate). In order to do this hoteliers should sell rooms at their maximum rate when demand is strong and seek to stimulate demand during low periods by offering lower prices.

Modern hotel management tools include computerization of the front office and reservations functions. CRS and PMS are capable of providing an analysis of historic demand patterns as well as accurate forecasts of future occupancy *on the books*. With this information at their fingertips, hoteliers are able to manipulate the rates they offer for future bookings in order either to stimulate demand (by offering low prices) for low periods, or to maximize revenues (by charging rack rate) for periods of strong demand.

The various modern GDS offered by airlines and other reservations service providers allow hotels to manipulate the rates and types of rooms on offer via the GDS for specific periods of time.

Yield marketing

Arguably, the next step in the overall marketing process will be yield marketing, linking the sales, marketing and reservation systems to the property management and yield management systems. Yield marketing will link customer responses to the hotel's advertising and promotional efforts. The hotel will be able accurately and quickly to measure and even anticipate the effectiveness and efficiency of marketing investments. As advertising and sales costs continue to increase, a yield marketing system will be essential in helping hotels achieve a specific and measurable return on marketing investments.

Product specification

That part of the guest experience which relates to physical specification (or to product specification) has had a material impact on profitability in both the revenue and cost dimensions.

Revenue implications

Grand or landmark buildings such as the Crillon in Paris, the Plaza in New York or the Ritz in Madrid have provided the opportunity to achieve higher than average profits because of their architectural style and ornate decoration, but have carried a penalty in terms of operational and maintenance costs.

After the grandeur and opulence of the architectural style of the Victorian and Edwardian eras, the design and specification of hotels fell under the influence of the engineers, economists and accountants. Efficient but rather compact hotels such as the Churchill and Hyatt Carlton Tower hotels in London are examples of this influence.

The renaissance in architectural significance in hotels was led by John Portman and others about 20 years ago; examples include the Hyatt Regency in Atlanta and the Acapulco Princess. Exciting and dramatic architectural statements have been pursued by many architects subsequently. Most recently, they have been adopted in the new Disney hotels in Orlando – the Dolphin and Swan theme hotels. In many cases, guests have been induced to pay a higher tariff for the privilege of staying in these buildings and this has contributed to a higher level of achieved profitability.

However, it must be observed that the achievement of higher operating profitability is normally a necessity since the development costs of these hotels is significantly higher than conventionally designed buildings.

Cost implications

In analysing the influence which product specification has on the difference in profitability between two hotels which are otherwise similar, a number of recurring issues become apparent.

1. Payroll costs tend to be adversely affected by bad spatial planning. For example, if kitchens are poorly located relative to the restaurants and conference areas, service staff cannot be used efficiently and a higher cost is required to deliver a particular standard of service.
2. Food, beverage and other consumable material costs tend to be higher than they should be where there are deficiencies in storage and thus security. This occurs particularly where receiving bays are remote from dry goods storage and refrigerators, or where there is insufficient space to keep secure all the consumable items which a hotel requires.

     Attention to detail in planning key operating areas, such as kitchens, can result not only in higher profitability through efficiency, but also improved morale. Planning the layout of a kitchen to recognize a production flow which addresses goods inwards–food preparation and cooking–service–return of crockery–dishwashing may ultimately be reflected in both kitchen and service staffing levels and food cost.
3. Property operation and maintenance costs are adversely impacted by poor spatial planning. Although attractive, large public areas and corridors require to be cleaned, heated, lit, furnished and carpeted.
4. Energy costs will tend to be higher in hotels which have large lobbies, banquet and public areas, particularly where energy-saving and management systems have not been implemented.

Whilst these reasons are likely to be the most significant in respect of a direct impact on profit, other issues, which might be described as service enhancements, can also impact profitability and performance, albeit indirectly. A guest's attitude towards a hotel can be impacted, positively or negatively, by the following issues which, individually, are relatively minor.

Such issues would include:

1. Poorly designed lighting systems, which are difficult for the guest to operate easily on arrival.
2. Inefficient or uncontrollable heating and ventilation systems.
3. Poor lighting quality and access to mirrors.
4. Poor positioning of a telephone and/or operating instructions.

Although individually trivial, such physical defects can be sufficient to encourage the guest to choose a competitor hotel on the next visit to that city.

Service delivery

As marketing guru Theodore Levitt of Harvard University said, 'Customers do not buy products or services so much as they buy expectations'.

At its simplest, the guest experience, which is what the hotel industry sells, is made up of the physical specification of the hotel plus service delivery. Having previously addressed physical specification issues, it is now relevant to turn to the contribution which service can make to superior profitability.

Service is the ingredient which transforms the physical accommodation facility into an experience – one way or another! Guests have expectations of service, whatever the quality of accommodation.

Figure 16.12 illustrates the relative importance attached to the product offered, relative to the service offered, at different levels in the marketplace. At the one-, two- and three-star levels, the physical specification of the accommodation itself assumes a greater priority in the purchase equation. At the four and five star level, service assumes an equal or greater priority, but is more likely to be the factor having the greatest influence on pricing, performance and profitability.

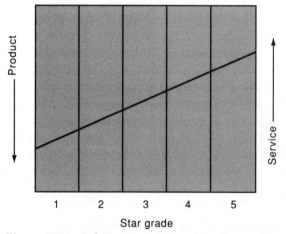

Figure 16.12 Relative importance of product and service to the guest. *Source:* PKFA

Life would be easier if guest expectations, for whatever category of hotel, remained static. Of course they don't. Rising consumer expectations are economic and social phenomena. Consumers and guests are more demanding because they are constantly being educated to be more sophisticated and thus are able to make better judgements. It is axiomatic that service becomes of greater significance in the guest experience in higher-quality hotels, because there isn't much provided in lower grades of hotels. In a one- and two-star hotel the expectation is limited to the check-in/check-out experience. At the upper end of the market, service manifests itself in so many more ways, from the interface with the doorman, to reception, porters, bar and restaurant waiters and room maids. However, even at the lowest level of expectation, the service must be delivered in a friendly, courteous, efficient manner. Research consistently reveals how very important the reception/check in experience is. A good or bad experience on check-in will carry a very heavy weighting in the guests' evaluation of their experience at that hotel.

When guests' experience of service falls short of their expectations in whatever grade of hotel, it is likely that those guests are vulnerable and may be lost to a competitor. They believe that they have had a poor-value-for-money experience. However, when the service delivery is equal to, or exceeds, the guest expectations then two things are likely to happen:

1. Premium pricing can be introduced, and
2. The occupancy of that hotel will tend to be above average.

Figure 16.13 illustrates the resultant concept of service premiums and service gaps.

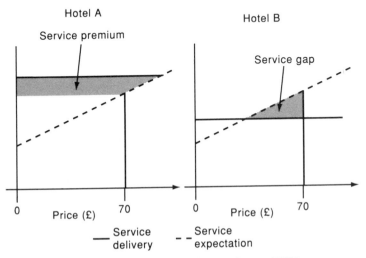

Figure 16.13 Service premiums and gaps. *Source:* PKFA

The evidence suggests that service excellence is a major contributor to enhanced profit because it supports higher revenue achievement in respect of occupancy and room rate. Those hotels enjoying greater profitability in similar market conditions have either closed or eliminated the service gap, or are consistently delivering service which exceeds guest expectations. In other word, 'a happy guest is relatively price-insensitive.'

How is the excellence on service delivery achieved? Service is difficult to deliver on a consistent basis because it is so ephemeral and, at the upper end of the market, has to be delivered on a large number of occasions in so many different locations in the hotel, every day.

Whereas service standards can be defined and specified in a manual, delivery can only be realized through a single-minded commitment by everyone in the company, from the top down. A number of the leading hotel companies are currently committing significant financial and human resources to quality management programmes which have a heavy focus on service delivery and guest interface.

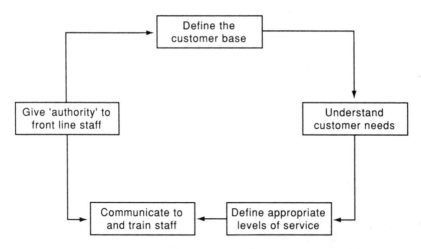

Figure 16.14   Service strategy. *Source:* PKFA

A service strategy, as illustrated in Figure 16.14, is one of the key techniques used by management to achieve this goal. This requires the hotelier to define clearly the target customer base and develop a clear understanding of their needs. From this, appropriate levels of service in all departments of the hotel can be specified. This creates the framework for staff training. If the product has been matched with clearly identified guests, then staff can be trained to meet and satisfy the needs of these guests. However, it is essential that responsibility and authority should be distributed down through the organization to the front-line staff. These are the people in regular day-to-day contact with guests who can therefore influence profitability. If staff are motivated, happy and working in the interests of the hotel, then the chances of guest satisfaction increase dramatically, and consequently so should revenue and profit.

Whilst it may be fair comment to characterize the focus of the hotel industry in the 1980s on the upgrading and respecifying of the physical product, the focus of the 1990s appears to be on improving service delivery, at all levels of the market.

In the context of the analysis of relative profitability between two otherwise similar hotels, the importance of the service element to obtaining premium revenues and providing a high profit potential should not be underestimated.

Excellent service providers appear to have a number of characteristics in common. This is a theme which emerges from one of the most successful management texts of the 1980s, *In Search of Excellence – Lessons From America's Best Run Companies* by Thomas Peters and Robert Waterman. The following example from this book illustrates this point particularly well. Thomas J. Watson Jr of IBM described the principles which helped build the company, as follows:

> In time, good service became almost a reflex in IBM. Years ago we ran an ad that said simply in bold type: 'IBM means service'. I have often thought it was our very best ad. It stated clearly exactly what we stand for. We want to give the best customer service of any company in the world... IBM's contracts have always offered, not machines for rent, but machine *services*... That is the equipment itself *and* the continuing advice and counsel of IBM staff.

Similarly, for hotel guests the experience is not only the product, it is the service delivery as well. The fact that companies like IBM were often regarded as market leaders in service should not surprise us. Their reputation was built on service, largely communicated through word of mouth, that is to say, satisfied customers telling friends and colleagues – the most powerful of all forms of promotion.

The key elements in the achievement of optimum service delivery, whatever the company, and whatever the quality of the product, are the same:

1. A commitment and active involvement on the part of senior management to quality service.
2. A strong orientation towards people.
3. A high level of monitoring, measurement and feedback.

Conclusions

In attempting to draw together conclusions from the preceding analyses, it is useful to consider the relative importance of the various critical success factors in arriving at the overall superior profit performance demonstrated by the *winners* in Figure 16.15.

Approximately 50 per cent of the profit uplift is revenue-based, whilst the balance is cost-based. The revenue-based superiority should logically be based upon superior marketing and service delivery, whilst the better cost performance is based upon greater operating efficiency and a better physical product specification. It is not feasible objectively to analyse the underlying causes without more detailed reference to the various individual hotels. Based on experience, however, the relative values presented in Figure 16.15 are a useful rule-of-thumb. An understanding of the areas offering the greatest potential impact for profit improvement will help management to focus most closely on those areas where the rewards are likely to be significant.

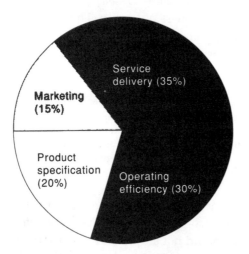

Figure 16.15   Relative importance of identified critical success factors. *Source:* PKFA

The complexity and interdependence of the issues and activities which contribute to superior profitability serve to emphasize that success is a journey rather than a destination. In an ever more complex and dynamic marketplace, hoteliers will increasingly be required fundamentally to re-evaluate their methods of generating revenues and the means of reducing costs.

References

Pannell Kerr Forster, EuroTrends Database, PKFA.

Peters, T.J. and Waterman, R.H. Jnr (1982) *In Search of Excellence*, Harper and Row.

Index

Hospitality Managers Pocket Book Series

Series Editor: Professor John O'Conner Oxford Brookes University

This series of pocket books is designed for managers in all fields of the hospitality industry, in particular, hotel, restaurant, restaurant and licensed house mangers. Each book can be used as a concise introduction or a portable reference source for working managers. Practical techniques are emphasised and concrete examples relevant to the hospitality industry feature throughout. No prior knowledge of the subject is assumed, and each book is written in an informal, accessible style. Students as well as managers will find the series a useful source of practical information.

- **Unique series for hospitality managers**
- **Portable, accessible format**
- **Emphasises practice rather than theory**
- **Features realistic examples throughout**
- **Combined reference source and introduction in one book**

Marketing

Books Published in association with Caterer and
Hotelkeeper magazine

Arnold Fewell,
Consultant
Neville Wills,
Managing Director, Gryphon Group Consultancy

Marketing provides a straightforward approach to marketing techniques, avoiding complicated jargon. The authors demonstrate how to improve sustainable profit and increase it year on year. Initially, the book looks at ways of analysing where your business is today, and a strategic review framework is then developed. Further chapters advise on how to make the tools of marketing work and how they can help your overall business objectives. Finally, there is a detailed section on creating a business plan, and a chapter on how to involve all levels of staff in the planning process. Throughout the book five examples of a hotel, restaurant, pub, staff restaurant and a fast food restaurant are used. '... avoids jargon and breaks the subject down into clear, practical techniques.'

CONTENTS: What is Marketing? Customer orientated management; Where is your business: Market research; Plotting the course; Product development and test marketing; Is the price right? The promotional mix; Advertising; Public relations; Sales promotions; Introduction to personal selling; Merchandising; Direct Marketing; Marketing and promotional calendars; The distribution network; Pulling it all together; the business plan; The re-analysis of your business; Index.

0 7506 0165 5

Successful Pubs and Inns

Michael Sargeant,
Tony Lyle

Successful Pubs and Inns plots a clear course towards successful innkeeping. It is intended for professionals already within the business and for those considering a licensed trade career. It will be of particular help to anyone considering leasing or purchasing a pub or inn. It is jargon free and written in an easy-to-read style. It can easily be used as a reference book as each chapter covers a particular aspect of the trade.

There are over 50,000 pubs and inns in the UK, which are either managed directly by brewers/pub owning companies or by self-employed tenants, lessees or by owners of free houses. These latter groups have become increasingly important due to recent changes in legislation and market conditions. This book will appeal to existing and potential licensees, especially those who find themselves solely in charge of their business. It will be of great value to anyone contemplating leasing or buying a pub or inn, with its clear message on initial selection and evaluation. The authors between them have considerable and relevant experience in pub operations and the brewing industry.

CONTENTS: Preface; So you want to run a pub?; What pub do you want? The choice is yours; Setting out your stall; Running the business; Customer care; Profit control; The perfect pint; Profit from food; The down the side; Keeping the Law; A way of life.

0 7506 1835 3

The Business of Hotels

S Medlik,
*Former Head of Department of Hotel, Catering and
Tourism Management, University of Surrey*

The fully revised edition of this well-known text by an experienced author, consultant and educator follows the structure and approach which has proved so successful since its first publication in 1980. The book examines the hotel as a business providing commercial hospitality. It focuses on markets, money and people, and uses examples from hotel operations throughout the world. This new edition is the outcome of a thorough revision of an established text. The new material includes a comprehensive profile the hotel business in the 1990's and includes data, quotes and extracts from a wide range of authoritative industry sources. This text is ideal for the practitioner - the owner, director or manager - the book can help to organise and formalise what they might have learnt in a less sympathetic way by experience and will contribute to a more balanced view of their business. Newcomers to hotels and others with a professional interest in understanding them should find the book a suitable introduction to the hotel industry.

CONTENTS: Basic Hotel concepts - Staying away from home; Hotel products and markets; Hotel policies, philosophies and strategies; Hotel guest services - Rooms and beds; Food and drink; Miscellaneous guest services; Hotel men and methods - Hotel organisation; Hotel staffing; Productivity in hotels; Hotel support and services - Marketing; Property ownership and management; Finance and accounts; Hotel dimensions - The small hotel; Hotel groups; International hotel operations.

0 7506 2080 3

Profit Planning

Published in association with Caterer and Hotelkeeper magazine

P Harris,
Oxford Brookes University

Ideal for hotel, restaurant and licensed house managers, this title focuses on profit planning, the major area of finance which the general manager needs to master. It looks specifically at the practical aspects of finance as it relates to the hospitality business, emphasising the 'how' rather than the 'why' and it contains a minimum of technical language. In particular, the book is designed to encourage confidence in the use of profit planning techniques, since many managers avoid using accounting information for fear of misinterpreting figures. Computer applications are included wherever necessary to speed up the process with particular reference to spreadsheets. The book emphasises the practical aspects of day-to-day profit planning.

CONTENTS: Key features of hotel and catering operations, Review of hospitality financial statements, Monitoring progress; Interpreting results; Understanding costs and revenue; Introduction to profit planning; Profit planning: the business mix; Pricing; profit improvement; Forecasting and budgeting; Controlling annual results; Using computer spreadsheets; Getting the information you need; Capital expenditure decisions.

0 7506 0223 6

Managing People

Michael Riley,
Lecturer, Department of Management
Studies for Tourism and Hotel Industries,
University of Surrey

Managing People provides a practical approach to applying management techniques in the 1990s. It will help professionals in the hotel and catering industry responsible for personnel and training. Managers will gain an understanding of vital aspects of people management.
Riley explores how aspects such as labour cost, utilisation, labour market behaviour and pay are inseparable from skills of people management, particularly in a labour-intensive industry. It is especially of relevance for managers with responsibility for personnel and training, though degree-level students will also find its non-prescriptive approach helpful

0 7506 2289 X